Literary Gaming

Literary Gaming

Astrid Ensslin

The MIT Press
Cambridge, Massachusetts
London, England

MIT Press books may be purchased at special quantity discounts for business or sales promotional use. For information, please email special_sales@mitpress.mit.edu.

This book was set in Stone by the MIT Press. Printed and bound in the United States of America.

Library of Congress Cataloging-in-Publication Data

Ensslin, Astrid, author.
Literary gaming / Astrid Ensslin.
    p. cm
Includes bibliographical references and index.
ISBN 978-0-262-02715-1 (hardcover: alk. paper)
1. Internet games—Social aspects—Philosophy. 2. Digital media—Philosophy.
3. Interactive multimedia—Philosophy. 4. Hypertext fiction—History and criticism—Theory, etc. 5. Fantasy games—Philosophy. 6. Play (Philosophy) 7. Intermediality. I. Title.
GV1469.17.S63E57   2014
794.8—dc23
2013029589

10 9 8 7 6 5 4 3 2 1

To Anton and Leo
and the playful worlds they inhabit

Contents

Acknowledgments

I would like to thank a number of people without whom this book would never have seen the light of day. First of all, thanks to Virginia Crossman, Katie Helke Dokshina, Margarita Encomienda, Susan Mai, and Doug Sery at the MIT Press for their help and advice throughout the reviewing and production process. I'd also like to thank my anonymous reviewers for their insightful and constructive feedback.

I received a lot of invaluable comments, encouragement, and support from a wide range of colleagues, students, academic peers, and friends. First and foremost, thanks to my long-standing friend and collaborator Alice Bell for her meticulous proofreading of earlier drafts of the manuscript. Further people who took their time to discuss aspects of this project, comment on draft chapters, look up references and games, and/or simply provide motivational support include, in alphabetical order: Saer Maty Ba, James Barrett, Ian Bogost, Serge Bouchardon, Joe Bray, Isamar Carrillo Masso, Amy Chambers, Geraint Ellis, Sonia Fizek, Alison Gibbons, Auriea Harvey, David Herman, Llion Iwan, Deena Larsen, Xavier Laurent, Brian McHale, Conor Mckeown, Andy McStay, Jason Nelson, Dan Punday, Raluca Radulescu, Samantha Rayner, Aaron Reed, Hans Rustad, Marie-Laure Ryan, Michael Samyn, Peter Paul Schnierer and his students at Heidelberg, Lyle Skains, Hans Stadthagen, David Trotter, and Jill Walker-Rettberg. Thanks also to those individuals and design teams who gave permission to reproduce various items in individual chapters:

- Deena Larsen for the screenshot of *Firefly* in chapter 4;
- Robert Kendall for the screenshot of *Clues* in chapter 4;
- Amanita Design for the screenshot of *Samorost 2* in chapter 5;
- Serge Bouchardon for the screenshots of *Loss of Grasp* in chapter 5;
- geniwate and Deena Larsen for the screenshots of *The Princess Murderer* in chapter 6;

- Jason Nelson for the screenshot of *evidence of everything exploding* in chapter 8;
- Gregory Weir for the screenshot of *Silent Conversation* in chapter 8; and
- Tale of Tales for the screenshots of *The Path* in chapter 9.

My biggest thanks, as ever, goes to Atik Baborie, who patiently endured my absent-mindedness and occasional panic attacks during a time when we busily prepared for and embarked on first-time parenthood, as well as to my parents, to whom I owe the fact that I completed the manuscript on time despite all the odds.

I realize that in a book like this a lot of important texts and authors have to remain unmentioned, although they more than deserve a place in it. Apologies therefore to all those digital writers, artists, game designers, critics, and scholars whose work should have but could not be included due to spatial constraints. I hope that the research presented will stimulate many ludoliterary analyses that will pay tribute, in their entirety, to the sheer plethora of fascinating creative artifacts that give rise to literary gaming as discussed in this book.

1 Introduction

1.1 Ludicity and Literariness in the Digital Age

"As we move into a situation where poetry is more electric and Net-oriented, and where videogames are maturing into their art possibilities, there will be more exploration of the meeting ground of poetry (and other arts) with games. Because games need to be literate, in some sense, to attain art in which language is handled with depth and precision, and poetry needs to move into the digital and find new ground rather than simply porting print to the digital."
—(Andrews 2007, 58)

This book is about literary gaming—a specific form of digital gameplay that happens when we interact with digital artifacts that combine so-called ludic (from Latin *ludus*: game or play) and literary (from Latin *littera*: alphabetic letter, or plural *litterae*: piece of writing) elements. In other words, it looks at a hybrid subgroup of creative media that has both *readerly* and *playerly* characteristics. Or, as you might say in more straightforward terms, this book is about the creative interface between digital books that can be played and digital games that can be read, and it suggests ways of combining both processes for users and analysts.[1]

In a sense, therefore, this book continues where art game designer Jim Andrews's prophecy left off in 2007 (see opening quote). I propose that future experimental creative practices in digital media will give rise to an ever-growing body of hybrid artifacts that blend verbal and other arts with videogame technologies. This fusion is urgently needed to grant creative writing a more contemporary, media-savvy outlook, as well as to expand and advance the artistic and critical significance of games.

Literary as used in this study is not an evaluative term. It does not entail any value judgment about the apparent creative merit or canonical potential of the texts studied. My selection of texts for close analysis is based on functional concerns, that is, how succinctly and reliably they allow me to illustrate the analytical methodology that lies at the core of this book. Hence, when I use the terms *literature* and *literary*, I refer to artifacts of verbal art in the broadest possible sense, where literariness in the sense of linguistic foregrounding is part of the authorial intention and where human language (spoken or written) plays a significant aesthetic role. In other words, this investigation includes only works that can be read in the sense of decoding letters, words, phrases, and other linguistic and semiotic signs and structures. Verbal art in the broadest sense is not bound to any particular genre, medium, platform, or technology it may be called poetry, fiction, or drama; it may be print-based or digital; and it may require the use of (e-)book technologies, personal computers (PCs), gaming consoles, or mobile devices. What all works of verbal art have in common, however, is an aesthetic concern with structural and thematic elements of their own form, genre, or medium, and the way in which they express this self-reflexive agenda can be described in terms of subversive play.

By the same token, *literary* in the sense of verbal art also always refers to the experience of reading a text that one recognizes or identifies as such. What happens in literary communication (Pettersson 2000, 4) is that fictional events, situations, etc. are represented verbally and "presentationally." This means "the reader is supposed to make himself acquainted with them and to somehow derive pleasure from doing so." Hence, literary communication involves a virtual contract or unspoken agreement between text and reader that presupposes that the latter is willing to engage with the former and all its formal and conceptual implications in order to be entertained in some way, shape, or form. As we shall see in this book, this engagement can occur with verbal art that is formally explicated and realized as such—for example, a *hypertext* poem or digital fiction—or indeed with verbal art that is embedded in or merged with other, dominant art forms, such as computer games.

Neither computer games nor digital (or electronic) literature are new phenomena as such. Research on both has proliferated in the past two decades, and we have reached a point where we can move away from making generalized comments on what it means to read or play digital as opposed to analog media, how literature and textuality have to be reconceptualized when the book is removed from the materiality of print, and how gameplay has to be redefined in the context of digital technologies. We have progressed from a first wave of digital literature and videogame criticism that provided definitions and important theoretical insights (e.g., Bolter 1991; Moulthrop 1991; Delany and Landow 1991; Landow 1992,

1997; Salen and Zimmerman 2004; Juul 2005; Egenfeldt-Nielsen et al. 2008) to a second wave of systematic, analytical scholarship that looks in detail at specific phenomena within both sectors and applies principles of literary and ludological criticism to individual genres or artifacts (e.g., van Looy and Baetens 2003; Pressman 2008; Ciccoricco 2007a, 2007b; Bell 2010; Bell et al. 2010; Simanowski 2011; Bell, Ensslin, and Rustad 2014; MacCallum-Stewart and Parsler 2007; Ryan and Costello 2012; Ensslin 2014b; Tosca 2014). This second-wave research confirms that both creative practices and the scholarship associated with them have reached a "mature" stage, as Andrews (2007, 58) aptly puts it. *Literary Gaming* is firmly rooted in the second wave and presents a new, systematic method for analyzing literary-ludic texts that takes into account the analytical concerns of both literary stylistics and *ludology*.

Importantly, we have to understand that we are not dealing with just any form of digital literature and videogames. Rather, digital literature as referred to in this book is digital-born, which means it is "written for and read on a computer screen that pursues its verbal, discursive and/or conceptual complexity through the digital medium, and would lose something of its aesthetic and semiotic function if it were removed from that medium" (Bell et al. 2010, n.p.). In other words, digital literature excludes at least two mainstream forms of digital media that we might otherwise associate with the term: e-books or any other paper-under-glass forms of digital writing that can be printed without losing their specific aesthetic appeal and distinctive interactive qualities; and videogames that we cannot read in the sense of close-read and close-play for their artistic verbal and ludological forms and contents. Clearly, most videogames contain written and spoken language, most typically in character dialogues, backstory descriptions, instructions, interface items, and *paratextual* materials (box blurbs, websites, commercials, and so forth). However, the vast majority of them do not use literary language (spoken or written) in the sense of verbal art as previously explained, and this book seeks to shed light on precisely the small but growing group of games that do.

Most existing research that combines digital literature, play, and games has approached the field from the literary side. Since the beginning of digital literature scholarship, scholars have focused, for example, on literary forms of hypertext (e.g., Landow 1992, 1997, 2006; Joyce 1996; Ensslin 2007; Bell 2010), *interactive fiction* (IF) and drama (e.g., Montfort 2003; Douglass 2007; Mateas 2004), network fictions (Ciccoricco 2007a), digital poetry (e.g., Glazier 2002; Block, Heibach, and Wenz 2004; Kac 2007), and other forms of electronic verbal art (e.g., Simanowski 2002, 2011). However, they have pointed out various playful interactions that these artifacts give rise to without placing them in a systematic ludological framework. Studies that have examined gaming as an aspect of reading digital literature of various kinds include Andrews's (2007) important yet generalized and eclectic essay on "Videogames as Literary Devices" and Kocher's (2007) typological yet insufficiently specific study "The Ludoliterary Cycle: Analysis and Typology of Digital Games."

Admittedly, some forms and specimens of literary gaming as understood in this book have been discussed eclectically in various related academic contexts, such as interactive fiction (Montfort 2003; Harrigan and Wardrip-Fruin 2007), electronic literature (Gendolla and Schäfer 2007; Hayles 2008; Schäfer and Gendolla 2010), cybertext and ergodic literature (Aarseth 1997; Ryan 1999; Eskelinen 2012), kinetic poetry and new media poetics (Morris and Swiss 2006; Simanowski 2011), new media arts, game narratives and digital performance (Wardrip-Fruin and Harrigan 2004; Ryan 2006; Ricardo 2009) and game art and/or writing (Compton 2004; Clarke and Mitchell 2007). However, there is to date no systematic, monographic attempt at studying the hybrid interface between literary (poetic, dramatic, and narrative) computer games and ludic electronic literature—a lacuna that this book seeks to fill.

Art game research, under which large umbrella concept the *game* aspect of literary gaming falls, is currently in a fledgling state, with a small yet growing body of research literature (Clarke and Mitchell 2007; Bittanti and Quaranta 2006; Catlow, Garrett, and Morgana 2010). Most of this literature focuses on the two main phenomena produced by the creative marriage between videogames and art: game art on the one hand and art games on the other. *Game art* refers to works of art that are inspired by videogame aesthetics and technologies but aren't games as such. They are typically displayed like other pieces of art in exhibitions and galleries and are akin to installations and participatory art. Leading game artists include Jon Haddock (*Screenshots*), Tobias Bernstrup (*Killing Spree*), Cory Arcangel (*NES Landscapes*), Joseph DeLappe (*Dead-in-Iraq*), Totto Renna (*Pixel Art*), JODI (*Jet Set Willy Variations*), and Brody Condon (*Fake Screenshot Contest*). *Art games*, on the other hand, are actual games—analog, digital, or both—that are developed by individuals or small teams of independent game designers and tend to have noncommercial or even anti-commercialist philosophies behind them. I shall elaborate on this group of videogames in various places throughout this book.

If we understand game art in its broadest sense as "any art in which digital games played a significant role in the creation, production, and/

or display of the artwork" (Bittanti and Quaranta 2006, 9), we may group certain works of ludic digital literature under its remit. Chapter 6 of Erik Loyer's (2001) "narrative poem" (Flores 2012) *Chroma*, for example, is set in a three-dimensional (3D) virtual environment that closely resembles the labyrinths of early 3D adventure games and first-person shooters (FPSs) such as *3D Monster Maze* (Evans 1982) and *Wolfenstein 3D* (id Software 1992). It is navigated via cursor keys and presents readers with a first-person *avatar*, whose location is also displayed on a dynamic map on screen. Nevertheless, despite its visual design and navigational functionalities, *Chroma* isn't a game with rules, challenges, targets, feedback mechanisms, victory and termination conditions, etc. It isn't driven by *ludic mechanics*, that is, the digitally programmed or analog mechanisms that afford gameplay. It is a digital poem that uses aspects of digital game design for its audiovisual aesthetic and corresponding phenomenological implications. In fact, as we shall see in various chapters throughout this book, the less a digital fiction or poem contains ludic mechanics proper—and I will explain the full meaning of this term in more detail—the less it can be considered game-like, or playerly, although it may be playful or game-inspired in its overall philosophy and implementation.

Literary videogames as understood in this book form a subgroup of art games, which contain or even foreground verbal rather than purely audiovisual art. None of the existing literature on art games focuses in any depth on this phenomenon. Similarly, book-length publications dealing with games, storytelling, digital fiction, narratology, software studies, and critical theory (Wardrip-Fruin and Harrigan 2004, Harrigan and Wardrip-Fruin 2007, 2009; Wardrip-Fruin 2009) have not shed any light on literary videogames as an independent object of study, with its own analytical tools and body of artifacts. Instead, narratologists and textuality scholars have been studying how games tell stories, create fictional worlds, and engage with a larger textual and media ecology (e.g., Jenkins 2004; Juul 2005; Ryan 2006, 2008; Jones 2008; Ensslin 2011a). This book therefore addresses the need for systematic analytical engagement with literary-ludic (L-L) hybrids that both manifest and challenge the possibility of fusing the seemingly alien worlds of gaming and literary close-reading beyond the study of *storyworlds* and the techniques of in-game storytelling. My aim is to map a distinctive body of such hybrid texts along a literary-ludic spectrum (see chapter 3), and to introduce and showcase a rigorous analytical methodology based on a profound and suitable critical framework.

The aforementioned body of hybrid artifacts is grounded in a conception of computer games (or elements thereof) as experimental literary arts. These include artifacts that employ letters artistically, kinetically, and multimodally as part of a digital *Gesamtkunstwerk* rather than following a rigid paper/print-under-glass trajectory. As mentioned previously, in this context *literary* has to be detached from print as its defining technology with respect to both production and reception. We are no longer talking about texts that are sequentially organized, that offer closure, and that are received largely on a two-dimensional page. Reading is no longer limited to the materiality and format of the codex, no matter whether it appears on paper or paper-under-glass (in the case of e-books). We no longer understand reading almost entirely in terms of turning or even scrolling pages. Literariness in the sense of twenty-first-century verbal art opens itself to an ever-changing array of interactive and multimodal practices. There is no one way of reading digital media. Digital literacy must involve the aptitude, ability, and willingness to adapt our interactive practices to every individual artifact, which may involve a wide range of heuristic and autodidactic practices, from learning-by-doing to studying manuals and literally rehearsing hardware and software usage.

Literariness, if and when applied to computer games, tends to be embedded in *ludic-mechanic* structures, much in the same way that *ludicity* in electronic literature is embedded in specific literary macrostructures, such as a multimedia novel or short story collection. Literary-ludic hybrids, then, aim to "knock . . . down the verbal structures of linear discourse and [to] melt . . . different poetics into a hybrid tradition" (Beiguelman 2010, 409). This tradition, or body of texts, is so varied and elusive that it precludes straightforward categorization: *prima facie* some of these texts appear to be poems, stories, novels, or dramas—yet upon closer examination their ludic features render them gamelike. Other texts may be referred to as games in the title or front matter yet turn out to be not just playerly but readerly as well. It is mainly for this reason that the title of this book is not *Literary Games*, because that would seem to exclude ludic e-literature. The more processual, phenomenological character of *Literary Gaming* allows for the integration of a wide range of hybrid phenomena which are experienced as a mixture of, or, indeed, clash between, reading and gameplay and whose specific form and interaction render them closer to either the literary or the ludic side of the L-L continuum.

Importantly, in computer games and gaming as literary art, narrative, dramatic, and/or poetic techniques are employed in order to explore the affordances and limitations of rules and other ludic structures and processes. These artifacts challenge the aesthetic of run-of-the-mill blockbusters like first-person shooter, adventure, racing, and role-playing games. They are designed to make players reflect on conventional aspects of games such as fast-paced action, rule-governed kinetic behavior, goal-directedness, and simplistic friend-and-foe binary thought. Their boundaries with playful digital literature are often fluid, and throughout the book I will demonstrate the wide spectrum of creative practices integrating various types and degrees of ludicity and literariness in digital media.

1.2   Ludic Books and Literary "Games"

As Spariosu points out in his seminal work *Literature, Mimesis and Play* (1982, 130), "literature has always been regarded, in our culture, as a 'higher' or a 'lower' form of play, and has consequently shared the latter's spectacular value fluctuations on the metaphysical stock-market." Despite those fluctuations, play and games as forms of human interaction and entertainment have had a difficult time being accepted in contemporary literary scholarship and tend to be viewed with a great deal of skepticism— much as film studies did in the 1950s. Similarly, games studies tends to be seen as a discipline more akin to media and cultural studies and is typically found in institutional isolation from English departments. To some degree, of course, this is understandable, because games as literary or verbal art, or hybrid forms of games and literature, used to be few and far between. However, the past decade has seen a proliferation of such digital media hybrids, and it is against this creative and cultural backdrop that this book seeks to correct the widely held view that games and literature do not really go together. It aims to draw attention to a new form of experimental literary art that is closely tied to digital media as a productive, receptive, and participatory platform, and that requires entirely novel ways of close play and reading.

Leaving aside the disciplinary and institutional implications of marrying literary communication and gaming, the idea of literary play has been researched quite extensively since the 1960s. Although theorists have often been insufficiently specific in their distinction between play and game and have tended to use the latter term to talk about the former, there is no denying that playful (print) literature has formed an important object of literary scholarship and debate over the past fifty years. While chapter 2 will go into more detail about play and games as philosophical, theoretical, and critical topics both within and beyond literary studies and ludology, I shall use this section to offer a broad survey of print literature as play between writer, reader, and text, interwoven with the scholarship that has sought to capture this phenomenon anthologically and theoretically.

Before I can do so, however, let me clarify a few terminological issues. I have mentioned previously that *play* and *game* are often used interchangeably, especially in literary scholarship. From a ludological point of view, this is highly misleading because games are a subform of play. Play can assume a wide range of manifestations. As Zimmerman (2004, 159) explains, it comprises three large categories: (1) gameplay, which is the formal play of games, such as board games, card games, sports, or computer games. This type of play follows rules and is both highly structured and goal oriented. (2) Ludic activities involve informal play—that is, any nongame behaviors that we commonly refer to as playing (around), such as kicking a ball from one person to another without applying the formal rules of football, children playing "Ring a Ring o' Roses," or wordplay and other forms of linguistic and literary creativity. Finally, being in a playful state of mind (3) is the psychological framework we adopt when we have fun, crack jokes, chuckle, cheer, and rejoice and therefore is much broader than the first two categories. In reverse order, then, the three categories encapsulate each other like Russian dolls: "Game play (1) is a particular kind of ludic activity (2) and ludic activities (2) are a particular way of being playful (3)" (Zimmerman 2004, 159). This important distinction has been neglected by much literary-ludic scholarship and has caused a lot of conceptual and terminological confusion as a result.

Games are the most structured and rule-bound form of play, and they are often described in terms of systems, or mechanics, which involve the rules, targets, actions, challenges, risks, rewards, victory, and termination conditions to which players have to commit. According to Suits (2005, 54–55), "to play a game is to attempt to achieve a specific state of affairs [prelusory goal], using only means permitted by rules [lusory means], where the rules prohibit use of more efficient in favour of less efficient means [constitutive rules], and where the rules are accepted just because they make possible such activity [lusory attitude]." Games tend to enable measurable progress, which may be reflected by levels, credits, gauges, scores, avatar development, and/or repository items. Both failure and success are normally integrated as possible outcomes, and upon completion some games allow replay and *respawning*. Therefore, gameplay, despite being a playful activity, can be and often is taken extremely seriously, and breaking the rules can lead to radical penalties such as disqualification, system errors, or simply failure.

Play, on the other hand, is a much broader and looser concept that can relate to games but more often than not refers to nongame activities, which are open, unstructured, and spontaneous and do not meet the game-ness criteria outlined in the previous paragraph. Hence, the so-called "games authors play" (Hutchinson 1983) aren't normally games in the narrow sense of the word but rather playful activities on the part of literary communicators (reader and writer), which can take a plenitude of manifestations and have a wide range of aesthetic effects. So whenever (most) print scholars talk about literary games, what they actually mean is literary play and the concrete formal and thematic manifestations that result from it in the history, or canon, of playful literature. I will look at literary play in more detail in chapter 2.

Among the earliest collections of playful literature are Isaac D'Israeli's *Curiosities of Literature* (1791–1817) and Ludovic Lalanne's *Curiosités littéraires* (1845), although their scope somewhat exceeds what contemporary ludoliterary scholars would subsume under literary play. D'Israeli's compilation, for example, comprises a plethora of essays on playful literary topics as diverse as Cicero's puns, ancient Greek and Latin *lipograms* and *anagrams*, purposeful *errata* in early print, and intertextuality ("connexions") in literary anecdotes. Despite the fact that play and games were not held in high scholarly esteem in the nineteenth century and were presented by both D'Israeli and Lalanne as marginal rather than mainstream phenomena, both works turned out to be very popular (Hutchinson 1983, 8) and had to be reprinted many times.

The first systematic compilation of literature as gameplay did not appear until the early 1960s, however, with Alfred Liede's two volumes of *Dichtung als Spiel* (Poetry as Game/Play) (1963).[2] As its subtitle (*Studien zur Unsinnspoesie an den Grenzen der Sprache, Studies into Nonsense Poetry on the Margins of Language*) indicates, Liede was mostly interested in nonsense and other liminal forms of poetic play, which he placed in the context of subversive and iconoclastic artistic movements such as Italian Futurism, Dadaism, and Surrealism. On his list of relevant genres are what he refers to as nonliterary games (nursery rhymes and adult wordplay in folk songs, proverbs, jocular epitaphs, and tall tales); literary "games" such as concrete and visual poetry, riddles, play on rhyme and verse, and letter, syllable, and word puzzles (e.g., anagram, lipogram, palindrome); and "larger games" such as parody, travesty, onomatopoeia, and *cento*. Liede's study covers poetry from the late Middle Ages (Abraham a Sancta Clara) to twentieth-century poets such as Christian Morgenstern and Hans Arp, and the literary forms that he illustrates with mostly German examples can be traced through various Western literatures.

A particular emphasis on French literature was made in a groundbreaking special issue of *Yale French Studies*, "Homo Ludens Revisited" (1968), which contains essays on a diversity of ludic texts, authors, and theories by a range of leading ludological and ludoliterary scholars such as Jacques Ehrmann, Roger Caillois, Eugen Fink, and Kostas Axelos. Ehrmann (1968), for example, focuses on the inextricable connection between play and reality, on the communicative essence of play and games, and on the fact that readers are both subject and object of literary play. Morrissette (1968) looks at structural "games" in Robbe-Grillet's novels (e.g., *Les Gommes* [The Erasers], 1953, and *Dans le labyrinth* [In the Labyrinth], 1959), and Lewis (1968) examines word "games" in La Rochefoucauld (e.g., *Maximes* [Maxims], 1665). Although the special issue lacks any sense of systematicity in the treatment of literary play, it marks an important stage in ludologically informed literary theory and criticism. It was duly followed by a number of studies focusing on various forms of literary play in the work of individual authors, including Nabokov's novels (Gezari 1971, 1974), Sterne's *Tristram Shandy* (Lanham 1973), Pope's *The Rape of the Lock* (Wimsatt 1973), Carroll's *Alice's Adventures in Wonderland* and *Through the Looking Glass* (Blake 1974), Gide's *Les Caves du Vatican* (The Vatican Cellars) (Steel 1971), Brecht's ludic theater (Esslin 1986), Chaucer's "The Miller's Tale" (Wilson 1986), Borges's short stories (Coleman 1986), Donne's *Elegies* and *Songs and Sonnets* (Guiness 1986), Eliot's "The Love Song of J. Alfred Prufrock" (Spariosu 1986) and Beckett's late plays (Cohn 1986).[3] Other studies examine entire literary trends, such as games and play in twentieth-century American fiction (Detweiler 1976) and "language games" in German concrete poetry (Prawer 1969).

As for works spanning national and linguistic boundaries, the postmodern novel has often been described as playfully deconstructive. In his reader-centric monograph *Theories of Play and Postmodern Fiction*, Edwards (1998) places the literary "playhouse of language" in the context of ludological reader response and deconstructivist theory. He emphasizes the centrality of the reader's participation in literary-verbal play found in novels ranging from Cervantes to Oulipo, Borges, Nabokov, Calvino, Barth, Pynchon, and Coover. In particular, Edwards focuses on Pynchon's clownery in *Gravity's Rainbow*, Barth's epistolary artistry in *LETTERS*, intertextual infiltration in Kroetsch's *What the Crow Said*, the feminist revision of the carnivalesque in Carter's *Nights at the Circus*, and Carey's bricolage of narrational unreliability in *Illywhacker*.

Having moved well into the second decade of the twenty-first century, it would be somewhat ill-advised for this book to presuppose a complete separation between print and digital in relation to literary gaming. This would repeat the myopia of much contemporary print scholarship, which still ignores literary technologies other than print. Furthermore, recent years have seen an increasing amount of copying and mashing of texts across different technologies, as well as adaptations of ludic print literature to digital media. Already, in the early 1990s, hypertext scholarship pointed to the structural similarities between digital hypertext (see chapter 4) and proto-hypertextual, nonlinear writing such as biblical glosses, encyclopedias, and fictional footnotes (Ensslin 2014a). More recently, experimental writing has been mapped across different media. For example, Marc Saporta's *Composition No. 1* (1961), a "book in a box," stores its pages as unnumbered loose leaves, and readers are expected to shuffle them like a deck of cards. A digital edition of *Composition No.1* for the iPad was published in 2011, with touch-pad movements replacing the physical shuffling of leaves. With a new generation of cross-media writers emerging on the horizon, a greater variety of explorative texts will become available—a variety that will implement both literary play and literary gaming as understood in this study. Be that as it may, the texts selected for analysis in this study are exclusively digital-born, simply because digital media are extremely well suited to experimentation with innovative forms of literature and games. This, in turn, is due to the fact that the underlying codes and algorithms of digital media are formulated along the lines of conditional statements and syntactic rules, which makes these texts executable—that is, they can be performed through on-screen interaction (Beiguelman 2010). Hence, digital media form an ideal starting point to any investigation of literary gaming.

1.3   Methodology and Structure

As we shall see throughout this book, literary computer games combine poetic and narrative techniques with serious, self-critical game design in order to explore the affordances and limitations of rules, challenges, risks, achievement-drivenness, and other ludic structures. Ludic digital literature, on the other hand, uses a wide range of ludic strategies, to different degrees of salience. As I will explore in more detail in the following chapters, these strategies break into three different types: (1) *cognitive ludicity*, which we know from ludic print literature as exemplified in the previous section; it involves mostly cognitive reading strategies, such as solving word puzzles or whodunit riddles, engaging in intertextual association, and mapping allegorical meaning onto one's own reality. (2) The second type of strategy is what I call ergodic ludicity, which involves not only cognitive but corporeal, kinetic interaction with the hardware and software of a computational system and requires, as Aarseth (1997, 1) puts it, "nontrivial effort . . . to allow the reader to traverse the text." (1) and (2) tend to co-occur when reading ludic digital literature, in which case I refer to them collectively as cognitive-ergodic ludicity. However, what I am particularly interested in here is (3) ludic mechanics, which occur in ludic-literary works that borrow from computer game technologies and structures such elements as rule-driven action, performance measurement, credit counts, winning and losing mechanisms, rewards, tasks, and challenges. Most digital literature does not contain elements of (3), and those works that do have not been theorized systematically by previous research—a gap that this book seeks to fill.

As indicated previously, a school of thought does not come of age until it has laid down its methodological foundations and proven that they are fully operable and replicable. For this reason, I shall map out an analytical methodology for works that involve various degrees and forms of literary gaming. This approach is an extended version of world-leading digital narratologist Marie-Laure Ryan's (2006) functional ludonarrativism, which coalesces narratological and ludological principles and seeks to show how they condition each other in digital narratives. Ryan's approach is neither elaborated in any of her theoretical works, nor does it include poetic artifacts beyond the narrative contents and structures of digital media. I therefore propose a more inclusive analytical framework called *functional ludostylistics*, which comprises elements of ludology, ludonarratology, ludosemiotics, and mediality. This toolkit has been induced from a corpus of over 130 works of L-L artifacts, compiled from both digital anthologies (most notably the *Electronic Literature Collections Volumes I* [Hayles et al. 2006] and *II* [Borràs et al. 2011]) and independently stored and accessible texts. I will elaborate on this toolkit in chapter 3, and its functionality will be showcased in the analytical chapters of this book.

This book is divided into two major parts. Part I introduces its core theoretical and methodological underpinnings. Chapter 2 begins with a concise survey of the development of philosophical thought on play and games from eighteenth-century German idealism to the present day. It examines a range of aesthetic and theoretical movements since the nineteenth century that have play (with forms, norms, and conventions) at their core and that use it more or less politically to innovate, protest, or revolutionize institutionalized forms of art. It will then go on to discuss some key ludological theories insofar as they have been adopted by literary criticism scholarship, particularly in the second half of the twentieth century. The chapter will also investigate in more theoretical detail the two digital art forms that blend into various forms of literary gaming: literature *born digital* and (literary) art games.

Chapter 3 moves from theoretical to textual matters and introduces, instead of a typology, a spectrum between ludic digital literature and literary games (L-L spectrum). This spectrum is designed so as to accommodate texts subsumed under the literary gaming concept and it shows their relative emphases on reading versus gameplay. It is based on the phenomenological distinction between deep and hyper attention, where the former is typically associated with reading and the latter with gaming. This is followed by a discussion of literary play versus literary game insofar as this dichotomy applies to digital media. The discussion then leads to the core of this chapter: an exploration of the interface between experimental digital literature and computer games. It will map out the aforementioned continuum between ludic digital literature and literary computer games, illustrating it with relevant digital media genres and individual texts. The final section of this chapter then details the functional ludostylistic toolkit for analyzing digital, literary-ludic artifacts, which forms the methodological basis of the ensuing analyses.

Part II, which comprises various close-readings/close-playings, gradually moves from the literary to the ludic end of the L-L spectrum, whereby the emphasis on literariness, or readerliness, is replaced or complemented, step by step, by an emphasis on playerliness. Chapter 4 analyzes four literary hypertexts exhibiting different types of play according to Caillois (2001)—alea, ilinx, mimicry, and agon. It shows that, with very few exceptions, ludic mechanics are not implemented in hypertext fiction and poetry, which tends to foreground cognitive and ergodic ludicity, instead.

Chapter 5 examines Serge Bouchardon and Vincent Volckaert's *Loss of Grasp* (2010), an online *hypermedia* fiction that implements cognitive-ergodic ludicity in capricious ways and exemplifies how the latest technologies help digital writers compose linear works that demonstrate a far more diverse pattern of ludic structures and activities for the playful reader than early forms of (hypertextual or hypermedia) digital fiction managed to do. The overall impression this evokes is that of far more immersive ludicity, which comes close to ludic mechanics yet does not actually involve any gameplay proper. The concept of heuristic ergodicity will be discussed as a core principle guiding cybertexts and ludic-mechanic hypermedia.

Moving further along the L-L spectrum, I shall then go on, in chapter 6, to close-read/close-play geniwate and Deena Larsen's Flash fiction *The Princess Murderer* (2003). It is a seminal artifact in a book on literary gaming because it features an actual ludic-mechanic element—a counting device called princess census. Equally importantly, it thematizes and problematizes narratologically the misogynist implications of commercial videogames, which tend to represent femininity in terms of either weakness (the damsel-in-distress) or hypersexuality (the femme-fatale), or, indeed, both.

With chapter 7 we reach the middle region of the L-L spectrum. This chapter contains an analysis of Aaron A. Reed's poetic interactive fiction *Blue Lacuna: An Interactive Novel* (2008), which looks at the ways in which the text combines ludic-mechanic structures and narrative strategies to evoke a fictional world of epic dimensions that can be permeated only if the words are played adequately, so to speak. In particular, I shall focus on character development and on ways in which the IF functionalizes aspects of prose language to facilitate play-reading and ludic-mechanic progress.

Entering the ludic side of the L-L spectrum, chapter 8 examines a phenomenon called poetic or poetry games, which are—as the term suggests—games that have to be played, first and foremost. Yet they also contain high levels of creative textuality—poetic and multimodal—that can be understood comprehensively only if players are willing to combine deep and hyper attention and/or revisit the text as often as it takes for their full phenomenological repository, or range of subjective experiences, to have taken effect. The work I shall examine to illustrate these processes and textual-ludic structures is Jason Nelson's poetic browser game *evidence of everything exploding* (2009).

The final analytical chapter studies a specimen of what I call literary *auteur* games—a type of art game that has its designer's stamp firmly imprinted on its audiovisual and interactive style and thematic preferences and frames itself as a game without necessarily following an explicit literary trajectory. As a result, literary structures tend to be less obvious in these games than in poetic games as outlined in the previous paragraph. *The Path* (2009) by Tale of Tales will form the object of my analysis, and I will demonstrate how subtle fictional-literary strategies are used to augment the game's genre-critical, self-reflexive agenda as well as its literary character.

Each analytical chapter will end with a discussion of where the given texts are located on the L-L spectrum in relation to other, comparable artifacts. The book will close with an evaluation of ludostylistics as an innovative analytical methodology, its affordances and limitations, and its place within contemporary ludology, media studies, and literary discourse analysis (stylistics and narratology).

On a final note, let me say a few words about how to read this book. At the opening of this introduction I mentioned that it brings together two large disciplines of research: digital gaming, or, more specifically, a subdiscipline of it (art games), on the one hand and digital literature on the other. Both disciplines tend to come with their own theoretical apparatuses and analytical toolkits: ludology and its accompanying analytical methodologies for the former and discourse analysis, New Criticism, stylistics, and narratology for the latter. While it is one of the main concerns of this project to reconcile these two seemingly divergent areas of study, this task doesn't come without challenges. The most obvious ones are terminological and conceptual. Hence, in order to facilitate reading and understanding, I have provided a glossary that seeks to both introduce and, where appropriate, repeat and condense definitions of terms that may not be familiar to either research community. Any italicized terms that are not defined in the text are defined in the glossary.

I Theory and Methodology

2   Playing with Rather Than by Rules

2.1   Introduction

This chapter aims to provide the theoretical foundation for this book. It outlines some core theories of playfulness and traces the development of philosophical thought on play and games from eighteenth-century German idealism to the present day. It examines a range of aesthetic and theoretical movements and schools since the nineteenth century that have play (with forms, norms, and conventions) at their core and use it more or less politically to innovate, protest, or revolutionize institutionalized forms of art. Among these movements are modernism, the historical avant-gardes, the *Situationists*, and various elements of structuralism and poststructuralism.

In this chapter I will look at how ludological theories and insights have informed literary criticism, particularly in the second half of the twentieth century. I shall review and critique some of the core critical writings on literary games and gameplay and contextualize them with contemporary trends in digital media, which evoke a very different notion of reader-text interaction and require a move from mostly cognitive ludicity to technologically implemented and cybernetically experienced ergodic ludicity and ludic mechanics. The chapter closes with an investigation of the two digital art forms that blend into various manifestations of literary gaming: literature born digital and (literary) art games.

2.2   Ludology and Its Philosophical Foundations

To a certain extent, play can be considered a paradigm of the modern age. It triggers creativity and innovation, subversive activities that may lead to the (temporary) reversal of power, and cultural forms of expression that may become characteristic of ethnic and national identity. That said, although the roots of our contemporary understanding of play as an essential element of human (and animal) nature and culture date as far back as the late eighteenth century, it did not enter mainstream scientific and scholarly discourses until the mid-twentieth century. More recently, the rapid growth and diversification of the gaming industry has coincided with (if not generated) a sharp increase in the awareness of the importance of play and games as constitutive elements of human nature and everyday life. This again has led to strongly ludic currents in society, such as the popularization of *pervasive gaming* (Montola, Stenros, and Waern 2009) and the *gamification* of work, education, politics, economics, health, and domesticity (McGonigal 2011).

The introduction of play as a theoretical and aesthetic concept into modern philosophy was done by Immanuel Kant,[1] who nevertheless maintained play's subordinate status to knowledge and truth, a stance that he inherited from Plato (Spariosu 1982, 22). Indeed, it is to Kant's aesthetic that we largely owe the idea that art, aesthetic judgment, and (cultivated) life are forms of play—a notion that saw its most comprehensive elaboration and systematization about 150 years later in the work of Huizinga (1962; see below). Due to Kant's contribution, "it became increasingly common to talk of play in positive terms as a form of liberation and creative fulfillment" (Pope 2005, 119) rather than in terms of a lowly activity, inferior to rational thought and serious everyday activities. Kant's concept is skewed toward fine art, the pleasure in which he brings down to the "feeling of freedom in the play of our cognitive faculties" (1911, §45; Wimsatt 1973, 358). His idea of free play between imagination and understanding, which is independent of other people's judgments, is, to Kant, a capacity shared by all human beings. Generally speaking, Kant's notion of play is a very broad one that applies to animate and inanimate things and beings, such as water, fire, muscles, and thoughts, to children's activities, and also to ethnic and other forms of ritual. Nevertheless, it appears in its most orderly fashion in fine art (Wimsatt 1973, 359).

In his aesthetical essays (*Über die ästhetische Erziehung des Menschen*, 1795/2006), Friedrich Schiller adopted the Kantian notion of art as play and developed play into an existential concept that reflected its vital importance for human nature. He emphasized the basic human need for play, also called *play drive* (*Spieltrieb*), which he considered the mediator between the *sensuous drive* (*Stofftrieb*) and the *formal drive* (*Formtrieb*). The play drive reconciles dialectical opposites of physical and rational forces, thus liberating humans from both moral and sensuous constraints and enabling them to achieve genuine aesthetic freedom. Schiller's famous insight, mentioned at the end of Letter XV, that "man only plays when in the full meaning of the word he is a man, and he is only completely a man when he plays" (Schiller 1795/2006, n.p.), therefore formed an important step toward the recognition of play as the foundation of human culture.

Friedrich Nietzsche rooted his idea of play culture in the Dionysian impulse, the purely self-interested will to power that has the capacity to both create and destroy entire civilizations (Spariosu 1982, 25). *World play*, according to him, determines the perpetual recurrence of events (Laxton 2011, 10–11). Similarly, the *Übermensch*, as embodiment of world play, also represents its most powerful player. In *Ecce homo* (Nietzsche 1908/2004, 53; emphasis in original), Nietzsche stresses the importance of irrational play, thus subverting the rationally driven concepts presupposed by Platonism and Kantianism: "I know of no other manner of dealing with great tasks, than as *play*; this, as a sign of greatness, is an essential prerequisite." Contrary to Kant and Schiller, Nietzsche's play concept is superior to reason and ethics. It is a dynamic idea that not only captures the totality of signification but, paradoxically, incorporates destructive indeterminacy as well. To Nietzsche, the entire world is defined by play because the world, to his mind, is an illusion rather than something based on scientific principles of truth (Laxton 2011, 10).

In his endeavor to develop the centrality of game and play even further than Nietzsche, Martin Heidegger (*Sein und Zeit/Being and Time*, 1927) put forward the concept of human reality as a game of being. He embraced Nietzsche's concept of the will to power as a vital prerequisite to human participation in the arbitrary, violent, ecstatic *Weltspiel* (world play), both as player and plaything (Spariosu 1989, 124; see also Slethaug 1993, 66). Placed in this agonistic, existentialist, and planetary context, the game of being is relevant to all areas of existence and affects common people's everyday lives as much as it does larger political schemes. Furthermore, the game of being is rooted in and mediated by language, which is used to construct and deconstruct human reality (see section 2.3).

Of particular importance to language and communication studies have been Ludwig Wittgenstein's studies of wordplay, in which he systematized the inextricable link between play and language. In his theory of language games (*Philosophische Untersuchungen/Philosophical Investigations*, 1953/2001), he compares language to a game of chess. He stresses that different types of chess figures take on specific functions only if the player has been initiated to their meaning and rules. These functions can be realized only in actual gameplay, depending on specific figure constellations. Put differently, for comprehensive linguistic and communicative understanding it is not enough to know the semantic meanings of words.

One needs to be familiar with the various meanings words can adopt in various situations and the social and emotive functions they may have in different contexts.

Equally importantly, Wittgenstein highlighted the difficulty of defining the word *game* because the meanings of different types of games overlap in different ways. The lack of a common denominator makes it almost impossible to identify a basic explanation that applies to board games, ball games, card games, gambling, Olympic Games, and so on. Indeed, according to Wittgenstein, games are best understood in terms of family resemblances between their various manifestations.

In *Truth and Method* (*Wahrheit und Methode*, 1960), Gadamer draws on Kant and Schiller by underlining play's vital importance to art "both in the sense of art as a playful exercise and art as lacking final goals or necessary purposes" (Slethaug 1993, 65). To him, both art and games are manifestations of play, and therefore art is less about playful structures than entertainment and spectacle. In art, the interpreter becomes the subject and the work the object of a higher-order game, which is "part and parcel of the artistic process from creation to interpretation" (Slethaug 1993, 65). This game is partly determined by rules, structures, and conventions and partly by the autonomy of play, which allows new forms and individual styles to emerge and develop.

Eugen Fink, a pupil of Heidegger's, systematized the latter's idea of play as a metaphysical foundation of human ontology. To Fink (*Spiel als Weltsymbol/Play as World Symbol*, 1960), play has three major historical and phenomenological elements: a metaphysical and ontological, a mythical or religious, and a symbolical or holistic function. In its second aspect, myth or ritual, play becomes an enhanced form of reality in which human beings imitate and thereby approximate the divine. Thus, Fink "reverses the Platonic dialectic of reality and irreality and shows that 'irreality' is in fact more 'real' than reality, because it is a mode of knowledge which comes much closer to Being than the 'natural' objects and phenomena" (Spariosu 1982, 27). The third, holistic, element sees play as a symbol of the world that doesn't imitate parts of life but "makes the Whole appear on a limited stage" (Spariosu 1982, 28).[2]

The aforementioned core philosophical concepts of play and game were synthesized and turned into comprehensive cultural studies approaches by Johan Huizinga and Roger Caillois.[3] In his groundbreaking work *Homo Ludens*, Huizinga developed Kant's and Schiller's ideas of play as the foundation of human nature and culture into a comprehensive theoretical treatise, thus sparking off the evolution of ludology as a subdiscipline of cultural studies. For Huizinga, culture emerges and manifests itself in play, a phe-nomenon whereby the latter precedes and determines the forms and shapes of the former, for instance, in religious rituals and contests. Play occurs in two main types: in a natural, primitive, irrational form, for example, in infant and animal play, and in a cultivated, cultural, rational form, which is "more distinct and articulate" (Huizinga 1962, 7) and includes sports, performances, masquerades, and other organized events. The former type produces culture (including poetry, music, and dancing), while the latter becomes a sign of culture once it has evolved.

Among Huizinga's most pervasive concepts is the metaphor of the *magic circle*—a spatially and temporally confined psychological condi-tion that players enter into when they embark on gameplay. The magic circle separates players from the outside world. It imposes its own rules and value systems that are radically different from gamers' actual worlds and that oftentimes defy even the rules of nature, such as gravitation and mortality.[4] In order to play successfully and to adapt to the rules and laws dictated by gameworlds, players therefore have to adopt a *lusory attitude* (see section 1.2). As Salen and Zimmerman (2004, 98), drawing on Suits (1990), explain, the term "describes the attitude that is required of game players for them to enter into a game. To play a game is in many ways an act of 'faith' that invests the game with its special meaning—without willing players, the game is a formal system waiting to be inhabited, like a piece of sheet music waiting to be played. This notion can be extended to say that a game is a kind of social contract." This social contract emerges from players' willing immersion into the gameworld and all the regulatory mechanisms it entails, and if the game requires more than one player to participate, such as multiplayer racing or shooter games or massively mul-tiplayer online role-playing games (MMORPGs), then this contract applies to all players and their interactions with the game and each other alike (Ensslin 2011a, 32).

Caillois' *Les jeux et les hommes* (*Man, Play and Games*, 1958/2001) both builds on and critiques Huizinga's theory of play. In his structural-ist approach to ludological forms, Caillois argues against Huizinga's over-emphasis on competition and rules in play. To reflect the diversity of manifestations play and games can adopt, he produces an often quoted classification of "games" (or rather play types) that distinguishes between *alea* (games of chance), *ilinx* (games causing "vertigo," or dizziness), *mimicry* (games of make-believe), and *agon* (competitive games). Equally importantly, he places unstructured play (*paidia*) and rule-based gaming or gameplay (ludus) on two opposite poles at both ends of a vertical axis. All four types of games can take on more or less rule-governed (ludus) and more or less arbitrary, unstructured forms (paidia). A combination of paidia and mimicry, for example, generates masquerades and other forms of playful disguises. Ludus and agon, conversely, combine a whole range of competitive sports and games, such as football, fencing, and chess.

Huizinga's and Caillois's theories were part of a historical surge in interest in play and games across disciplines in the twentieth century. Modern science, for example, began to study play both in the sense of an object of scientific examination and as a methodological tool, thus reflecting a more playful, aesthetic attitude toward its objects of study. Biologists began to see play as an important factor in processes of *hominidization* (evolutionary developments from primates to humans). Play as a tool for learning, exploration, and creativity came to be seen as either equally or, indeed, more important than work, for instance, by developmental psychologists like Jean Piaget. Game theory, a method used by applied mathematicians to study systems and effects of decision making and strategies, came to be used as a theoretical backdrop for investigations into a wide range of economic, political, cybernetic, human, and animal behaviors. It would go beyond the confines of this book to explore applications of play across disciplines in a comprehensive way. In what follows I will therefore limit myself to what is most important for this book: the application of play concepts and theories in and to art and literature.

2.3   Playfulness as Aesthetic Tool and Weapon

This section looks at a number of theories and artistic movements that have used games and play as aesthetic tools of subversion and transgression. In their most extreme forms, these theories and movements have used playfulness as a political weapon against received opinion, dominant ideologies and policies, and the institutionalization and capitalist commercialization of art.

The two movements that tend to be associated most strongly with aesthetic innovation and subversion are modernism and the avant-garde. Bürger (1984) argues against the common trend to conflate the two terms, both historically and conceptually. Modernism, in his plausible opinion, has at its core the shift in artistic emphasis from content to form. It refers to and plays with the constructedness of traditional artistic structures and goes against conventional forms of artistic expression by means of estrangement, distortion, irony, and the grotesque. Politically and historically, however, modernism did not have a proactive agenda. It was and is largely concerned with aesthetic questions and allied to institutionalized forms of representation, such as museums, concert halls, and the publishing industry. Conversely, the historical avant-garde, in its various movements (e.g., Dadaism, Surrealism, and Fluxus), saw itself and its artistic processes and products as a proactive political tool to attack art as an autonomous institution within bourgeois society. While the historical avant-gardes failed to eliminate or impede the institutionalization of art, they "did destroy the possibility that a given school [such as realism] can present itself with the claim to universal validity" (Bürger 1984, 87). Thus, avant-garde playfulness is by definition more confrontational, shocking, politically explicit, and agonistic than its modernist counterpart.

Another important concept relating to aesthetic and subversive playfulness is Situationist détournement. The Situationist International was an international political and artistic movement of the 1950s and 60s whose ideas were inspired by Marxism and early twentieth-century European avant-gardes. Two of their key aesthetic concepts and methods include *dérive* and *détournement*. Dérive literally means drifting, which Guy Debord (1958/1981, 51), a key Situationist thinker, understood to be "a mode of experimental behaviour linked to the conditions of urban society: a technique of transient passage through varied ambiences." Drifting through space without any intention to follow a certain direction or path opens up possibilities of free exploration and experimentation, of spatial and temporal free play, as it were. Détournement, on the other hand, combines the concepts of appropriation and subversion. Its most common translation, *diversion*, is somewhat ill-conceived in that the English term suggests some kind of evasive agenda. What détournement does refer to, however, is the exploration of new ways of using commodity goods and the values attached to them in the sense of "an all embracing reinsertion of things into play whereby play grasps and reunites beings and things" (Vaneigem 1967, n.p.). Thus, détournement is conceptually akin to bricolage and deconstruction (see next paragraph) and particularly suited to games and other ludic activities as tools for artistic processes of dissolution, appropriation, reassembly, and subversion more generally.

Playfulness became a particularly salient principle in twentieth-century criticism and practice. Among the most significant poststructuralist theories are Bakhtin's idea of the *carnivalesque*, Lévy-Strauss's concept of *bricolage*, and Derrida's concept of *deconstruction*.[5] In *Rabelais and His World*, Bakhtin (1984) investigates late medieval and early Renaissance forms of social play and games. During this period carnivals and fairs offered platforms for common people to protest—in disguise—against political and clerical agendas.

As Slethaug (1993, 65) puts it, Bakhtin's idea of the carnivalesque can be seen as "Heidegger as read by Marx: the 'world play' must be subjected to parody in order to create new kinds of games." Thus, art in the broadest sense of the word can use play and games as aesthetic weapons to undermine and overcome the restrictions of mainstream policies and confront them with alternative forms of expression.

Lévy-Strauss's idea of bricolage (*The Savage Mind*, 1966) refers to the skill or practice of assembling new structures from pieces found and recombined arbitrarily. These playful new combinations of otherwise dissociate elements—linguistic or otherwise—reflect a subversive attitude toward the alleged orderliness of language and other semiotic systems, as well as toward static meanings, beliefs, and identities. Indeed, bricolage in the sense of "a process of textual play, of loss and gain," which "cuts up, makes concrete, delights in the artificial," which "knows no identity, stands for no pretense of presence or universal guise for relative truth," (Flam 2003, 388) becomes the main language of criticism and aligns closely with deconstructivist principles of reading.

Particularly influential to literary criticism and practice have been Jacques Derrida's thoughts on play and game. In "Structure, Sign, and Play in the Discourse of the Human Sciences" (1978) and *Of Grammatology* (*De la Grammatologie*, 1967), he borrows Bakhtin's idea of using play and game to deconstruct hierarchies and power structures within Western society. Derrida privileges play over game, as the latter is more restrictive because of its rule-bound, structuring qualities, and therefore more prone to political and social abuse. Of particular importance in Derrida's work is his notion of free play, which he considers a key counterforce to Western philosophical logocentrism. The restrictive nature of logocentrism lies in "a belief in some ultimate 'word,' presence, essence, truth or reality which will act as the foundation for all our thought, language and experience" (Eagleton 2008, 113). According to Derrida (1978, 289), the fixity inherent in logocentric thought determines what is and isn't acceptable, thereby restraining play at its core. He replaces the idea of a center with that of supplementarity, of "infinite substitutions" of the signified that cause "movement of signification" and a dynamic, ever-changing concept of meaning.

Having examined some core artistic movements and critical theories that placed play at the heart of their pursuit of innovation, subversion, or even political upheaval, let us now move on to how ludicity in the sense of play and game concepts has affected contemporary literary culture and theory.

2.4   Games, Play, and Literature

When you read a poem, you make something different of/from/with it than the next person, just as two playings of a game may differ. (Andrews 2007, 55)

The 1960s, 70s, and 80s saw a surge of academic interest in playful literature, driven partly by the growing importance of play across disciplines and theories (see section 2.1) and partly by a tendency toward playful structures in postmodernist fiction and other literary and artistic genres (Edwards 1998). That said, the late twentieth century didn't yet see the popular ludic mood arising across Western society that we have seen in the past five to ten years. This popularization of ludicity has been driven largely by the exponential growth of the gaming industry and the concomitant changes in popular media usage.

Previous research into the so-called "games" authors play has focused mainly on print. I've put "games" in quotes here because a more suitable term for the sort of activities undertaken by readers and writers of ludic print literature is playful activities: literary play between reader, writer, and text (in various combinations depending on the type of play). As discussed in chapter 1, games are in many ways contrary to the boundless, capricious activities normally associated with literature as play. Indeed, gameplay is an extreme subtype of ludic activities, one that is highly regulated and structured (Zimmerman 2004, 159). As Wimsatt (1973, 359) puts it, "[s]ometimes we play games; at other times, as when we gambol, or romp, or swim, or walk in the woods, or yodel, or doodle, we are just playing." Yet the latter often transforms into the former as rules and conventions are introduced into initially arbitrary play, thus creating a system or mechanics for players to adhere to.

When Bruss, in "The Game of Literature and Some Literary Games" (1977, 158), mentions interaction as a necessary criterion of a "literary game," she isn't referring to the kind of interactivity afforded by games proper, either analog (board games, ball games, etc.) or digital. After all, physical interaction between reader, writer, and print text is mostly limited to turning pages, albeit multidirectionally. The main interaction that does happen between readers and writers of print literature is of a cognitive kind, and the so-called contest between those players (Bruss 1977) is nowhere near as equal as many ludoliterary theorists claim it to be. What can be said instead is that writers produce ludic texts in order to leave them as playthings for thus-inclined readers, who are then supposed to read playful meanings into them. The author-reader relationship is therefore by definition an asymmetrical one that places the author in the powerful role of the puppet master. The reader, on the other hand, while surely having "a role to play . . . [is given] a fairly passive role: to pay attention, to understand, perhaps to think . . . but not to act" (Adams 1999, n.p.).

Therefore, the "games" authors play with readers and texts do not equate to gameplay in a narrow, ludological sense. Rather, the playful readerly activities afforded and demanded by ludic print literature can be characterized in terms of cognitive ludicity, which happens primarily in readers' (and writers') minds as they interact with a text (see chapter 1). Ludic (print) literature in the traditional sense therefore does not provide the ludic mechanics (the rules, challenges, risks, actions, and rewards that form the system of the game) needed for an artifact and users' interactions with it to merit the terms *literary game*, *gameplay*, or *gaming*.

In view of the above observations, Andrews's (2007) claim at the beginning of this section seems somewhat superficial in that it attempts to bring literary reading and gameplay on an equal footing based on the observation that individual readings of both phenomena are bound to differ between individuals. They surely do, but so do readings of other media and artifacts, and the degree to which the experiences of readings vary is less dependent on the choice of medium than on the authorial agenda driving the production and reception of any aesthetic artifact, as well as the broader inter- and extratextual context of the reader. In fact, playing the same game twice is far less possible than reading the same text twice, as the structures of games inherently enable if not demand variety, plurality of choices, and exploration rather than a carefully designed trajectory. Thus, when we talk about different readings of the same text, we tend to refer to different interpretations in the sense of hermeneutic processes. Different playings of a game, conversely, tend to result in entirely different games, with outcomes as varied as winning or losing, gaining and/or losing lives, credits, and other countable units, radically different navigation options, and, as a result, a large diversity of experiences of the gameworld per se. We might say that the rules and structures of a game open up an almost infinite array of gameplay experiences, which are far more diverse phenomenologically than different readings of a standard (print) text—no matter how literary its intent.

That said, literary texts are reliant on rules and other forms of regulations as well, or else we wouldn't be able to read them. At the very least, they use human language in more or less coherent and standardized, creative, and explorative ways. Jorge Luis Borges (1943, quoted in Hutchinson 1983, viii), who is renowned for his playful, postmodern fiction, writes about the "rules" of literature as a game: "Literature is a game with tacit conventions; to violate them partially or totally is one of the many joys (one of the many obligations) of the game, whose limits are unknown." Put another way, breaking the rules dictated by linguistic and literary conventions is, to Borges, part and parcel of being a writer. Clearly, his notion of game is a lot broader than commonly agreed ludological concepts, yet what is important here is that literature has the intrinsic quality of subverting its own conventions, of experimenting with structures for the sake of entertainment (entertaining both the reader and the writer). So while the so-called rules of literature cannot really equate with those needed to play a game, the subversive spirit conveyed by playful writing finds its ludological cognate in the sort of computer games under investigation in this study, that is, art games that seek to undermine the expectations brought toward them by players in order to entertain or, rather, engage players, in a (self-) critical and/or satirical way.

Based on his research into twentieth-century American fiction, Detweiler (1976, 48–49) suggests three different types of literary phenomena where games and literature intersect: (1) playful fiction, which is characterized by "exuberance and exaggeration, that appears spontaneous and casually composed (even though it is not), that is usually funny, and that does not portray a particular game, or play a game with the reader." Print examples of type (1) include fiction by Richard Brautigan (e.g., *The Abortion*, 1971) and Donald Barthelme (e.g., "The Glass Mountain," 1970). Type (2) is fiction that features games of various types, mostly to provide an allusion to, or allegory of, the main plot, character(s), and imagery. Sports have proven to be a particularly popular focus, especially in 1960s American novels such as Robert Coover's *The Universal Baseball Association* (1968) and Joyce Carol Oates's *With Shuddering Fall* (1964). Detweiler's final category (3) is very similar to Bruss's concept of games that authors play with readers through puzzles or jokes (see also Hutchinson 1983). Examples of this type include Susan Sontag's literary puzzle *Death Kit* (1967) and Nabokov's jocular *Pale Fire* (1962). Hardly any literary artifact represents only one of the above categories but rather mixtures of two or three of them, with one tending to be more salient than the other(s).

Bruss (1977) derives the essence of what she calls literary games partly from ethological insights into the main features of play as observed in humans and other animals and partly from mathematical game theory. She breaks literary play into three types: competitive (between author and reader), collaborative (ditto), and mixed motive (a mixture of the two former types). She locates the main difference between cooperation and competition in the distinction between hint and clue, which often co-occur in literary writing and create a tension between interdependence and conflict between reader and writer. The main problem with Bruss's approach is a conceptual one: she notoriously conflates play and game, and her idea of literary game applies to literally every piece of narrative fiction. After all, the interplay between cooperation and conflict is present in most fictional works as readers have to fill semantic gaps during the reading process. It is therefore hardly surprising that Bruss herself admits at the end of her essay (1977, 170) that "[e]ven the notion of 'game' itself may eventually prove too narrow, suggesting as it does a finite set of rules, a well-defined playing space, clearly ranked preferences, and conscious calculations. Perhaps literary games will come to seem too limited and too confining in their own right." This is indeed true, considering the fact that games are a subset of play and defined by a relatively fixed set of characteristics.

In *Games Authors Play,*[6] Hutchinson (1983) develops Detweiler's (1976) and Bruss's (1977) idea of authors' play with readers through contest further: he elaborates on the competitive relationship between author and reader, or narrator and narratee. This playful agenda challenges readers to take an active part in the reading process, most typically by solving puzzles (enigma, e.g., whodunit?); by tracing parallel meanings, for instance, through allegories, metaphors, or intertextualities; and more generally by engaging critically with narrative devices, such as self-conscious, multiperson, or unreliable narrators. Again, however, games and playful activities are presented as quasi-synonymous by Hutchinson, which creates a conceptual dilemma that he shrugs off by saying, "[o]f all games known to man, those in literature would seem to rely on rules the least" (1983, 5).

Another important type of literary play is the play with and on words, which includes a range of conventional stylistic tools and is particularly characteristic of poetic language. As Prawer (1969, 71; see also Hutchinson 1983) puts it, "[p]oetry and play are closely related, and many fascinating and happy games may be played with the phonic and graphic substance of language." Yet literary wordplay, particularly in poetry, goes far beyond the confines of conventional playful poetic forms (e.g., lipograms and palindromes), figures of speech (e.g., oxymora and pleonasms), puns (e.g., homonyms and homophones), and linguistic imagery (e.g., metaphors and similes). It is the very essence of poetry to assign new meanings to words, to implement phonemic and graphemic material so as to depict extralinguistic meanings in a multisensory way, and to create nonstandard combinations and constellations of word material so as to evoke multilayered, ambivalent, and often ambiguous meanings and emotions.

Drawing on typologies of play proposed by Caillois (2001; see section 2.2), Detweiler (1976), and Spariosu (1982), we may divide literary play into different categories, although most artifacts subsumed under this term exhibit attributes that match more than one of these categories. The first and broadest category is, broadly termed, freedom, which is linked to arbitrariness and irrationality: we find random, aleatoric structures (which work on the basis of chance), for instance, in multilinear fictions and Oulipian poetry (where readers can combine the lines of sonnets in whatever fashion they like, for example). Ilinx (or vertigo) is the sort of dizziness we feel when reading such artifacts as labyrinth poems, puzzling texts ("Jabberwocky" or the Möbius strip of John Barth's "Frame Tale"), or literary installations. Mimicry (role-play) is found in texts featuring unreliable narrators (where readers have to make an effort to un-mask the identity of a liar, psychopath, or schizophrenic). Agon broadly refers to some sort of contest between reader and writer, but it can also be a contest within the text (e.g., a game of chess, which incidentally is mostly also a parallel).

Finally, and this is something I'd like to add to the debate, there is *rhythmos*, which is Greek for rule, harmony, and rational order. This comes closest to Caillois' notion of ludus and relates to artifacts in which the mechanics of rules, challenges, rewards, winning, and losing form the structural foundation of the player's activity. Nondigital examples of this type are few and far between, yet in Persian culture there is a popular parlor game called Mosha'ere, "where one player recites a line of poetry, and a second player must then recite from memory another poem in which the first letter of its first word is the same as the last letter of the last word of the line recited by the previous player. Whoever fails to come up with a fitting line is eliminated" (Milani 2008, 652). Another rare example of analog literary gaming is Uta-garuta, a Japanese card game, in which players have to speed-match poetry lines written on cards to complete a full poem. The idea of rule-based literary gameplay, which gives rise to literary games proper, forms a gap in the research literature, perhaps because the sort of literary games most people can think of are strictly speaking language or word games like scrabble, crossword puzzles, or hangman.

Against this theoretical backdrop, it is important once again to emphasize that the concept of literary gaming as used in this book refers to games proper, or elements thereof: games that exhibit specific ludic mechanics and implement them through digital technologies. These ludic mechanics can either be embedded in a (digital-born) literary work or form the basis of an art game featuring literary (poetic, narrative, or dramatic) structures and strategies. As mentioned previously, most literary games we know from print aren't exactly games in the sense of rhythmos—they may play with the rules and structures of language, but they tend not to embed literary structures in ludic mechanics or vice versa. Hence, it may come as little surprise that there hasn't been much research into literary games in the narrow sense of games featuring literary structures. It is only recently, with the evolution of digital media as a platform for artistic and creative experimentation, that true literary-ludic hybridity has begun to flourish and proliferate, and it is within this context that literary gaming can now be studied systematically.

2.5 Literature Born Digital

Digital textuality is an all-pervasive phenomenon in the twenty-first century. It captures any textual processes and products performed and received in and through digital media. When it comes to books or literary texts in the digital sphere, most people will automatically associate them with commercial trends and think of e-books, that is, books that are produced for print and have also been made available in electronic form, which allows us to read them online and/or on various types of e-readers. For the commercial publishing industry, publishing print books in this so-called paper-under-glass form is still the financially safest option, if not more lucrative than selling actual print copies, which incur printing, storage, and distribution costs.

Digital literature operates on the basis of computer code and is read on an interactive screen. This means that text becomes a fluid object that cannot be read with the same degree of phenomenological reliability as that afforded by print technologies. It is reliant on the functionalities offered by digital media, such as hypertextuality, haptic interaction, *multimodality*, and, of course, ludicity (game-ness). A term coined by Hayles (2005) to designate the dynamic, mutant nature of digital textuality and aesthetic human–machine interaction more generally is *intermediation*. The ever-morphing existence of digital texts requires new concepts of materiality and textuality that are far less bound to the hapticity of the artifact as tangible product (book and print) but inextricably connected to its medial contexts and connotations. Textuality becomes a pluralistic idea and the work of art an "assemblage" of instantiations.

Early forms of digital literature include interactive fiction and hypertext. Almost entirely text based, in the sense of consisting almost exclusively of typescript, IF and hypertext fiction are programmed or scripted in specially designed software—such as Inform for the former and Storyspace for the latter. Both depend aesthetically on the specific affordances of their individual productive and receptive platforms: IF needs a compiler to transform code into natural language and an interpreter in order to be presented as finished products that reader-players can interact with. Hypertext needs, for its representation, a browser or a specifically designed offline writing and reading tool, such as Storyspace. IF is "read" by entering commands into text windows, which trigger new text chunks and, in an ideal world, narrative progression. Hypertext, on the other hand, is based on text chunks connected by hyperlinks into networks, and readers navigate it largely by clicking on overt or covert hyperlinks. Chapters 4 and 7 will focus on hypertext and IF, respectively, in more detail.

Whereas the beginnings of IF and hypertext date back to pre-Web decades (the 1970s and 80s), the 1990s saw the evolution of web browsers and graphics editors. These developments moved previously typescript-based digital literature into the age of multi- and hypermedia. Both IFs and, in a more pronounced fashion, hypertext became audiovisual, including still and animated images and sound. By the same token, interactivity transformed from entering text commands and clicking on hyperlinked words to a wide array of possible reader actions, such as drag-and-drop, roll-over, point-and-click, and various keyboard functions. The number of functional and metaphorical uses to which the mouse and keyboard can be put has increased immensely since the early 1990s, and it is now common practice to specify the type of technology or software used by an artifact to mark its genre: for example, Flash fiction, Storyspace fiction/poetry, Twitter fiction, and CAVE poetry.

Furthermore, it is common practice among digital writers and artists to develop software tools specifically for individual artifacts and the specific aesthetic effects they are supposed to evoke. One poignant example is Kate Pullinger, Stefan Schemat, and babel's (2004) crime mystery *The Breathing Wall*, for which a software called Hyper Trans Fiction Matrix was developed that releases narrative information based on the reader's breathing rate and depth (Ensslin 2009, 2011b). It works in connection with a headset, and readers have to place the microphone underneath their nostrils to allow their breathing rate and intensity to be measured and translated into narrative information.

The Breathing Wall also shows how digital textuality, when used in aestheticized form, tends to be nontrivial in its demands on the reader. Indeed, readers are integrated in a cybernetic feedback loop which requires them to develop and use a range of receptive and interactive mechanisms that are physiological, kinetic, and cognitive, to different degrees of intensity. This idea of non-trivial text interaction in digital media is generally referred to as *ergodicity* (Aarseth 1997). If, in addition to its ergodic nature, a digital text not only integrates but, indeed, thematizes and/or problematizes (parts of) the human body, its functions, and its limitations vis-à-vis the reading task at hand, it becomes an example of *physio-cybertext* (Ensslin 2009, 2011b) and *The Breathing Wall* is a key specimen of this genre.

In the past decade, digital writers have increasingly experimented with ergodicity and ludic mechanics to see how they might be embedded in literary artifacts, and to what aesthetic effects. Whereas ergodicity emerges from a broad range of interactive utilities, ludic-mechanic design tools are used specifically to afford gaming activities such as scoring points, racing against time, hitting, shooting, or collecting objects, and other types of challenges that have to be met in order to proceed in a game. Clearly, the borderlines between cognitive and/or ergodic ludicity and ludic mechanics aren't always as clear-cut as they may seem. My analyses will therefore demonstrate the broad variety of textual manifestations of literary play and gaming ranging from minimal ludic mechanics and maximal cognitive-ergodic ludicity to its exact reverse.

2.6 Art Games versus Game Art

By the second decade of the twenty-first century, computer games have become a well-established art form represented by a global industry whose turnover exceeds that of both Hollywood and the music industry. Since the years leading up to the boom of the gaming industry and the proliferation of commercially oriented, run-of-the-mill genre blockbusters from the 1990s onward, there has also been a steady increase in independent game design and development that has given rise to a wide range of noncommercial artifacts such as art games, online adaptations and parodies of classic platform games and shoot 'em ups, serious games (for education and health), and politically and socially critical newsgames.

There is little doubt that games have to be primarily played rather than read, listened to, or watched. That said, in order to play games, classic decoding mechanisms have to be codeployed, such as reading the rules in manuals and quest directives on screen, listening to nonplayer characters give instructions and hints, and interpreting the navigational iconicity, symbolism, and indexicality of interface design. The ways in which characters and gameworlds are depicted audio-visually have an important effect on players' thoughts, emotions, and attitudes—both within the magic circle and in actual life. Indeed, it is the normalization of ludic and representational features in particular that makes for computer games' subversive potential, be it for pure enjoyment or overt criticism. By the same token, fan culture, *hacktivism* (a blend between "hacker" and "activism"), indie and art game development, and other potentially deconstructivist metaphenomena now serve as an arena for social, linguistic, and aesthetic practices drawing on, problematizing, and subverting games, gameplay, and their wider social and discursive contexts.[7]

This quasi-iconoclastic experimentalism literally *détourns* aspects of commercial game development and gamer culture, that is, it appropriates ludic structures and reassembles them into new gaming architectures and practices in playful, subversive ways. As Dragona (2010, 27) puts it, "[u]sing play as a practice to transcend rigid forms and to break constraints is a distinctive feature of today's game-based art. Artists working in the field are playing with the rules, rather than playing by rules; they modify or negate instructions, structures, aesthetics and norms, seeing contemporary gameworlds as a reflection of the contemporary digital realm."

It is indeed this nexus between art and digital games that forms the aesthetic backdrop to literary gaming as understood in this book. However, the concept of games as art used here needs to be further refined. According to Adams (2007, 257), "the vast majority of what the game industry does is not art, but popular culture. Art . . . is not sold in toy shops. But the fact that most of what the industry produces is merely popular culture does not preclude the interactive medium from being an art form." In other words, it cannot be denied that videogames as entertainment media have developed into an art form in their own right, with specific conventions, artistic styles, and awards. Nevertheless, to qualify as Art with a capital "A," they need to have some kind of artistic, critical, and/or self-reflexive agenda intended to make players reflect on their medial, textual, interactive, material (or otherwise) nature. In short, games have to be conceptualized as art in order to qualify as art games, a designation that mostly means they are not intended for unreflected mass consumption and commercial profit making. This also implies that these sorts of games tend to be produced by very small groups of developers, sometimes even just one person, with very tight budgets and a strong sense of auteurship.

As mentioned in chapter 1, art games have to be distinguished from game art, whereby the latter term denotes "any art in which digital games played a significant role in the creation, production, and/or display of the artwork. . . . The resulting artwork can exist as a game, painting, photograph, sound, animation, video, performance or gallery installation" (Bittanti and Quaranta 2006, 9). Art games, on the other hand, are "videogames specifically created for artistic (i.e., not commercial) purposes" (7). They are often humorous and/or critical, challenging, for instance, cultural stereotypes, social or political matters, or détourning aspects of the mainstream (gaming) culture in which they are embedded. They "explore the game *format* primarily as a new mode for structuring narrative, cultural critique. Challenges, levels and the central character are all employed as tools for exploring the game theme within the context of competition-based play" (Cannon 2003, n.p., emphasis in original), whereby competition itself is often manipulated, suppressed, and/or presented as a ludic fallacy.

With the exception of interactive fictions and text adventures, computer games tend to be predominantly audiovisual rather than linguistic in nature. Language is therefore far less foregrounded than in experimental forms of digital literature such as hypertext fiction. That said, recent experimental forms of art games and digital experimental literature have merged visual, ludic, and literary design techniques and materials. As showcased by *Grand Text Auto* (a pun on the name of the mainstream console game *Grand Theft Auto*), a group blog run by interactive fiction writers, digital artists, writers and theorists, indie game developers, and other aesthetic new media experts, it is part and parcel of the impulse behind the "ludic turn" to bring together "interactive fiction, net.art, electronic poetry, interactive drama, hypertext fiction, computer games of all sorts, shared virtual environments, and more" (*Grand Text Auto* 2003–2013), thereby inspiring innovative creative practices as well as critical and analytical thought.

In computer games/gaming as literary art, then, literary and poetic techniques are employed in order to explore the affordances and limitations of rules. Literary gaming (as well as other forms of art games) implements Bogost's (2007) concept of *procedural rhetoric* in that it involves artifacts—part game, part digital literature—that are persuasive: their ludic mechanics and semiotic structures are designed in such a way that they afford and demand critical, reflexive, and meditative play and seek to persuade the player, through algorithmically grounded interactions, to understand and internalize their artistic and aesthetic message.[8] In the next chapter, I shall take a closer look at these hybrid artifacts and propose a typology that is grounded partly in technological elements and partly in psychological aspects of player-reader interaction.

3 Between Ludicity and Literariness

3.1 Introduction

This chapter follows on from my earlier research into computer games as experimental literature (Ensslin 2012a), in which I have drawn up a tentative typology, or rather textual spectrum, of digital ludoliterary artifacts. Here I shall further develop and elaborate this spectrum and illustrate it with examples of the wide range of artifacts under investigation.

With games studies established as an academic discipline, scholarly debate has moved from general, or generic, theories about digital games and gaming to a second wave of research dealing with more specific ludological and analytical concerns, game genres, and individual games and franchises (see also chapter 1 for a discussion of close-play as one such analytical concern). The past five or so years have seen a proliferation of monographs and edited collections on such diverse and specialized topics as games and spatiality (e.g., Nitsche 2008; Gazzard 2012); gaming, discourse, and communication (Ensslin 2011a, Paul 2012); players and gamers (e.g., Crawford 2011; Lankoski et al. 2011); online gaming (e.g., Taylor 2006; Crawford, Gosling, and Light 2011); casual and mobile games (e.g., Juul 2010; Reichle 2012); persuasive games (Bogost 2007); newsgames (Bogost, Ferrari, and Schweizer 2010); and also specific game titles and franchises such as *World of Warcraft* (Corneliussen and Walker Rettberg 2008) and *Grand Theft Auto* (Garrelts 2006). Similarly, as outlined in chapter 2, several book-length studies on the interfaces between games and art have appeared in the past decade. They aim to document the growing cultural impact of the games industry as well as the broad spectrum and historical development of "Art" (with a capital A) inspired by and involving game development (Clarke and Mitchell 2007; Bittanti and Quaranta 2006; Catlow, Garrett, and Morgana 2010; Getsy 2011).

As discussed previously, literary gaming involves hybrid literary-ludic artifacts, some of which may be considered specific forms of either game art if they are inspired by or contain elements of ludic mechanics; others are verbal art games, and still others are simply playful, ergodic artifacts that do not involve gameplay in the narrow sense of the word. However, gameplay and reading do not exactly attract each other phenomenologically like opposite magnetic poles. In fact, *literary gaming* is a somewhat paradoxical term because literature and computer games are two entirely different interactive, productive, aesthetic, phenomenological, social, and discursive phenomena. That said, I aim to demonstrate that some qualities of literary computer games and ludic-experimental digital literature are indeed compatible, especially considering how the digital medium enables semiotic multimodality, rule-drivenness, playability, relative agency, and interactive variability in various combinations and to various degrees. Similarly, the texts under investigation in the second part of this book seek to combine reading and gaming in ways that give rise to innovative forms of reception and interaction. The aesthetic effects achieved under this remit range from fluid, nondisruptive, almost *culinary* experiences to seemingly irreconcilable clashes between different styles of media consumption and their concomitant ruptured effects on the receptive process.

In what follows, I will first introduce the psychological concepts of deep and hyper attention (Hayles 2007), which form the phenomenological foundation to the previously mentioned digital gaming spectrum. I then move on to a discussion of literary play versus literary game insofar as this dichotomy applies to digital media. The textuality and mediality of digital games will be a major focus of this discussion. I shall then go on to explore the interface between experimental digital literature and computer games and map out a continuum between ludic digital literature and literary computer games. I offer a survey covering poetic, interactive-dramatic, and fictional artifacts and genres that locates them in their respective positions on the literary-ludic spectrum. The final section of this chapter then introduces my methodological toolkit for analyzing digital, literary-ludic artifacts, which I refer to as functional ludostylistics.

3.2   Cognitive Frameworks for Reading and Gameplay

When we play games, and specifically digital games, we tend to engage in a different cognitive style than when we read books. These cognitive styles are called hyper attention and deep attention, respectively. According to Hayles (2007, 187), deep attention "is characterized by concentrating on a single object for long periods . . . ignoring outside stimuli while so engaged, preferring a single information stream, and having a high tolerance for long focus times." These single objects tend to be traditional media such as novels, paintings, radio dramas, and even films. Clearly, we can easily become fully engrossed in a book or a TV show; we may even spend entire nights reading in order to reach the end of a suspenseful novel. However, what distinguishes deep attention from hyper attention is that the latter is likely to become an artificial primary need, which is likely even to replace, or suspend, the need for food, drink, sleep, or other basic human urges. Furthermore, it "is characterized by switching focus rapidly between different tasks, preferring multiple information streams, seeking a high level of stimulation, and having a low tolerance for boredom" (Hayles 2007, 187). Although the distinction between the two cognitive styles is not as clear cut as it may seem *prima facie*, it is a useful working theory when we try to conceptualize the main phenomenological differences between reading and gaming. Videogames offer all of the elements listed in Hayles's definition of hyper attention: they tend to require multitasking, engage the player in more than one mode of information (written and spoken language, sound, still and moving image), stimulate multiple senses and physiological processes at the same time (including haptic hardware interaction), and they tend to be designed in such a way as to prevent boredom, mostly by confronting players with ever trickier challenges, faster-paced action, and more desirable rewards. In fact, in extreme (albeit rare) cases players spend days, if not weeks, suspending natural basic needs for the sake of hyper attentive (online) gameplay, which may lead to dehydration, sleep deprivation, and, in the most infamous cases, death by exhaustion and/or heart failure.

Unlike maximally immersive, mainstream blockbuster games, literary and other art games are designed so as to allow players to enter the magic circle without fully suspending disbelief or developing a permanent state of hyper attention. Instead, these games tend to make players take a critical metastance toward the artifact and their own interaction with it. Put differently, they confront players with the seemingly irreconcilable clash between hyper and deep attention, which in some cases means they have to choose between the two to either play the game successfully or close-read it to comprehend its literary forms and meanings. As will be shown throughout this book, literary computer games and ludic digital literature (as well as numerous other ludic-artistic hybrids) draw on the distinction between cognitive styles in order to expose and undermine gamers' uncritical willingness to subscribe to commercial games' textually and algorithmically encoded (racist, sexist, classist, capitalist, etc.) ideologies and the aggressive thoughts and violent behaviors they can incur.

Similarly, this clash in cognitive styles calls out for new reading and gaming strategies that facilitate both successful gameplay and in-depth close reading and approach both gaming and reading from a *metaludic, metafictional* point of view. These new strategies go beyond rereading, revisitation, and revision (cf. Ziegfeld 1989; Douglas 1994; Ensslin 2007; Ciccoricco 2007a), which we engage in, for instance, when seeking to find a sense of closure in nonlinear hypertext narratives. Indeed, literary gaming strategies involve a much wider range of literacies (Gee 2003), as well as the willingness to approach a digital artifact with a different mindset each time we start play-reading it afresh.

More specifically, while we need to activate processes of hypothesizing, gap-filling, decoding, and inferring from perceived semiotic material when we read, we additionally have to engage in complex processes of decision making, strategy development, in situ learning, navigation, orientation and exploration, problem solving, cognitive and kinetic action and reaction, as well as multimodal communication (Wideman et al. 2007; Ensslin 2011a) when we play computer games. Furthermore, each literary-ludic artifact exhibits radically different medial and interactive features, which means we have to learn not only their rules but, more generally, how to work the game-text, which includes handling hardware components (mouse, keystrokes, etc.), understanding the interface logic, and navigating the gameworld, which can range from abstract, simplistic, and pixelated 2D to highly sophisticated, spatially expansive 3D environments.

Finally, the evoked clash of hyper and deep attention is likely to cause a self- and medium-critical metastance in player-readers. When engaging with ludoliterary hybrids, we are made to reflect on the expectations with which we commonly approach both videogame play and reading, to learn about our own gaming and reading styles and preferences, and, ultimately, to become more enlightened self- and medium-critical consumers. We are encouraged to meditate on the designers' artistic agenda, the intertextual links they might wish to activate in us when we engage in literary gaming, and the interplay between form, receptive process, and textual meanings more generally.

3.3   *Viewing Axolotls*—Approaching the Ludic in Digital Literature

In section 2.4, we established that most existing theories of so-called literary gaming have in fact dealt with the broader issue of literary play in the sense of playful activities between writer, reader, and text. As Edwards (1998) explains, play not only produces and constitutes cultural productions including literature but, in fact, helps us understand the core principles at work in aesthetic processes such as choice, chance, risk, linguistic and semiotic creativity, fluidity, serendipity, difference, pluralism, and social (inter)action: "[p]lay is always already interplay, and against ideas of solitariness and singularity, fixed positions, simple binarism, privilege and truth" (xii). Hence, literature as a creative phenomenon can be equated to literary play more generally, as the latter is deeply ingrained in writerly, readerly, and textual processes.

Literary games, on the other hand, have to be seen as a highly regulated, rule-bound, and structured subtype of literary play. They are therefore not a subtype of fiction, poetry, or drama but are, indeed, a particular type of game that embeds literary elements but has conceptual and interactive emphasis on the ludic structures of the artifact at hand in addition to the aesthetic effects and processes it evokes.

Surely, one might argue that literary texts follow certain rules as well—at the very least, they are subject to the rules of language, communication, and genre. On the other hand, however, we rather tend to ascribe literariness to texts that do the exact opposite—that creatively subvert linguistic, communicative, and genre conventions in order to achieve effects of *ostranenie* (defamiliarization, see Shklovsky 1917/1998), often coupled with humor and satire. Put differently, these texts quite literally play with the conventions of language and genre, and literary play suspends the communicative and textual rules it sets out to follow.

Still, the distinction between playful literature and literary games is not as clear-cut and binary as it may appear. In fact, the affordances of digital media in particular allow writers, game designers, and artists to experiment with a wide range of expressive forms of textual interactivity. These give rise to a plethora of ludoliterary hybrids and beg the question of how, where, and by whom these artifacts are supposed to be received: alone or in groups; at home or in museums and exhibitions (online or off); by aficionados and experts of experimental art, the general public, heavy gamers, and/ or literary and art critics (to name just a few). The latter question requires a research project in its own right that would take into account the wide spread of literary-ludic hybrids documented in this book and expand this research in the direction of empirical reader-response research. For now, however, I will concentrate on the textual foundations of literary gaming.

As indicated previously, literary gaming as understood in this study spans a large spectrum of digital texts that combine literary (poetic, narrative, and dramatic) and ludic elements. *Ludic* here ranges from the kind of cognitive playfulness exhibited by ludic print literature to ludic mechanics, with the latter operating either as an element of a ludic digital "book" (fiction, poem, or drama) or as the technological implementation of the rules of a literary game proper, that is, an artifact that has to be played, first and foremost. To illustrate how both cognitive-ergodic ludicity and technologically implemented ludic mechanics may operate in a work of digital literature, I shall briefly look at Regina Célia Pinto's Flash fiction *Viewing Axolotls* (2004), which is mainly a readerly (rather than playerly) artifact yet integrates a variety of ludic techniques and mechanisms.

Viewing Axolotls is a web-based hypermedia text that remediates Julio Cortazar's 1956 short story "Axolotl." In the original print fiction, a *homodiegetic* narrator tells the story of how he (himself) transforms into an axolotl (a salamander species that does not undergo metamorphosis from larva to mature adult stage) in the course of his frequent visits to a Paris zoo. At the decisive metamorphic moment the initial homodiegesis is replaced by dual *diegesis*, as the homodiegetic narrator (now an axolotl) starts to talk from the first-person point of view about his human alter ego (in the third person). This pronominal shift simultaneously marks unification and alienation between human and animal, as the process of trying to understand the animal has been cut short by embodiment. Thus, the story can be read as a comment on both the transformative, communicative, and affiliative power of art as well as the impossibility of comprehensive understanding and closure: "It occurs to me that at the beginning we continued to communicate, that he felt more than ever one with the mystery which was claiming him. But the bridges were broken between him and me, because what was his obsession is now an axolotl, alien to his human life" (Cortazar 1956).

The digital *Viewing Axolotls* has eight main sections, one of which ("visual narrative") is an audiovisual representation of the physical approximation and transformation from human to animal. Textual interaction in this section happens via clicking on hyperlinked words or images, and it is left to the reader's discretion when to switch from one section, or *lexia*, to the next. Hence, this part of the text is a ludic digital fiction in a figurative (Andrews 2007, 56) or cognitive-ergodic sense. The play effect lies in the imaginative reworking of Cortazar's original, which includes the way the text is broken into chunks and coupled with multimodal effects such as sound (background noises resembling those of a zoo), still and animated image, and interface interaction via point-and-click. Words highlighted as hyperlinks take the reader outside the narrative: "panther," for instance, opens a text box displaying a section from Rainer Maria Rilke's poem "The Panther," which is thematically and atmospherically related to "Axolotl" and evokes a critical stance toward restricting freedom and identity expression. The reader is in control of the reading process throughout the visual narrative, and the text's playfulness is perceived through the magic realism conveyed in the original story as well as through a range of multimodal and playful-interactive elements, such as "playing" (mimicking) an avatar woman in the sense of moving her shadow around via mouse or cursor keys.

The "game" section of the text contains the only genuine ludic-mechanic element. It asks the reader to engage in an aleatoric minigame (rolling dice), and it imposes a set of rules for the player to follow that connect the aleatoric dice game with a symbolic agon against the computer. The reader must choose three axolotls in an aquarium in the right order and thereby produce the word sequence "view—fog—comprehension."

Yet another section engages readers in a playful art exercise: it allows them to draw and animate their own "view" of the story and to send the product to the author herself. This kind of playful activity clearly does not involve any ludic mechanics but rather draws on human creativity as a playful tool for expressing individuality and selfhood.

In all, the reader of *Viewing Axolotls* becomes an agent in various playful, symbolic processes, including both cognitive-ergodic playfulness and, to a lesser extent, ludic mechanics. Thematically, the text's ludicity (in the sense of both play and game) symbolizes the human-animal fusion and the transformative power of art referenced in the original verbal narrative. At the same time, the text translates these processes into references to core digital media philosophies (Lister et al. 2009) such as the bridging of actuality and virtuality and the technical imagination (Flusser 1997).

3.4   The Literary-Ludic Spectrum

As the preceding example shows, digital media afford highly complex expressive processes that make it impossible to talk about a ludoliterary artifact either as a straightforward game or a straightforward piece of literature. In fact, rather than falling neatly into generic or typological categories, ludoliterary texts exhibit various degrees of hybridity and proportions of literary and ludic elements. These textual elements are closely aligned with their phenomenological aspects (outlined in section 3.2): literary elements are more closely associated with deep attention, and ludic elements with hyper attention. The two types of attention aren't exact binary opposites but rather a matter of degree of attention. Further, as we shall see in my analytical chapters, some ludic fictions and art games deliberately prevent or critique hyper attentive gamer behavior. Experiencing them is therefore a far more complex, multilayered process than the deep vs. hyper attention distinction might suggest. In lieu of a straightforward typology, I therefore suggest a phenomenologically grounded continuum of literary-ludic hybrids spanning the full spectrum from experimental digital literature containing game-like features (ludic digital literature, also called literary end of the spectrum) to computer games with poetic, dramatic, and/or fictional qualities (literary computer games, also called ludic end of the spectrum) (see figure 3.1).

Ludic digital literature (LDL), which sits toward the left of the vertical dotted line in figure.3.1, is primarily read and foregrounds overstructured (or deliberately understructured) oral and/or written language. "Overstructured" here refers to the formalist and structuralist idea that literary and particularly poetic texts tend to exhibit specific stylistic devices, such as phonological, morphological, or syntactic patterns, that are used to emphasize a specific formal and thematic concern (dark vowels, for instance, reflecting a gloomy mood). Likewise, literary language can be deliberately plain, or understructured, again to highlight a specific writerly agenda (reflecting, for example, the language of a child or uneducated adult). However, ludic digital literature also features ludic elements, as exemplified in the previous section (3.3 *Viewing Axolotls*). *Ludic* here refers to both/either cognitive and/or ergodic ludicity and/or ludic mechanics, whereby cognitive-ergodic ludicity is placed nearer the literary than the ludic end of the spectrum than ludic mechanics. Similarly, the more ludic mechanics an LDL text contains, the closer to the median (marked by the dotted line) it tends to sit.

At the other end of the L-L spectrum, that is, to the right of the dotted line in figure 3.1, are specimens of literary computer games (LCG), which

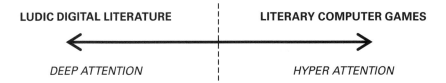

Figure 3.1
Literary-ludic continuum, combined with the spectrum between deep and hyper attention. The vertical line marks the conceptual boundary between texts that are primarily read (to the left) and those that are primarily played (to the right).

are primarily played and often explicitly referred to as games in their title or front matter. Yet they also feature some distinctive poetic, dramatic, and/ or narrative-diegetic elements, thus demanding deep as well as hyper attention and requiring close reading or, rather, close play for deep understanding, analysis, and reflection.

In what follows, I will move from the extreme left (literary) to the extreme right (ludic) of the spectrum, outlining ten types, or genres, of literary-ludic digital media and explaining why they tend to inhabit a specific place on the L-L continuum.[1] Figure 3.2 shows a schematic approximation of where I would place these ten genres on two comparative lines indexing degrees of literariness and ludicity (on a scale between 0 and 10). The graph shows roughly where the two lines meet: in literary interactive fictions and drama (see type [7] below). It also indicates that, at the time of writing, the literary side of the L-L spectrum is a lot more developed and diverse than the ludic side, and that the relative rise in ludicity strikes me as significantly steeper to the right of the median, as we move closer toward the ludic end of the spectrum.

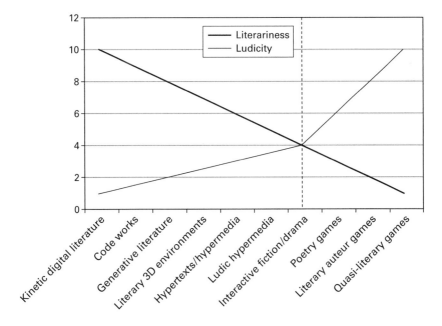

Figure 3.2
Degrees of literariness and ludicity. The vertical, dotted line (median) marks the conceptual boundary between (readerly) digital literature and (playerly) games.

(1) **Kinetic digital literature** such as Bill Marsh's *Landscapes* (2002), Young Hae Chang Heavy Industries' *Dakota* (2002), and John Cayley's *Windsound* (2001) tends to feature animated texts and comprise audiovisual text movies, which limit ludicity to a merely cognitive interaction with a text's forms and meanings.

(2) **Code works** such as Flash-based code movies (e.g., Giselle Beiguelman's *Code Movie 1*, 2004/2006) and Perl poetry generators tend to restrict ludicity to a purely cognitive play with the reader's expectations of literary conventions and the functions of source code as a purely algorithmic versus procedural and poetic stylistic tool. In some cases, such as Nick Montfort's "Computer Hat" (from *ppg256* series, 2008/2011), the performance of the text involves collecting words from a physically present audience, much like a magician's hat trick. Again, however, the playfulness lies less in the reader's actual gameplay than in active audience involvement in the text's creation.

(3) **Interactive generative literature** such as geniwate's Shockwave poem "Concatenation" (2006) and Nanette Wylde's story generator *Storyland* (v.2, 2004/2006) requires readers to take an active role in generating new poetic sequences, typically by mouse-click or mouse-over. Hence, the ludicity of these works lies primarily in the cognitive play with novel combinations of words and other linguistic sequences. However, there is no occurrence of ludic mechanics in the sense of technologically implemented, rule-based gameplay, and kinetic ergodicity appears only to a very limited degree compared to a hypertext poem, for example.

(4) **Literary 3D environments** may occur on a two-dimensional computer screen, such as Dan Waber and Jason Pimble's Java-based visual poem "I, You, We" (2005/2006), or in a physical 3D environment, such as the CAVE works created at Brown University—for example, Noah Wardrip-Fruin et al.'s *Screen* (2003). The latter requires readers to stand in the middle of the CAVE cube and physically play with words that are flocking around them: they can touch them with their hands and send them back to the walls or even break them apart. However, the text does not involve any actual ludic mechanics that would integrate the reader's actions in a gameplay environment. Ludic text interaction is therefore limited to cognitive and ergodic play.

(5) Examples of **literary hypertexts and hypermedia** include Deena Larsen's poem *Firefly* (2002),[2] Robert Kendall's poetic thriller *Clues* (2001–2008), Shelley Jackson's feminist hyperfiction *Patchwork Girl* (1995), and Richard Holeton's surrealist *Figurski at Findhorn on Acid* (2001). I shall discuss these texts and their respective ludoliterary qualities in the next chapter. Suffice

it to say here that hyperlinking and other interactive technologies make the reader part of individual text creation, which is generally perceived as authorial play with the reader and readerly, exploratory, ergodic play with the text. While it normally does not involve ludic mechanics proper, I will include a controversial counterexample of this rule-of-thumb in chapter 4.

(6) The first genre of ludic digital literature that occasionally features ludic-mechanic elements is **ludic hypermedia literature**. Works that come under this label cover a wide range of phenomena, from what have elsewhere been called *cybertexts* to texts that feature actual ludic mechanics, such as minigames, explicit game rules, challenges, rewards, and/or interface items such as performance meters. My concept of cybertext (see Ensslin 2007, 22–24) applies to digital literature that plays with the reader by giving the software code a considerable degree of control of the reception process without suspending interactivity. It refers to ergodic digital texts that are programmed in particular ways as autonomous *text/machines* (Aarseth 1997), which assume power over the reader by literally "writing themselves" rather than allowing readers to control their own trajectory. The term *cybertext* was originally coined by Espen Aarseth, who roots it in his alternative model of textual communication (1997, 21). This medium, instead of being a sign-oriented model, places the "text/machine," a mechanical rather than metaphorical concept, at the center of the communicative triangle. The text/machine is symbolically surrounded by the (human) "operator," the "verbal sign," and the material "medium" that disseminates the text. These three elements engage in a complex interplay with the text and each other, resulting in a variety of textual manifestations, depending on which element is emphasized most strongly. Consequently, readers become part of a cybernetic feedback loop, which operates on the basis of mutual stimulus and response between machine and operator. Inspired by other ludoliterary genres such as videogames and MMORPGs, cybertext writers use the latest achievements in hypermedia technology combined with a variety of plug-ins that add interactive, playful elements to the text. Examples of ludic hypermedia literature include Stuart Moulthrop's *Hegirascope* (1997), Urs Schreiber's *Das Epos der Maschine* (Machine Epic) (1998), and, more recently, Serge Bouchardon and Vincent Volckaert's *Loss of Grasp* (2010). *Hegirascope* features tightly timed links, which cause lexias to change at a rapid pace (every 18 seconds in version 1.0) without giving the reader a chance to take control via mouse-click or to close-read them. *Das Epos der Maschine* consists of autonomously moving text that appears, vanishes, expands, diminishes, and wanders across a highly interactive but simultaneously elusive interface. A close reading of *Loss of Grasp* will be offered in chapter 5.

Examples of ludic hypermedia literature that feature ludic mechanics include Kate Pullinger and Chris Joseph's episodic "digital novel" *Inanimate Alice* (2005–2009) and geniwate and Deena Larsen's ludic Flash fiction *The Princess Murderer* (2003; see chapter 6). *Inanimate Alice* features a range of minigames that have to be played to progress with the story, and *The Princess Murderer* adopts elements of game interface design to subvert aspects of game culture.

(7) The middle ground of the L-L spectrum is inhabited by specimens of **interactive fiction** and **interactive drama**. These types of ludic texts are impossible to pin down as either primarily readerly or playerly. This is because the gameworld is created almost exclusively through written text, and readers cocreate and interact with the narrative by entering commands and other language sequences in a text line that then triggers further text. Among these texts is a specific (and rather recent) type of IF that seeks to reflect on the genre's linguistic contingency and commonly underexplored poetic potential.[3] Some striking examples of such literary IFs include Nick Montfort's *Ad Verbum* (2000), which satirizes its own generic qualities and the linguistic competence and creativity of its players, and Aaron A. Reed's epic *Blue Lacuna: An Interactive Novel* (2008), one of the longest and most meditative, lyrical IFs currently in existence. A close analysis of *Blue Lacuna* will be provided in chapter 7.

An oft-quoted example of interactive drama is Andrew Stern and Michael Mateas's award-winning *Façade* (2005).[4] It operates on the basis of artificial intelligence (AI) and the ludolinguistic mechanics and cybernetic processes of interactive fiction. *Façade* follows the representational and rhetorical conventions of social or even naturalist drama, but expands the fourth wall to draw the player into the action (cf. Conway 2010). Players are required to become entangled in marital conflict by talking to the audio-visually represented protagonist couple, making suggestions as to how to improve their relationship, and mediating between them. Elusive input such as "This is none of my business" is not accepted by the parser, and the player is drawn haphazardly further and further into the argument. Players key in conversational turns to converse with the characters via keyboard, but, unlike conventional IFs, they can also use the arrow keys to navigate or use the mouse to collect and utilize in-game objects.

(8) Moving into the ludic half of the L-L spectrum, we now start looking at primarily playerly artifacts, that is, texts that have to be played, first and foremost, that clearly exhibit ludic mechanics, and that are mostly referred to as games in their titles and/or subtitles. The most prolific genre in this range has been kinetic, visual, and concrete **poetry computer games** (see

also chapter 8 for a close play of Jason Nelson's *evidence of everything exploding* [2009]). These artifacts replace—either fully or partially—the kind of graphical elements we know from standard videogames (player-characters, enemies, obstacles, and cursors) with linguistic material, or, indeed, they mix graphical and poetic-linguistic elements. In so doing, they foreground and critique players' hyper attention and replace it phenomenologically with textual material that requires deep attention for in-depth understanding and intertextual referencing.

(9) **Literary-fictional "auteur" computer games** (art games that exhibit idiosyncratic features that are closely associated with their individual designers) employ 2D and 3D audiovisual elements as their primary modes of representation but feature sophisticated linguistic elements such as quotes from the Western literary canon, verbal rather than graphical cursor devices, dramatic dialogue, interior monologues, epistolary elements, and subtextually rich dialogue patterns or poetic interludes. Examples include the semi-surreal graphical adventure role-playing game (RPG) *To the Moon* (Freebird Games 2011), Jonathan Blow's narrative-philosophical platform game *Braid* (2009), and the gothic RPG *The Path* (Tale of Tales 2009a). This last game, the literary appeal of which rests within the subtleties of its textual and metadiscursive layers, will form the analytical core of chapter 9.

As we have seen earlier in this section, the closer we move toward the outer margins of the literary-ludic spectrum, the less straightforward it becomes to identify clearly the ludic in digital literature (for instance, in the case of kinetic and generative poetry, which does not feature any ludic mechanics and exhibits a limited degree of ergodicity) and vice versa (in the case of some art games that feature almost no verbal art). On the extreme ludic side of the spectrum, we may even be able to accommodate what we might call (10) **quasi-literary games**, that is, games that represent in-game literary technologies such as books (e.g., *Myst* [Miller and Miller 1993] and *Syberia* [Sokal and Microïds 2002]) or that intertextualize and/or remediate canonical literary texts. *Tradewinds Odyssey* (Sandlot Games 2009), for instance, satirizes Homer's *Odyssey*, and the *Fable* series (Lionhead Studios 2004–2010) intermediates various medieval Anglo-Saxon epics. Indeed, intertextuality and transmediality are characteristics shared by many ludic digital fictions and literary computer games, and the more critically, creatively, self-reflexively, and satirically their intertextual origins are interwoven and referenced either explicitly or subtextually, the more "literary" they tend to appear. According to the definition of literariness introduced in chapter 1, however, only those texts that notably "play with" the rules of their own form and genre and show an artistic commitment to the written or spoken word are included in this study as far as the ludostylistic analyses are concerned.

To come to a more consolidated understanding of digital gaming and the textual features needed for an artifact to be referred to as ludic digital literature or literary computer game, I shall now introduce the analytical toolkit underlying the analyses in chapters 4 through 9. This toolkit has been induced from a large body of literary-ludic hybrids (approximately 130 artifacts) that I read/played as part of my research for this book, and its components can be understood to constitute the basic elements of digital media subsumed under the concept of literary gaming.

3.5   Approaching Functional Ludostylistics

Recent years have seen the publication of a number of book-length works on how to close-read digital literature, and digital fiction in particular (Van Looy and Baetens 2003; Ensslin 2007; Ciccoricco 2007a; Ensslin and Bell 2007; Ricardo 2009; Bernstein and Greco 2009; Bell 2010; Simanowski 2011; Bell, Ensslin, and Rustad 2014). This so-called second wave of digital literature criticism marked an important step toward recognizing the analytical-critical potential of noncommercial verbal art in the digital sphere, and helped establish the field of digital literature criticism within the larger disciplines of literary and media studies. Similarly, ludologists have produced methodological toolkits for analyzing games as ludic-textual artifacts within their wider discursive, textual, and socio-cultural contexts (e.g., Consalvo and Dutton 2006; Dovey and Kennedy 2006).

However, as games studies is branching into ever more differentiated subdisciplines, new methodological approaches are needed that are tailored to the specific artifacts at hand (see, for instance, Fizek [2012] on analyzing player-characters in computer role-playing games). While there have been a range of attempts at close-reading—or rather close-playing—ludoliterary digital media (e.g., Montfort and Moulthrop 2003; Ciccoricco 2007b; Kocher 2007; Schäfer 2009; Ensslin 2012a, 2012b, 2014b; Ensslin and Bell 2012), no comprehensive, synthetic approach exists to date that combines literary-stylistic and ludic analytical tools in a systematic fashion. Kocher's (2007) "ludoliterary cycle" probably comes closest to such an undertaking, yet her focus is simultaneously more and less inclusive than the approach taken here: on the one hand, she includes under the label "ludic forms of storytelling" not only hyperfiction—which is one of many genres on the literary side of the L-L spectrum discussed here—but also a wide range of what I would call nonliterary, commercial narrative games and virtual environments such as run-of-the-mill adventure games (*Monkey Island* or *Runaway: A Road Adventure*), interactive movies (*I'm Your Man* or *Swiss Love*), society simulations (*The Sims*), and role-playing games (*World of Warcraft* or *Baldurs Gate II*). Furthermore, Kocher does not include any poetic or dramatic artifacts, which renders her ludoliterary typology less inclusive and somewhat misnomered.

To address the lacuna left by previous research, I propose an analytical toolset called functional ludostylistics, which integrates elements of narratology, poetics/stylistics, semiotics, mediality, and ludology. In doing so, I draw on Ryan's tentative idea of "functional ludo-narrativism," which suggests a methodological framework that "studies how the fictional world, realm of make-belief, relates to the playfield, space of agency. By connecting the strategic dimension of gameplay to the imaginative experience of a fictional world, this approach should do justice to the dual nature of video games" (2006, 203). While Ryan herself doesn't explicitly flesh out this framework, she proposes a number of methodological strategies required to synthesize ludological and narratological analyses:

1. examining the "heuristic use of narrative" (Ryan 2006, 200) that relates to the ways in which game design (i.e., mechanics and narrative elements) facilitates learning, for instance, through object and level design, or training sequences and their narrative embedding;

2. looking at the ways in which narrative elements and strategies feature in videogames, such as game scripts, action sequences performed by players, noninteractive narratives (cut scenes, text boxes, voice-over back stories), narratives used as rewards (cut scenes, clues, unlocking new levels/storyworlds), nonplayer character (NPC) narratives, and player narratives;

3. investigating narrative structures, such as the storylines in games of progression (Juul 2005), *embedded narratives* (Jenkins 2004), and narratives of emergence (Salen and Zimmerman 2004);[5]

4. analyzing how the player is embedded dynamically in the *story arc*, for instance, through a first-person avatar, its biography, and its psychological framework;

5. examining what type(s) of plot a game exposes, including epic (event and protagonist-centered), tragic (relationship and conflict-centered), and epistemic (mystery and solution-oriented) plots (Ryan 2008);

6. comparing the fictional world with the rules of the game, for instance, through object interaction and its meaning in relation to the gameworld and mechanics;

7. closely related to the previous point: focusing on the relative coherence between rules and narrative, and whether the narrative helps the player

understand and learn to master the rules, moves, and actions required to succeed;

8. and evaluating the extent to which the actions and events produced by the rules tie in with the logic of the fictional world in which they are embedded.

Clearly, this list applies only to a limited range of videogames, namely those that come with a solid narrative framework (such as adventure games and RPGs). It excludes games with more abstract interfaces and representations, such as *Tetris* or *Bejewelled*. It also neglects poetry games, as outlined in the previous section, and more generally the complex multimodal, literary-linguistic structures exhibited by literary computer games and ludic digital fiction. My own analytical approach, which I've defined as functional ludo-stylistics, builds on Ryan's catalog while also widening the potential range of primary texts from purely narrative games to games (narrative, abstract, and poetic) that integrate verbal art and digital literature (of any genre) that features ludic structures. As shown in table 3.1, I suggest four main analytical components for this framework: (1) ludology, which analyzes ludic mechanics such as rules, gameplay, game architecture, victory and termination conditions, risks and challenges, feedback, agency, and game genres (see Adams 2010), but also types of play from paidia to ludus and from ilinx to rhythmos (Caillois 2001); (2) ludonarratology, which studies aspects of in-game narrative (which applies to poetic and dramatic as well as narrative games), game-story relationship, and external narrativity;[6] (3) ludosemiotics, which examines aspects of interface design, verbal language, text and discourse, procedural rhetoric (Bogost 2007; see chapter 2), and multimodality; and (4) mediality, which looks at technological, material, and medial elements such as platform, hardware, software, ergodicity (nontrivial interactivity), and textuality, that is, the ways in which the text at hand interrelates to other texts and media. Of particular importance for ludoliterary analyses are the stylistic components of this scheme, which are listed under "verbal language" and relate to segmental and supraseg-mental linguistic structures inherent in the poetic, narrative, and dramatic language used in individual texts.

What is important about literary gaming and its various textual manifestations is the fact that experiencing them involves a complex array of ludic, narrative, semiotic, and medial elements. Similarly, every ludoliterary artifact requires for its analysis its own idiosyncratic selection of tools from this menu. As we shall see in the following chapters, the ludostylistic toolkit does not work equally well with all types of so-called ludic digital literature. More specifically, those ludoliterary texts that do not exhibit any

Table 3.1
Tabular overview of functional ludostylistics.

Component	Aspects	Examples
Ludology	Rules	Game mechanics; aims and objectives; tools and methods
	Gameplay	Player actions, moves, and hardware/ software interactions
	Game architecture	Level structure; progress
	Victory and termination conditions	Winning and losing; number of lives; game ending
	Risks and challenges	Threats; dangers; obstacles; difficulty levels
	Feedback	Rewards; penalties; feedback code
	Agency	(Illusory) player agency; freedom; sandboxing; choice
	Game genre	For example, platform, shooter, adventure, role-playing
	Types of play	Paidia, ludus; agon, mimicry, ilinx, alea (Caillois 2001), rhythmos
Ludonarratology	In-game narrative	Game/storyworld (settings, props); points of view; showing vs. telling; player-character/avatar; cutscenes; backstory; voice-over; NPCs; plot types
	Game-story relationship	Coherence; consistency; narrative level design
	External narrativity	Player narratives, for example, playthroughs, walkthroughs; metaleptic narratives; transmediation
Ludosemiotics	Interface design	Graphics; art work; gameworld; 3D/2.5D/2D; settings and props; menus
	Verbal language	Written vs. spoken; foregrounding; stylistic considerations: poetry—prose— dialogue; segmental and sentential levels of linguistic analysis
	Text and discourse	Textual macrostructure; linearity; discursive and social embedding; context and subtext; pragmatics (speech acts, implicature, etc.); themes, topics, and argument structure; cohesion and coherence; monologue vs. dialogue
	Procedural rhetoric	Algorithmic encoding of rhetorical purposes (e.g. educational; polemic; religious; see Bogost [2007])
	Multimodality	Semiotic modes other than language (image and sound) and their relationship with linguistic elements; clusters; complex meanings and their social and aesthetic embedding; haptic interaction

Table 3.1 (continued)

Component	Aspects	Examples
Mediality	Platform	PC; console; mobile device; online/offline; data carrier
	Hardware	Keyboard; mouse; controller
	Software/program code	Flash; Shockwave; Java; HTML; php; C++ . . .
	Ergodicity	Nontrivial interactivity (Aarseth 1997) caused by specific coding mechanisms
	Textuality[7]	Self-reflexivity; remediation; intermediality; paratextuality; transmediation; and other intra- and intertextual processes

ludological elements in the sense of ludic mechanics (rules, gameplay, risks, challenges, rewards, and feedback) cannot, strictly speaking, be close-played using ludostylistics proper. They may well invoke playful readings and be analyzed using aspects of mediality, multimodality, narratology, stylistics, and even types of play, yet they fall short of the literary gaming concept as proposed in this book. The following analyses (chapters 4 through 9) will showcase ludostylistics in action and demonstrate in a replicable way the extent to which the ludostylistic toolkit can be applied to a multitude of ludic digital texts.[8]

II Analyses

4 "The Pen Is Your Weapon of Choice": Ludic Hypertext Literature and the Play with the Reader

4.1 Introduction

This first analytical chapter examines a specific type of digital literature which has often been described as "play(ful)" (e.g., Fauth 1995; Morgan and Andrews 1999; Millard et al. 2005) and/or (being like) a "game" (e.g., Fauth 1995; Luce-Kapler and Dobson 2005; Rustad 2009; Bell 2010). Literary, or "serious" hypertext, as it is often called, is one of the earliest genres of digital writing. Its beginnings date back to the late 1980s, when media-savvy writers and scholars turned their attention to burgeoning home computer technologies and started exploring how and to what degree hypertextuality might be exploited for writerly and readerly (or, in Landow's [1992] terms, *wreaderly*) purposes.[1] This happened even before the launch and popularization of the World Wide Web in the early to mid-1990s. Early offline technologies for producing and receiving hypertext fiction and poetry include Storyspace, Intermedia, and Hypercard, and some of them are still in use today. More recently, however, hypertext fiction and poetry have been produced almost exclusively for the web, and access to these works tends to be open.

It is hardly surprising that of all digital media technologies, hypertext comes closest to the printed book. In its purest form, it consists of typescript and allows only a limited scope of ergodic interactivity. This interactivity is mainly restricted to the ways in which text chunks (lexias) are hyperlinked into complex textual networks, and the nonlinear aesthetic it gives rise to both puzzled and fascinated an entire generation of scholars and writers, mainly in the 1990s and early 2000s.

It is mainly due to hypertext literature's subversive and nonculinary aesthetic that this form of digital writing has never reached a popular audience. In this sense, it is akin to print texts, from Sterne to Saporta, that defy closure and challenge readers formally and thematically. As Bruss (1977, 155–156) puts it in her own terminology, these literary games are disconcerting to those who approach them looking for mimesis, emotive force, or formal beauty, [and therefore] they are often described in negative terms: antiliterature, antipsychologism, nonsense, eccentricity, shapeless and incoherent. And some games do deliberately frustrate "positive" expectations . . . : Borgesian fragments, Robbe-Grillet's "pointless" expositions, the slippery metamorphoses of Nabokov, and the autodestructive paradoxes of Queneau become suddenly less disconcerting when viewed as interaction rather than as eccentric objects.

What I seek to demonstrate in this chapter is the extent to which hyperfictions and hyperpoems can be regarded as literary games. I argue that, with very few exceptions (see section 4.5), literary gaming in the sense of operating ludic mechanics does not actually happen when reading hypertext literature (see also Koskimaa 1997/1998). Instead, readers engage in a highly complex form of cognitive-ergodic playfulness, which can take various forms and have diverse aesthetic effects. As I will argue methodologically, many core elements of ludostylistics cannot be applied to these texts, which places them closer to the literary than the ludic end of the spectrum, not least because the texts prevent any form of hyper attention.

To show how various theoretical concepts of play (rather than game) apply to select hypertexts, I offer four close readings, each focusing on one type of play as proposed by Caillois (2001).[2] Deena Larsen's hyperpoem *Firefly* (2002) exhibits aleatoric playfulness; readers of Richard Holeton's *Figurski at Findhorn on Acid* (2001) are exposed to a surrealist form of ilinx; the subtle workings of mimicry are at play in Shelley Jackson's *Patchwork Girl* (1995); and Robert Kendall's *Clues* (2001–2008) exemplifies agon in the form of enigma. The chapter will close with a discussion of where these texts are located on the literary-ludic scale, and for what reasons.

My analyses cover the following elements of the ludostylistic toolkit (see table 3.1): from the ludological "drawer," I use agency and types of play. Since these texts aren't games in the narrow sense of the word, they do not contain any of the other ludological elements that could be taken into consideration, with the exception of Kendall's *Clues* (see sections 4.5 and 4.6). Ludonarratologically, I examine the storyworlds that form the narrative settings of the texts and how these physical and psychological backdrops match the texts' formal properties. I look at who speaks, and to whom, and how the narratives are interwoven with the hypertextual structures and playful readings they evoke. The ludosemiotic drawer will provide me with tools for analyzing the texts' multimodal interfaces, as well as some of their key verbal and discursive structures. Finally, the medial analysis will comprise aspects of platform, hardware, software, ergodicity, and textuality. In the readings I offer it will become clear that most of these aspects are interlinked, so while my enumeration may appear like a checklist, analytical reality requires a far more synthetic approach.

4.2 Alea: Deena Larsen's *Firefly*

"A tale told in 180 degrees of separation," Deena Larsen's online Flash-based *Firefly* (2002) is a lyrical poem telling a personal story, or rather reflection, of loss, memory, and loneliness from an agendered lover's first-person point of view. In select verses of the largely arbitrary reading puzzle, as well as the final lexia of the poem, the reader learns about the likely reason for the speaker's solitary musings: unrequited love vis-à-vis a male companion, or lover, to whom the speaker refers pronominally either in the communal "we" form or the aloof third person, "he":

Silence between us occupies
eons as he signals again
in my breath's absence
I do not know how
to answer him

This pronominal ambiguity causes a referential tension between addressivity (in the case of the collective first-person plural pronoun) and narrative distance (in the case of the third-person singular pronoun). This tension is reflected in the poem's subtitle, "180 Degrees of Separation," which references both a straight connecting line between speaker and addressee and oppositionality between the two poles, or ends, of the same line, which separates them from each other.

Metaphorically, the addressee is represented as the eponymous firefly, a symbol of hope and human warmth but also of vulnerability and ephemerality. The illustrative stanza in figure 4.1 can therefore be read as an allegory of the unhappy love story the speaker relates in the personal narrative, where the object of love is metonymically represented in terms of "wings trembling" and a "dark body fl[ying] off toward other lights."

On clicking the directional arrow in the sixth stanza (shown in the bottom right-hand corner of figure 4.1), the reader reaches the final lexia, which cannot be played with or modified but rather reveals the communicative and emotional dilemma underlying the speaker's frustration: "For what he has to say is not for me." This closing sentence expresses the idea underlying the whole poem: no matter how we combine and reassemble verses into stanzas, the central meaning we are trying to retrieve, personified by the firefly-man, will remain obscure and elusive.

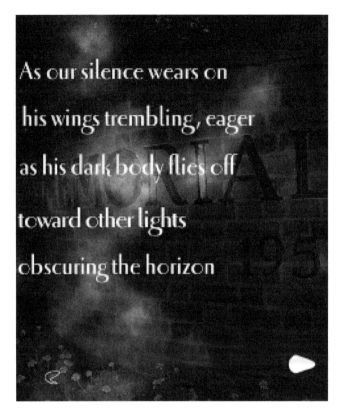

As our silence wears on

his wings trembling, eager

as his dark body flies off

toward other lights

obscuring the horizon

Figure 4.1
Screenshot from *Firefly* (Larsen 2002).

The poetic text is set against a photographic background depicting a series of images of a memorial site. The reader does not learn about the exact geographical location or symbolical meaning of the memorial and is therefore led to link it multimodally to the speaker's reflexive musings. The green shading of text and background suggests a sylvan environment—the most common habitat of fireflies, as well as a popular retreat for lyrical poets.[3] The allegorical insect greets the reader in the form of an animated word (*firefly*) in the poem's opening lexia, fluttering about the screen before it settles in the same navigational position as the green arrows in the remaining lexias (figure 4.1). It is thus a likely reference to the speaker's physical inspiration for the poetic monologue—a nightly encounter with the insect that has triggered associations with a lost lover. Yet the buzzing, fleeting movement also reinforces the text's playful, aleatoric atmosphere.

In its formal approach, *Firefly* is, according to Larsen (2008), "a 'true' hypertext in that it cannot be read linearly." Although the reader has the option of moving from stanza to stanza without modifying them, the poem's lyrical and narrative depth emerges only through activating alternative lines in a quasi-arbitrary rather than linear fashion. Thus, reader agency is limited to mashing up lexias; the directionality of the text, however, is preprogrammed and cannot be altered in the reception process. In this respect, *Firefly* can be considered an intermedial reference to Raymond Queneau's Oulipian *Cent mille milliards de poèmes* (A Hundred Thousand Billion Poems) (1961), a print-based, cut-up sonnet cycle inviting the reader to combine individual lines of each poem so as to form a potential whole of 1,014 different sonnets.

As the author describes, *Firefly* is "a poem 6 lines long with 5 stanzas. However, each line is also 6 lines 'deep.' Click on the line to uncover ulterior meanings" (Larsen 2008). By "deep" and "ulterior," Larsen means the alternative semantic meanings and aesthetic effects underlying and caused by each displayed line, which can be swapped with the other five options by exploratory and playful clicking. Since readers cannot predict the effect that their new combinations of lines will have on the meaning of each stanza, their play with poetic forms and meanings is based on chance and can therefore be compared to a metaphorical rolling of dice, or alea (Hutchinson 1983, 6; Detweiler 1976). The ludic element of *Firefly* is therefore less a built-in input and output mechanism than a subtle, subtextual expectation formed by readers as they engage in playful, interpretive interaction. Finally, the process of constructing, or rather selecting, their own personalized narratives out of the combinatory material has a meditative effect, which in turn parallels the speaker's mindset. Thus, deep reader attention gradually turns into a flow-like state (Csikszentmihalyi 1990) that focuses readers' minds on the meditative qualities of the text without allowing them to develop a hyper-attentive cognitive style.

4.3   Ilinx: Richard Holeton's *Figurski at Findhorn on Acid*

This section looks at a hypertext that instantiates Caillois's (2001) notion of ilinx, or vertigo, which is in other words a form of youthful, paidiac play with the reader that involves physical or metaphysical forms of dizziness, confusion, or bemusement. Hutchinson (1983, 6) sees "a sense of 'vertigo' in works where the reader is subjected to constant attempts to surprise, puzzle or confound him." Techniques used to achieve such effects may include, for example, *metaleptic* intrusions of characters into the *extradiegetic* world of the narrator (as in Flann O'Brien's *At Swim Two Birds*). Yet even a simple pun can cause temporary confusion or bemusement, particularly when it is integrated in a text that plays with language more generally. In Lewis Carroll's *Alice in Wonderland*, for example, the Mouse tells Alice that "Mine is a long and sad tale!" Alice misunderstands "tale" in terms of its homophone "tail" and imagines the Mouse's story in the sense of words formed typographically into a mouse's tail.

The experience of reading literary hypertext has often been described negatively in terms of "cognitive overhead," "serendipity," or being "lost in hyperspace" (Conklin 1987; Kuhlen 1991), or, more positively, in terms of "uncertainty, anticipation and curiosity" (Cuddon 1999, 883). Leaving aside any value judgments that tend to accompany both positions, the confusion and bewilderment resulting from hypertextual nonclosure and nonlinearity can be considered a generic feature of this type of writing. Feelings of ilinx are therefore ingrained in the medium itself and form part of readers' expectations when embarking on a reading "session" (Rosenberg 1996).

That said, some literary hypertexts set out to evoke particularly strong feelings of ilinx by adding to the formal structure specific semantic elements that further augment readerly confusion and bemusement. A prime example of this double ilinx is Richard Holeton's surrealist Storyspace hypernovel *Figurski at Findhorn on Acid* (2001). The narrative involves three protagonists (the convict Frank "Many-Pens" Figurski, who has killed his PhD supervisor, Professor Quentin Kingsley; The No-Hands Cup Flipper Nguyen Van Tho; and the journalist and double-crossdresser Fatima Michelle Vieuchanger), three locations (Findhorn, Scotland; Port St. Lucie, Florida; and the *Star Trek* Holodeck), and three objects (Spam, LSD, and a Mechanical Pig), and is organized temporally in terms of a timeline. The tripartite structure (character—place—object), which is reflected in the title, is curiously reminiscent of the way most digital games are structured—in terms of units (characters and props) and settings. However, this does not mean that readers are exposed to ludic mechanics proper. Nor does the relatively high level of agency afforded by the hypertext structure translate into meaningful narrative choices. Rather, readers are made to navigate the text in a playful, open-minded way that allows for surprises at various levels of storytelling. Individual reading paths often end abruptly without going into narrative detail. They seem generally disconnected semantically (a textual representation of the reference to "Acid" [LSD] and similar hallucinogenic drugs), and despite readers' committed attempts at creating a coherent mental image of the text, they will almost inevitably be disappointed (Bell 2010, 150).[4]

As I have pointed out elsewhere (Ensslin 2007, 89), starting with one of the three major characters is perhaps the most insightful approach to reading *Figurski*, as readers learn about the characters' biographies, their motivations, and, most important, their obsessive relationships with the Mechanical Pig. The three protagonists compete to take possession of this proto-robotic automaton, whose symbolic and subconscious significance is only gradually revealed to the bemused receiver. During the protagonists' final encounter in 2000 at Findhorn, they inadvertently "merg[e] into different components of the same character, taking on aspects of one another's personality" (3.2.01). Subsequently, all three are presented on the Holodeck in an ultimately permutational form, swaying between egos and alter egos, between actual and model identities. Figurski becomes Ted Streleski, on whose murder case he modeled his own, Nguyen transforms into his master cup flipper, Eugene Zanger, and Vieuchanger experiences the bewildering feeling of physically turning into a man (rather than simply cross-dressing as one—who pretends to be a woman).

Beginning with the time element, the reader is presented with a timescale of actual historical and biographical events that convey the contrived and ambiguous sense of reality underlying the narrative. In the course of the reading process, it becomes clear that many features are interconnected via psychoanalytically conceived associations that, more often than not, surface in surrealistic, traumatic, utterly nonsensical actions on the part of the protagonists. The historical story unfolds over a period of several years, starting in 1993 and directly succeeding Figurski's release from prison. He finds the mysterious Mechanical Pig on a beach near Findhorn, Scotland,[5] unaware of its material and historic value and of the fact that two malicious antagonists (Nguyen and Vieuchanger) are feverishly tracking the antique. This realistic narrative ends in December 2000, that is, shortly before the publication of the hypertext. This date marks the final meeting of the main characters in order to reassemble the previously disassembled original Pig, the parts of which they have equally distributed among themselves.

Figurski embeds multimodality in subtle ways. Graphics and photographs mostly illustrate elements mentioned in the text, as well as adding comic, surprising pastiche features to the novel (e.g., the Wing Tips onlineshopping commercial, [034]). However, pictographic and photographic elements only occasionally carry their own, isolated meaning. In the majority of cases, they are employed intersemiotically to underline concepts featured elsewhere in the novel.

In terms of textuality, *Figurski* contains a wide range of text types underscoring individual characters' backgrounds and activities. It combines fictional prose with dramatic dialogue and poetry, as well as nonfiction texts such as email exchanges, oral conversations (in Scottish youth slang), and conference abstracts (Bell 2010, 151). This seemingly random array of genres adds to the ilinx effects of the novel as unsuspecting readers are left wondering how to jigsaw them together into a coherent textual ecology—before they come to realize that coherence is the last thing they should worry about. By the same token, the "staccato style of the narrative" (Bell 2010, 153) is likely to produce humorous effects as it evokes intertextual links to various Monty Python productions (Eastgate Systems 2008). The text's playfulness therefore derives from its surrealist conceptual and formal design, which is intended to confuse and bewilder its readers, thereby evoking a feeling of mental vertigo.

4.4 Mimicry: Shelley Jackson's *Patchwork Girl*

In its most straightforward uses, mimicry, or *mimesis*, as a ludic principle refers to various types of imitation, exhibition (Huizinga 1962), and simulation (Caillois 2001; see also Detweiler 1976). Most typically, this involves the iconic or symbolic representation, emulation, recursion, or repetition of textual content in the formal structure of an artifact, or vice versa. Chess, for instance, not only is an agonistic interaction between two players but also operates on a mimetic level "as sublimated [symbolical] warfare" (Detweiler 1976, 59). Perhaps the most obvious form of mimicry in print literature happens in so-called concrete, or visual, poems, such as Eugen Gomringer's "silencio" (silence, 1954). The piece consists of five lines, each depicting three instances of *silencio* except for the middle line, which omits the second instance of the word, thus creating a gap at the very center of the poem. This can be read as a moment of poetic silence, or more symbolically as a welcome moment of peace in a world flooded with telecommunications and noise.

Hypertext as a formal principle has often been described metaphorically in terms of a labyrinth (of possible pathways through the text; e.g., Keep, McLaughlin, and Parmar 1993–2001), a spider's web (of links in which it is easy to get lost; e.g., Millon 1999, 89), or a patchwork quilt (of patches, or text chunks, sown together into a fragmented whole; Dicks et al. 2005, 170). It is the latter image that lies behind the main theme of Shelley Jackson's cyberfeminist hyperfiction *Patchwork Girl; Or, a Modern Monster* (1995). The work is a feminist take on Mary Shelley's gothic novel *Frankenstein; or, The Modern Prometheus* (1818/1998). It features "Mary Shelley herself" as narrator, telling the story of her own female monster, which is constructed by readers of the text—literally by "sewing together" text chunks into a subjectively coherent, albeit open-ended, whole. The monster embarks on an adventurous journey of spiritual maturation and physical decomposition in the "a story" chapter. That said, this mostly linear element of the novel contrasts with four other chapters ("a graveyard," "a journal," "a quilt," and "broken accents") that are nonlinear in concept and structure and provide the reader with material for assembling the monster's body by symbolizing the text in the mind.

Jackson uses Eastgate's Storyspace software for the writing and reading environment, which carries with it a specific aesthetic that keeps the text self-contained, that is, without any external links. The text is represented in Storyspace's characteristically small, mostly typescript-based windows, or lexias. It contains some pictographic devices, the most important being a body map in the "a graveyard" chapter of the chaotically assembled, eponymous female monster, whose individual body parts are graphical links to the life stories and tragic deaths of the deceased women to whom they used to belong. This map lends the metaphorical, quilted text-body iconic form and readers are invited to assemble the body by clicking on its various parts. The "scars" (Seidel 1996, quoted in Landow 2006, 239) holding the limbs together in a makeshift way visualize the hyperlinks loosely connecting the text patches in readers' mental representations of this narrative. The fact that the scars gradually dissolve in "a story" serves as an allegory of the fluidity of narrative meaning in hyperfiction as well as of female writerly identity in cyberspace.

More generally, hypertextual structures are used in *Patchwork Girl* to mimic and subvert the Frankensteinian idea of the composite, synthetic body that, in the original print novel, reflects human fears of the unpredictable, destructive powers of modern science. More specifically, Jackson's feminist transmediation of Shelley's text transfigures the monster from male constructedness and fixity to feminist deconstruction. In so doing, Jackson highlights the positive, liberating powers of *écriture féminine* in the imaginary environments of cyberspace, the ideal abode and ultimate postmodern frontier of contemporary feminist writers (Ensslin 2005, 2007).

The patchwork metaphor runs through the text, which literally pieces together quotations from a plenitude of sources "in an intuitive, crazy-quilt style" [sources].[6] These sources are both fictional and theoretical, the former mostly intertextualizing Shelley's *Frankenstein* and the latter drawing on a range of feminist and deconstructivist critical writings, such as Derrida's *Dissemination* (1983), Shaw and Darling's *Female Strategies* (1986), Walker Bynum's (1991) *Fragmentation and Redemption: Essays on Gender and the Human Body in Medieval Religion*, and Miller's (1986) *Poetics of Gender*.

The author's central concern is the symbolical corporeality of hypertext. Its pastiche-like and multilayered form mimics that of a Frankensteinian monster patched together: "[e]ach patch in Jackson's quilt is composed of various other patches, various other texts, from theoretical to fictional, from pop cultural to hearsay, sewn together to form either a sentence or paragraph" (Raz, quoted in Landow 1997, 199). Hypertext, according to Jackson (n.d.), represents "the banished body. Its compositional principle is desire. It gives a loudspeaker to the knee, a hearing trumpet to the elbow . . . . Hypertext is the body languorously extending itself to its own limits, hemmed in only by its own lack of extent. . . . You could say that all bodies are written bodies, . . . all lives pieces of writing." This allegorical remit suggests parallels to social constructionism and the way in which people, and particularly women, construct their identities on the basis of media representations of idealized female bodies, and the resulting peer pressure relating to ideal female performativity (Butler 1990). Jackson's hypertext offers an alternative to this commodifying, self-destructive body image by showing how a specific textual principle allows (female) writers and readers to mimetically construct and deconstruct text and body, thus forming fluid, dynamic, and, therefore, liberating images of corporeal subjectivity.

In terms of ludicity, the text plays with various levels of representation and symbolism and invites readers to engage creatively with its nonlinear structure, thus forming different yet mutually complementary readings in each reading session. Readerly agency is limited to clicking links, albeit in any order, and to forming mental representations of the text in any given sequence and combination. Nonetheless, *Patchwork Girl* is not a literary game as such because it refrains from displaying or implementing any rules, rewards, or other ludic-mechanic structures, not least because the resulting rhythmos would ruin the deliberate openness and fluidity that the text offers the reader.

4.5   Agon: Robert Kendall's *Clues*

A striking case of literary play dominated by figurative agon (contest, or "cooperative conflict," between author and reader; see Hutchinson 1983, 1; Detweiler 1976) is Robert Kendall's poetic hypertext detective fiction *Clues* (2001–2008). It sends its readers on a mystery quest, which audio-visually suggests a standard noir detective thriller. Yet the text itself turns out to be a largely self-reflexive, metafictional piece of nonlinear writing focusing on its own textuality and the reader's interaction with it.

The literary investigation takes place multimodally, as image, sound, and some elements of text work together to reveal information about the allegorical setting of the mystery and the musings of the narrator. The thus-depicted setting superficially evokes the atmosphere of a typical Hollywood noir movie: labyrinthine corridors through buildings, dilapidated suburban alleyways, a mysterious park, suspicious (yet often meaningless and noninformative) characters, and objects (e.g., a car, a wastepaper basket, a letter, a gun, a wall painting). While one would normally expect these objects to yield evidence and the characters to hold information, or clues, this is not necessarily the case here. Red herrings seem to be just as common as actual clues, and collecting them randomly will almost inevitably lead to playerly failure. The soundtrack, which is reminiscent of Hitchcock films, creates an eerie atmosphere, augmenting the impression of there being an actual murder to solve—an impression that turns out to be false.

In terms of narrative discourse, the reader enters into a virtual dialogue with the text through second-person address. Apostrophes like "Want me to fill in blanks for you?" and "If there's really a 'you,' what about the 'I'?" blur the ontological boundaries between text world and real world (see also chapters 6 and 9) and place the reader-narratee in a fictional conversation with a narrator who seems omniscient with respect to the crime (or whatever else forms the core of the enigma) and exposes the reader's ignorance and naivety. On the other hand, however, the narrator confronts the reader with the question of the ontological status of narrator and narratee and whether the apostrophic addressee is a "[r]eal person" or is simply used as a "[r]hetorical device."

Clues frames itself discursively as a "game" and does meet a range of ludic criteria while still maintaining its emphasis on digital literariness. The prologue encourages the reader to "Play the words. / Crack the text. / Win the game," thus suggesting some sort of word game, crossword, or encoded message. Similarly, the entry page provides a link to "the Game" and "the Rules." The former opens a text window that tells readers that they can save their reading at any time by returning to this page. This is facilitated by a specific software called Connection Muse that tracks reading history and allows readers to continue where they left off previously. This function is reminiscent of saving a player's current position and level in a videogame. The paradoxical "Rules" lexia disappoints reader-players' expectation of encountering gameplay proper by explaining that "[t]here are no rules" and subverting the apparently negative connotations of the word *rules* thus: "Well, perhaps there are, but 'rules' is such an ugly word, isn't it? Let's just say there are no rules except those of communication, knowledge, and identity. What I present to you here instead is an offer, an invitation—just a few suggestions in terms I'd like to think you can't refuse." Thus, the authorial narrator, adopting the perspective of an *implied author*, introduces literary play as a voluntary cognitive-ergodic pleasure to which readers may or may not willingly submit themselves. If they do, the text is likely to reward them with complex and possibly humorous layers of meaning; if they don't, they will not lose the so-called game, but they will not gain anything from their interaction with the text, either. This strategy places the text firmly within the tradition of literary agon—the competition between author and reader as outlined by various ludic print literature scholars (e.g., Detweiler 1976; Hutchinson 1983)—particularly in relation to novelistic, self-referential tendencies since *Tristram Shandy* and *Don Quixote* as well as literary whodunits. The agon featuring in these works is based on readers' communication with the text and the knowledge structures they form by inferring and guessing, using the clues provided by the textual puzzle.

The hypertext structure provides an element of choice and decision making, which is an important aspect of gameplay proper. Readers can click on doors to enter rooms and obtain clues. However, they will discover during the reading process that any narrative devices such as setting, props, plot, and character are purely figurative devices for self-reflexive reading and poetic communication and that "The pen is your weapon of choice," as the text tells them. The true riddle therefore lies in interpreting the text's metafictional and metapoetic layers of meaning and rediscovering one's own role in the literary communication process.

Similarly, the reader's search for referential meaning is duly penalized: On clicking a pop-up human face, for instance, an error message appears (figure 4.2) that reprimands readers for looking for embodied characters rather than appreciating the poetic reflexivity of the text. Readers are thus once again admonished to use their imagination to create links between self-referential and figurative meaning and to appreciate the poeticity of the text itself rather than look for a good story or a coherent narrative gameworld.

The eponymous clues are pieces of fictional and poetic advice readers collect like tokens or credits by clicking on objects in the storyworld. In the "Rules" lexia the narrator advises that "You must uncover every clue to win the game. Your score (in the upper right-hand corner) will be your constant traveling companion. (We'll leave aside for now the question of whether winning or losing represents the superior outcome.) " Hence, the text contains an objective, as well as victory conditions, which are core for games of various kinds. The victory conditions are both explicated and sidelined at the same time—winning the game seems possible yet potentially meaningless.

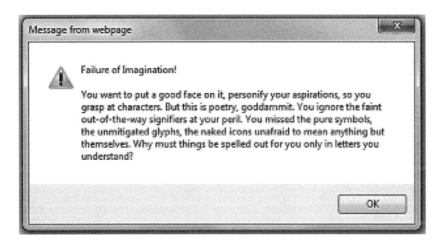

Figure 4.2
Corrective error message on how to read *Clues* (Kendall 2001–2008).

The clues, which *prima facie* may seem like a pseudo-reward element, ultimately do turn out to be key to successful literary gameplay. They have to be collected like repository items, and the core challenge is to distinguish them from red herrings, which lead to error messages, looping pathways, and, ultimately, failure. Whenever the reader finds him or herself entering the park without having collected all clues, they are told they have lost the game, with the following proviso: "Have you really lost? It's your game, so can't you just adjust the rules?" Reading is therefore represented as a game whose rules depend on the reader rather than the writer, and although it is evident that collecting an insufficient number of clues will lead to superficial failure, the reading generated by a prematurely terminated trajectory is ultimately as valid as a superficially successful gameplay session.

The nongame aspect is underscored by the successful ending, which confronts readers willing to risk continuing the quest with the following final instructions:

You want to keep looking?
Then shut down the system.
Let the time and place
drain from the screen.
Let the circuits unload their reasons.
Let the network fade into solitude.
Let the metaphors discharge.
Now take what's left and begin.

Rather than being given the closure effect of having won the game, typically announced by a familiar system message (e.g., "You've won!"), readers are instead encouraged to muse on the emotions and meanings the text has evoked in them and to remove all narrative and technological paraphernalia to search for and create one or more mental images of the text and its meaning(s) independently in their imagination.

4.6   Discussion

Having studied four eclectic hypertexts in separation, I shall now reflect on literary hypertext's degrees of ludicity and literariness more generally and map the four exemplars onto the L-L spectrum. It will become clear that the distribution of text genres depicted in figure 3.2 is a simplification of what is in fact a far more complex picture. As we have seen in the four readings offered in this chapter, individual specimens of one and the same digital media genre are likely to occupy a more diverse spread on the L-L spectrum than one might assume. Hence, I suggest a modification or, rather, refined version of the graph depicted in figure 3.2 that illustrates more precisely where the four texts sit in terms of their relative emphases on literariness and ludicity (figure 4.3). Importantly, the two curves are not intended to designate any value judgments with some texts being more literary and hence more artistically valuable than others. Instead, they depict an approximation of the degree to which individual texts (and/or genres) emphasize ludicity and literariness and the extent to which we can apply either more or fewer analytical elements from the ludological and ludonarratological drawers of the ludostylistic toolkit.

As shown in figure 4.3, the four hypertexts discussed in this chapter are relatively equal in their emphasis on literariness. They all exhibit similar degrees of "readerliness," self- and medium-reflexivity, verbal language versus other modes, and elements of linguistic foregrounding. However, on the ludicity scale there is a significant discrepancy between the largely cognitive-ergodic features of *Firefly*, *Figurski*, and *Patchwork Girl* on the one hand and the distinct ludological qualities of *Clues* on the other. The three former texts largely play with the reader's imagination and explorative, combinatorial capacities: *Firefly* requires meditative immersion into the musings of the hapless lover and allows readers to recombine poetic verses into personalized stanzas. Thus, readers interact with the text in a largely aleatoric way, subjecting themselves to high levels of chance. *Figurski* causes feelings of bemusement and amusement in readers. Its surreal storyworld and highly unpredictable narrative structure continually surprise readers,

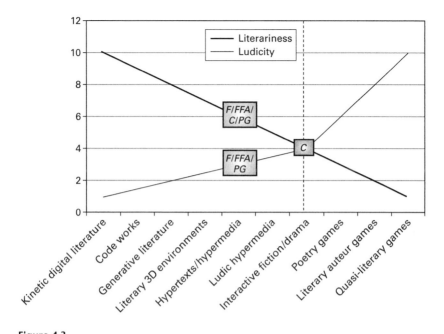

Figure 4.3
The four hypertexts located on the L-L spectrum. *F* stands for *Firefly*, *FFA* for *Figurski at Findhorn on Acid*, *PG* for *Patchwork Girl*, and *C* for *Clues*.

leading them into a mental state akin to dizziness or vertigo. *Patchwork Girl*, finally, uses mimicry as a tool for representing hypertextuality in terms of the Frankensteinian female body, which the reader has to assemble by reading individual lexias in any given order, much like a jigsaw. This element of parallel, as Hutchinson (1983) would call it, is complemented by an intricate intertextual network of fictional and nonfictional reference that, in their totality, mimic the liberating qualities of écriture féminine in virtual space.

Conversely, *Clues* frames itself discursively as a game rather than a poem or novel, and more so than any standard literary enigma or whodunit narrative tends to do. The directive apostrophe to the reader, "Play the words. / Crack the text. / Win the game," on the title page places the text on the middle ground between reading and gaming. Instead of playing *with* words, which would relate to standard literary play, it uses the transitive verb *play* + DIRECT OBJECT, which tends to be used for ludic-mechanic games (*to play* chess, football, computer games, etc.). "Crack the text" and "Win the game" refer to further transitive ludic-mechanic activities, signifying the solving of concrete (rather than metaphorical) puzzles and, more important, the act of winning, which is atypical of literary communication but key to gaming. Clearly, the content of Kendall's text is metafictional and almost devoid of any extratextual meaning, and it is mainly the symbolical, pseudonarrative gameworld evoked by the graphics and the audio that lends the text the feel of an actual detective thriller. Nevertheless, *Clues* displays a range of formal ludic mechanics that situate it considerably closer to the ludic end of the L-L spectrum than the other three hypertexts: readers are made to collect clues for credits, they can win or lose the game, they can save the game to return to where they left off at any given time, and they have to meet the challenge of developing reading strategies that will help them avoid the risk of accruing red herrings rather than real clues.

The ludic features of *Clues* create considerably higher levels of hyper attention in the reader than those in the other three hypertexts discussed here do. In fact, impatient readers may go as far as to skip long passages of text for the sake of finding the most effective strategy of navigating their way to a successful finish. This is particularly likely to happen as soon as the reader-player has developed a mental image of the text's metafictional content, which means they are ready to move from deep- to hyper-attentive interaction. Since interaction with this text combines close reading and gaming in roughly equal measure, I have placed *Clues* exactly on the median line between the literary and the ludic end of the L-L spectrum (figure 4.3). This brings it close to literary interactive fiction and drama, although, as we shall see in chapter 7, in relation to text genre the picture again isn't as straightforward as it may seem.

The core conclusion to be drawn from this chapter is that a purely generic approach to ludoliterary hybridity is likely to lead to theoretical and analytical oversimplification. Instead, ludostylistic analysis should look in detail at individual specimens rather than generalize about entire groups of seemingly similar texts. For this reason, in the remaining chapters of this book I will concentrate on individual artifacts and treat them at considerably greater depth than I have been able to in this chapter. This approach is intended to do justice to the distinct ludoliterary idiosyncracies exhibited by the chosen artifacts and to showcase how in-depth ludostylistics may be executed in a replicable and convincing manner. Links to comparable texts will be drawn as appropriate, mostly in the discussion sections of each chapter.

5 "Love Poem or Break Up Note?" Ludic Hypermedia Fiction and *Loss of Grasp*

5.1 Introduction

Three of the four hypertexts analyzed in the previous chapter (*Figurski*, *Patchwork Girl*, and *Clues*) are digital fictions, a large and diversified genre of digital literature that has narrative structures at its core. It is therefore akin to other forms of digital narrative, such as narrative videogames, interactive television, and digital (pictorial) storytelling.[1] That said, digital fiction is a type of verbal (rather than audiovisual) narrative art and supplements its linguistic features with a wide range of multimodal, kinetic, and ergodic elements. In this chapter we examine a specific type of digital fiction that uses the affordances of hypermedia programming for a variety of aesthetic purposes. Most important, it makes readers feel they're being played with rather than playing literary games as such.

Like digital literature more generally, digital fiction has its "structure, form and meaning . . . dictated by and in dialogue with the digital context in which it is produced and received" (Bell, Ensslin, and Rustad 2014, 4). This means that digital writers choose the technologies for creating such artifacts carefully, as the software and hardware will shape both the production process and the experience of reading/playing digital fictions. Technologically there has been a historical shift from first generation hypertext fiction through second generation hypermedia to what I have elsewhere called third generation cybertext (Ensslin 2007, see chapter 3, section 3.4) and, more recently, fourth generation social media fictions (Rustad 2012).[2] Strictly speaking, however, the term hypermedia, when used more broadly, also covers examples of both third and fourth generation digital fictions due to its reference to the multiple, diverse, fluid, and flexible modes of representation and interaction afforded by contemporary digital literature.

The focus of this chapter and the next is on so-called ludic hypermedia fiction. As outlined in chapter 3, there are various types and manifestations of this genre. Among the most important ones are cognitive-ergodic hypermedia, cybertext, and ludic-mechanic fictions. Cognitive-ergodic hypermedia (hypermedia that combine cognitive and ergodic ludicity, as explained in section 1.3) have evolved technologically, conceptually, and aesthetically from hypertext fiction and expanded the genre by implementing new software technologies such as Flash animation, 2D and 3D graphics, photography and film, sound, voice, and music. Semiotically, this has resulted in a vast array of multimodal artifacts and analytical approaches that have embraced the theories, tools, and techniques of multimodal discourse analysis and semiotics. Typical examples of cognitive-ergodic hypermedia fictions include Stefan Maskiewicz's *Quadrego* (2001), Jason Nelson's *Dreamaphage* (2003, 2004), Christine Wilks' *Fitting the Pattern* (2008), and Kate Pullinger and Chris Joseph's *Flight Paths* (2010). Reading these texts requires nontrivial effort on the part of the reader, yet the resulting play with the reader does not go beyond fully reader-controlled interactions with the text such as clicking for new screens or zooming via mouse-over.

Cybertext fictions are closely related to and implemented mostly as part of cognitive-ergodic hypermedia. My own concept of cybertext refers to texts that play with the reader by giving the software code a considerable degree of control of the reception process, but without suspending interactivity. As discussed in section 3.4, cybertexts are coded so as to expose readers to the apparent whims of the source code, creating an agonistic situation between reader and text/machine (Aarseth 1997).

Finally, ludic-mechanic fictions include elements that create a gaming situation, either in conflict with or complementing the reading process. Such elements typically include minigames, explicit game rules that have to be followed while traversing the text, challenges, rewards, and/or interface items that emulate (and often parody) commercial videogame interfaces and discourses. Chapter 6 will showcase this genre by analyzing one particular text that not only integrates ludic mechanics in a multiperson narrative but, indeed, critiques unreflected gamer behavior thematically.

This chapter will examine a cognitive-ergodic ludic hypermedia fiction that merits the term cybertext to some extent. This is because some segments of it seem to play with the reader by writing themselves, thus reducing readerly control while at the same time appearing to augment it. Serge Bouchardon and Vincent Volckaert's award-winning *Loss of Grasp* (2010) tells the story of a man who has lost grasp on his life, and the structure and interactive design of the narrative reflect this feeling, allowing readers to relate to the protagonist not only cognitively, through reading the text, but in a more comprehensive, sensory, and emotional way through haptic interaction and what Bouchardon (2014) calls "gestural manipulations."

In what follows, I will begin by discussing a ludological principle that permeates digital interactive art, including visual arts, games, and literature, and is particularly salient in cybertexts and ludic-mechanic hypermedia. Heuristic ergodicity, as I refer to it, applies to texts that have to be "learned," as it were, to be read/played meaningfully. Many of these texts do not contain any instructions or guidelines for the user. Instead, the heuristic process is mostly characterized in terms of learning by doing (i.e., systematic or haphazard haptic interaction), logical reasoning, and decoding the signs given by the interface. How this principle applies to *Loss of Grasp* (*LoG*) as well as to other ludostylistic devices used in the narrative will then form the analytical core of this chapter. Once again, the chapter will close with a discussion that places *LoG* on the L-L spectrum and contextualizes it with other, comparable ludic hypermedia fictions.

5.2   Heuristic Ergodicity in Games and Digital Interactive Art

In *Avatars of Story* (2006, 200; see chapter 3, section 3.5), Marie-Laure Ryan suggests a ludological, "game-centered" approach to the narrative analysis of videogames. Her catalog of guidelines proposes, first and foremost, that analysts should "[i]nvestigate the heuristic use of narrative." In other words, they should look at how gameplay creates a "game-story" and how players learn the rules, moves, and mechanics of a game by navigating and interacting with the gameworld and its objects and characters, either devoid of or in combination with the instructions given in the user manual.[3] This also involves players' knowledge of the real world, which they translate into and map onto the fictional world of a game. Seeing a car in the gameworld, for instance, triggers logical reasoning: this object probably either can or, indeed, needs to be driven, pushed around, opened, closed, smashed, or stolen, according to the ludic principles and narrative logic of the specific game at hand. The exact array of possible interactions with an in-game object usually needs to be explored through trial and error, and reapplied and/or modified when encountering similar objects later on in the game.

Hence, heuristic ergodicity relates to the specific ways in which digital texts demand and facilitate learning in the reader, player, or user through nontrivial interaction with their structures.[4] It is particularly pertinent in game design (in the sense of mechanics, interface textuality, and narrative architecture), where players learn what to do in order to make progress, through level-ups and other advancements. In games, heuristic ergodicity manifests itself most typically through object and level design, interface clues, training sequences, and the ways in which they are embedded in the gameworld. In level 1 of *Prince of Persia* (Ubisoft 2008), for example, the Prince meets the mysterious Princess Elika. He follows her as she runs away, and as he encounters various obstacles in the landscape, the interface tells the player through written instructions what key strokes to apply (in the PC version) to jump across chasms, climb up and across rock faces, and fight enemies using a range of moves and weapons. At the same time, the player-character is exposed to similar challenges repeatedly, thus enabling the player to practice and internalize the newly acquired moves so that they become second nature for future, more challenging levels.

Written or spoken instructions that are presented in voiced-over or superscripted ways are common in commercial videogames. After all, they are designed so as to facilitate player learning without foregrounding the learning process. Heuristic processes are embedded smoothly within the game narrative. Players acquire new skills and knowledge almost subconsciously, and the instructions given tend to follow the sole purpose of maximizing player progress. This is not the case, however, in some more artistically inclined digital media. Amanita Design's Flash art game series *Samorost* (Dvorský 2003, 2005), for example, does not feature any written or spoken instructions. All the player has in front of him or her is a purely graphical interface (including musical soundtrack) depicting a meticulously crafted, miniature fantasy world whose rules and logic are partly borrowed from the player's actual world (e.g., gravity, organism growth and movement, and various types of flora and fauna). Yet the particular mechanisms and processes governing this world have to be learned by players through the heuristic ergodicity programmed into the game text. Players have to explore the gaming interface by moving the cursor across the screen to find interactive elements that aren't specifically marked. Progress can be made in this multilayered narrative puzzle only if and when those interactive elements are activated in a certain order following a specific pattern, and the logic of this pattern becomes apparent only in the course of gameplay.

The initial conflict driving the plot of *Samorost 2* (Amanita Design, 2005), for example, is triggered by the player rather than being part of the backstory. This is, incidentally, another unusual design feature that differentiates the narrative architecture of this art game from run-of-the-mill blockbusters. The interface of chapter 1 shows a fantasy/science fiction landscape: an imaginary planet inhabited by a small, peace-loving man that is invaded by aliens at night (figure 5.1). The aliens set out to steal some pears from the little man's garden, and as the player seeks to stop them by clicking on the man's guard dog, the aliens take the animal away, too. This sets the scene for what is to come: the little man, dressed in a white nightgown and cap, witnesses his dog being kidnapped and runs downstairs to follow the alien spaceship in his own airborne vehicle.

The next scene (or level) shows the two spaceships landing on the aliens' planet. In trying to make the little man disembark from his space craft, the player finds the figure is clickable. However, as soon as the man has left the vehicle, he is entangled in one of the surrounding plants. To free him, the player has to run the cursor over those interface items that are most likely to be interactive. However, though the plants' leaves are fully interactive and fly off when clicked, this type of activation turns out to be inconsequential for the game plot. Moving a little woodworm that is sitting on one of the trees to the tree holding the protagonist via drag-and-drop, conversely, causes the insect to sit down and gnaw on the wood, thus releasing the little man. He walks off toward the next scene, which shows something resembling a hollow tree. Inside the tree are a cauldron and a variety of taps, funnels, and bottles. From studying the entire setting and its interactive components, the player works out that he or she has to find a way to run water into the cauldron and mix it with seeds from the nearby poppies in order to feed a large anthropomorphic snail, which has been hammering away on its own metal shell. Having drunk the water, the snail falls asleep, allowing the little man to steal its hammer and move back to the previous scene, where he uses the hammer to wake the robot guarding the entrance to the aliens' cave. Until this moment, the player is unlikely to guess why the little man needs to drug the snail, or that he requires the hammer to activate the robot. In other words, the reasoning needed to work out the pattern governing the logic of each scene in the game narrative always appears partly random, as the rules underlying the gameworld do not become transparent until they are revealed by a carefully integrated cut scene.

As we have seen, the logic underlying the narrative architecture of *Samorost 2* is driven by both realism and fantasy. The rules that the player must infer from interface interaction can be transferred from other point-and-click games only to a minimal degree, and they only partly follow the likely expectations of the player. Indeed, I would argue that heuristic ergodicity in the *Samorost* series operates at two levels: in the first, players use their standard cognitive, sensory, and haptic repertoire to decode the interface, mostly through trial and error; in the second, however, the player is exposed to the highly peculiar, witty idiosyncrasies of the gameworld, and he or she

Figure 5.1
Interface of *Samorost 2*, chapter 1.

learns about its internal mechanisms and its characters' thoughts and motivations in a quasi-random fashion. This combination of intentionality and surprise, coupled with meticulous audiovisual design and execution, is, to my mind, what constitutes the main artistic appeal of the *Samorost* series.

In the following section, I shall examine, along with other ludostylistic principles, how the concept of heuristic ergodicity applies to a work of ludic digital fiction. Of core importance here are, of course, linguistic elements in the text and the playful ways in which readers interact with them and other semiotic elements.

5.3 Analyzing *Loss of Grasp*: Fallaciousness, Heuristic Ergodicity, and Cybertextuality

Déprise/Loss of Grasp/Perdersi (2010) is a trilingual online Flash fiction by Serge Bouchardon and Vincent Volckaert, a French digital writing and hypermedia design team. The narrative tells the story of a man—a husband and father—losing grasp on his life and identity in six short scenes, meant to be "played and acted in a private reading" (Bouchardon in Rettberg and Tomaszek 2010). The first scene opens with a black interface, voiced over by a female voice saying "Welcome. Press the hash key" and "Congratulations" after the reader has done so. This starts off the homodiegetic narrative, told by the protagonist, who is reflecting on his disillusionment with life ("How can I have a grasp on what happens to me? / Everything escapes me. / Slips through my fingers. / Objects, people. / I feel I've lost control."[5]). This is followed by what sounds like an automated phone message, which asks readers to choose when to have "the meeting: in ten years, press one; in three hours, press two; now, press three." Pressing any key will trigger a message by the same female voice saying "It's time for the meeting," overlaid with a soundtrack that is reminiscent of various Nintendo games.

Scene 2 answers the question of what kind of meeting is referred to here: it is set back in time and sees the narrator reflecting on the moment he first met his wife: "The woman in front of me seemed so perfect, I was flabbergasted." His inability to say anything coherent is represented by speech recognition software output misrepresenting various utterances spoken by Bouchardon himself, such as "What do you do fall and evening?" instead of "What do you do for a living?" The questions the narrator feels he has to ask "to reveal" his future wife are subsequently combined by the player, via mouse-over, to reveal a photograph of her, little by little, much like a jigsaw or the brushstrokes producing a painting. However, despite all the knowledge he gains about her throughout their marriage, he finds that he "never got to know her truly."

Scene 3 is set twenty years after their first meeting when, one morning, the narrator finds a note from his wife. It reads rather differently depending on the cursor position: moving the mouse to the right will render the text as a love poem; moving it to the left reverses the order of the lines, transforming the text into a break up note.

In scene 4 the narrator moves on to thinking about his son, who has recently shown signs of detachment and disappointment in his father. Reading an essay on heroism written by his son, the narrator understands that between the lines the young man is accusing his father of not being a role model or hero figure for him, of not knowing him or sharing any common interests with him. He concludes his son has stopped loving him, which adds sorely to his frustration.

Scene 5 then moves on to the narrator's reflections on his own self-image, which seems to "escape" and "fail" him. Here the text is combined with distorted photographic images of the reader (recorded via webcam), which he or she can pull and drag in all directions, thus emulating the narrator's fleeting and damaged sense of self.[6]

As the narrator sets out to "take control again" in scene 6, an empty box appears on screen into which the reader can type using the keyboard. Whatever keys he or she activates, however, the text presented on screen ends up typing itself in the same preprogrammed way:

I'm doing all I can to get a grip on my life again.
I make choices.
I control my emotions.
The meaning of things.
At last, I have a grasp . . .

Hence, contrary to what the wording of this passage seems to suggest for the protagonist, the auto-typing mechanism renders the wreader powerless vis-à-vis the preprogrammed text machine. Mapped onto the diegetic level of the text, this shows that the protagonist's attempt at resuming control of his life ultimately fails and the grasp he seems to have regained is, after all, an illusion that is bound to fail to materialize.

In what follows, I offer a close reading of *LoG*, focusing in particular on the following elements from the ludostylistic toolkit: (1) Ludology: since this text is not a videogame and therefore doesn't exhibit any ludic mechanics as defined earlier in this book, I shall concentrate on how the text plays with the reader in a cognitive-ergodic sense. Of specific significance here are elements of illusory agency (MacCallum-Stewart and Parsler 2007) and what I call aleatoric fallacy. (2) Of particular interest from the ludonarratological drawer is how the protagonist's "loss of grasp" is portrayed through narrative voice and its interplay with (3) ludosemiotic elements such as interface design and multimodal interaction, and especially the "gestural manipulations" coded into the text (Bouchardon 2014). Finally, from the mediality drawer (4) I shall select, as announced in the previous section, heuristic ergodicity as a specific subtype of Aarseth's (1997) broader concept. I will examine the cybertextuality of *LoG* in the sense of how parts of the text literally write themselves (Ensslin 2007) while projecting reader agency (see previous paragraph on scene 6). Furthermore, I shall look at how intertextuality and intermediality are used to evoke the illusion of playing a game, for instance, through the satirical use of voice-over, soundtrack, choice, and feedback. Once again, these analytical tools will not be ticked off, as it were, in a strictly consecutive fashion. Instead, they will be woven together in the analysis to reflect the text's creative interplay of carefully designed and collated stylistic elements.

As mentioned previously, *LoG* is not a game in the ludic-mechanic sense of the word. Rather, it is a digital fiction that plays with the reader in a cognitive-ergodic fashion. "Functionally, the interface itself plays games with the user by erasing certainty and interrupting conventional usability" (Heckman 2011, 10). Yet there is more to *LoG*'s ludicity than this. "Erasing certainty" may be refined by looking at the ways in which the text uses illusory agency (MacCallum-Stewart and Parsler 2007), that is, how it projects false impressions of reader freedom. *Prima facie*, readers of *LoG* seem to have a significant degree of agency. In scene 1, for example, they are given three choices as to when to have "the meeting." It turns out, however, that all three options lead to the same narrative continuation, frustrating reader expectations vis-à-vis the conditionality of the plot and the playability of the narrative. Yet simultaneously it reinforces the message that the reader enacts, through reading *LoG*, the narrator's weariness and loss of control.

Another element of cognitive-ergodic ludicity in *LoG* is what I have termed aleatoric fallacy, or the illusion of complete randomness, for instance, in automated text generation. A large part of the fictional text is written in individual lexias, or short phrases or sentences, displayed one at a time. Whenever the reader touches a lexia with the cursor, the text is jumbled up at high speed like a randomized text generator. The text generation process, however, cannot be stopped at any given moment. Rather, readers have to wait after mousing over each dynamic lexia until it comes to rest on the next preprogrammed static lexia (see figure 5.2 for an example). This play with the reader's assumed freedom to randomize text is the essence of aleatoric fallacy in *LoG*.

Actually, fallaciousness is a trope that pervades both the content and form of *LoG*. The blurb tells readers both that the text manifests a "play on grasp and loss of grasp," and how it "mirrors the reader's experience of an interactive digital work" (Rettberg 2011). Hence, as the narrator-protagonist talks about losing control of his life, the reader is made to perform this feeling interactionally by experiencing loss of control of the interface. In scene 1, the dynamic lexias, or "slippery texts" (Heckman 2011, 9), represent the protagonist's impression that his life is slipping away from him. To illustrate his futile attempts at regaining control, the dynamic lexias are interspersed in one instance with a fully clickable, static text link saying "I control my destiny." This apparent increase in character control and reader agency is signaled by a change from cursor arrow to hand. All following lexias are dynamic again but combined with a more multimodally interactive interface, including a meditative soundtrack and dreamlike, colorful shapes on screen that the reader seems to create as he or she continues to mouse over it (displayed as a long streak of white in figure 5.2). Finally, at the end of scene 1, the cursor hand changes to a text cursor when the reader reaches

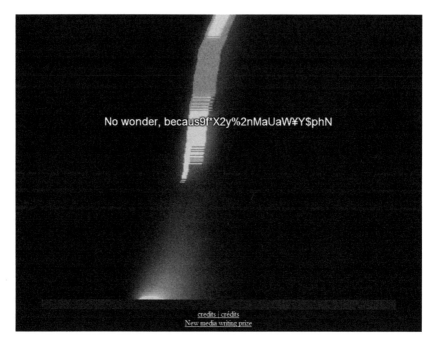

Figure 5.2
A dynamic lexia in scene 1 of *LoG* is coming to rest on the sentence "No wonder, because I had chosen them."

the emotional turning point in the narrator's monologue. This point marks a change in mood from being confident and in control ("I control my destiny. / I am the king of the world. / I will become what I want. / I followed my own path. / I browsed beautiful landscapes. / No wonder, because I had chosen them. . . .") to being disillusioned and confused: "Everything escapes me. / Slips through my fingers. . . ."

In a recent essay, Bouchardon (2014) introduces the concept of gestural manipulations as an analytical tool for digital fictions and other interactive narratives. Starting from the assumption that "all clicking is interpretive" (Bouchardon 2014, 160; see also Jeanneret 2000), he suggests a refined view of how readers interact with digital media through a "repertoire of gestures" (Bouchardon 2014, 161–162), the use of which depends on the physical device used to interact with a particular digital text (a PC, tablet, or mobile phone, for example). To Bouchardon, analyses of gestural manipulations happen at five different levels: (1) the gesteme (an individual move, such as a key stroke or mouse click, linking haptic move and interactive interface item), (2) the acteme (a sequence of individual gestemes combining to form a larger unit of gestural meaning, such as drag-and-drop or pull-and-release), (3) the semiotic unit of manipulation (abbreviated as SUM, meaning the sum of identical or similar actemes and their semiotic function), (4) media coupling (the particular conventional and nonconventional functions and meanings of SUMs in their individual medial context), and (5) interactive discourse (the level of digital text in context, and the functions of gestural interactions seen against this larger backdrop).

Bouchardon (2014) is particularly interested in unconventional media couplings used to parallel form and meaning in a creative digital text. The blurred reader faces in scene 5 of *LoG*, for instance, show an unconventional use of webcam manipulation software. Whereas this type of technology normally serves its users as a highly entertaining type of leisure activity, here it is used to represent the protagonist's distorted sense of self. The aesthetic effect of blurring the photographic images is that "even the character's own image seems to escape him. . . . [The reader] can distort and manipulate it. The character/reader thus 'feel[s] manipulated'" (Bouchardon 2014, 127) by the gestural interactions coded into the text.

Bouchardon's concern with mediality is reflected in a number of further stylistic elements in the text. *LoG* intertextualizes a range of other media. Earlier in this section I mentioned elements of choice (when to have the meeting), which are intrinsically ludic mechanic. Yet here the reader's ludic expectations are undermined, as all three choices lead to the same continuation of the plot. The female voice over in scene 1 is allusive of automated telephone discourse, which tends to lead to high levels of frustration because the caller has little or no control of the remote communication process. Similarly, the same automated female voice says "Congratulations" after the reader has pressed the hash key. This kind of feedback can be seen as an intermedial reference to videogame discourse (Ensslin 2011a). It is reinforced by the Nintendo-like electronic soundtrack that evokes associations of portable device games such as the *Super Mario* series (Nintendo 1985–2012) and *Cooking Mama* (Office Create 2006). However, once again, the positive feedback, even coupled with the uplifting soundtrack, doesn't lead anywhere, least of all to a sense of (re)gaining control of the interactive text.

Having looked at a range of ludostylistic elements in *LoG*, let me now close the hermeneutic circle by returning to two concepts discussed in earlier parts of this chapter: heuristic ergodicity and cybertextuality. To recapitulate, heuristic ergodicity relates to the specific ways in which digital texts demand and facilitate learning in the reader, player, or user through nontrivial interaction with their structures. Learning here refers to acquiring knowledge and skills about how to "operate" a particular digital fiction that is using interactive and semiotic elements in highly unconventional ways, mainly for aesthetic, satirical, and parodic purposes. In this respect, heuristic ergodicity is commensurate with Bouchardon's idea of unconventional media coupling, where default interactive elements are put to nondefault uses, the meanings and functions of which have to be read into the text by readers themselves. One particularly poignant heuristic-ergodic section in *LoG* occurs in scene 3 when the protagonist talks about a note (either a love letter or break up note) he has received from his wife. Depending on where the reader places the cursor on the interface and in which direction he or she moves it, the text will move either upward or downward and its meaning is either positive (in the sense of a love letter) or negative (in the sense of a break up note; see figure 5.3). Multimodally, this ambiguity is reinforced by gestural manipulations of the soundtrack: the famous Habanera from Bizet's *Carmen* is playing and depending on the position and movement of the cursor, the music will be slowed down or sped up, played forward or backward, or blurred into an incomprehensible tangle of noise. Thematically, the Habanera is an aria about the rebelliousness of love and the impossibility to "control" it. Thus, it parallels both the main theme of *LoG* and its formal execution by the reader, who finds it impossible to read the letter in a coherent fashion.

In fact, we might argue that some passages of *LoG*, such as the one described in the previous paragraph, go as far as to subvert heuristic ergodicity. Scene 3 makes it impossible for readers to learn how to operate the interactive text as it offers two equally plausible yet diametrically opposed

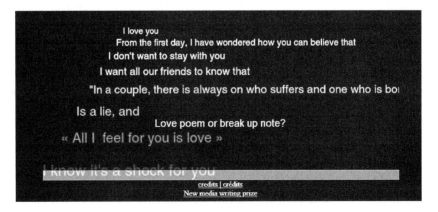

Figure 5.3
Screenshot of the love letter/break up note in scene 3 of *LoG*.

readings—love or separation. Indeed, this navigational impasse, which parallels the protagonist's emotional condition, forms the structural core of *LoG* and is therefore key to its macrotextual understanding.

Lack or loss of control is a trope that is further instantiated by the cybertextuality inherent in *LoG*. To recapitulate, cybertexts are ergodic digital texts that are programmed in particular ways as autonomous text/machines (Aarseth 1997) that assume power over the reader by literally "writing themselves" rather than allowing readers to control their own trajectory (Ensslin 2007). The most salient cybertextual element of *LoG* is the interactive text box in the final scene. Using the keyboard, readers can type any sequence of characters into it, only to find that their input will inevitably be converted to the pre-scripted monologue quoted earlier in this section ("I'm doing all I can . . ."). Thus, although the reader seems empowered by the text to participate in the narrative by "wreading" into it, this turns out to be an illusory impression and readers literally lose any sense of participatory control of the text. This, of course, parallels the narrator's illusion that he has regained a grasp on his life, and the cycle of disillusionment begins afresh.

5.4 Discussion

Loss of Grasp, like many of Bouchardon's digital works, détourns the ways in which digital media tend to be used by default, often for commercial purposes. By making his readers reflect on their actions and interactions with the interface, he questions their submissive attitude toward digital media consumption. Seemingly unmarked gestural manipulations like dragging-and-dropping, mousing over, and keyboard input are converted into non-conventional media couplings and transfigured into symbols of subversion. "[W]hile eschewing any sort of overt political content" (Heckman 2011, 6), the subversive potential underlying his creative and theoretical work brings Bouchardon in line with other avant-garde artists and writers. Not only does he use digital technologies to "make it new," but he transforms the digital interface into a creative platform to critique institutionalized media interactions and fossilized consumer behavior.

The "play" with conventional interactional gestures outlined in the previous section situates *LoG* firmly in the cognitive-ergodic area of the literary-ludic spectrum. In contrast to literary hypertext, ludicity in the sense of play with the reader here is a lot more varied as it is linked to many types of gestural manipulations and their multimodal realizations. As discussed in section 5.3, technological and semiotic references to digital gameplay are present, yet they turn out to be illusory and parodically motivated. Phenomenologically, this creates a ludic attitude in the reader, who is encouraged by the sheer variety and fluidity of interactions as well as the brevity of lexias and multisensory stimulation to read on in a playful yet deep-attentive fashion.

It is partly due to this brevity of lexias that the degree of, or focus on, readerliness is significantly less than that of literary hypertext as discussed in chapter 4. There is far less written text to read than in most hypertext fictions. Its advanced use of hypermedia makes *LoG* much more multisensory and multimodal, combining written and spoken text with music and other sound effects and a wide range of interactive visuals and coded gestural manipulations. One could argue that its increased multimodality replaces the strong focus on written language characteristic of hypertext fiction and poetry and moves digital fiction so far away from print culture that it becomes more akin to videogames and other interactive audiovisual media. For these reasons, I have placed *LoG* closer to the ludic half of the L-L spectrum than *Firefly*, *Figurski*, and *Patchwork Girl*, yet not as close as *Clues*, which focuses more on the reader's play of the poetic whodunit game and its rules.

Compared to other contemporary hypermedia fictions,[7] such as Kate Pullinger and Chris Joseph's *Flight Paths* (2010) and Christine Wilks' *Fitting the Pattern* (2008), *LoG* exhibits a much greater variety of ergodic tools, as well as a level of cybertextuality that highlights textual play with the reader. *Flight Paths* (*FP*) is a short, episodic narrative revolving around Yacub, a refugee from Pakistan, and Harriet, a housewife living in a wealthy London suburb. They meet in a supermarket parking lot as Yacub mysteriously survives falling off the plane on which he was hoping to enter the country as a stowaway, and the narrative's main focus is on the bizarre cultural encounter between its two protagonists. *Fitting the Pattern or Being a Dressmaker's Daughter A Memoir in Pieces* (*FtP*) is an autobiographical narrative told by a woman who reflects on her relationship with her mother. In the style of écriture féminine it explores the link between women's writing and the gendered metaphor of textile, and how the two notions impact the subjectivity and body image of the narrator.

FP mostly follows the traditional hypertextual interaction pattern of clicking links, and *FtP* largely operates via mouse-over. The focus of both these texts is more on the symbolical content expressed linguistically and multimodally than on interactional variability and playability. *FP* does have a ludic element to it, as represented in its latest episode ("Jack meets Yacub"). Here the plot sees Yacub meeting Harriet's teenage son, Jack. Their two contrasting worlds (Jack's wealthy London background versus Yacub's impoverished refugee status) meet in an imaginary videogame session. The ludicity thematized in the narrative is instantiated, if at all, through continuous mousing over the digital interface (this is also the case in *FtP*, albeit with a greater diversity of narrative interface metaphors). This constant mouse movement drives the plot forward, so to speak, as it releases individual lexias, or text chunks, to be displayed on screen. Nevertheless, there are no rules to follow, choices to make, levels to win, or similar ludic-mechanic parameters, and hence there is no actual gameplay involved in reading *FP*. We might therefore say that both *FP* and *FtP* are placed slightly more to the left of the ludicity scale of the L-L spectrum than *LoG*, roughly colocated with *Figurski*, *Firefly*, and *Patchwork Girl* (see chapter 4): their focus is more on literary semiotics and cognitive-ergodic ludicity than on playable tools, and they maximize readability through high levels of interactivity and brief, poignant chunks of verbal information.

As far as literariness is concerned, I have placed *LoG* higher than *FtP* and *FP*. This is because Bouchardon and Volckaert play with language not only in a conventional, poetic, and/or multimodal sense but, indeed,

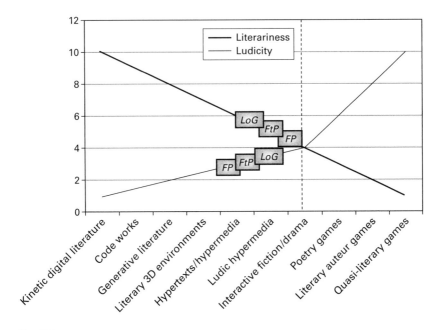

Fig. 5.4
Loss of Grasp (*LoG*), *Flight Paths* (*FP*), and *Fitting the Pattern* (*FtP*) located on the L-L spectrum.

technologically, for instance, through quasi-randomization, poeticized speech recognition output, and manifested *ekphrasis* (words literally making up the narrator's wife's portrait). Finally, *FtP* is more literary than *FP* because the language used in it is distinctly more poetic and verbose, whereas *FP*'s main original goal was to provide a straightforward narrative plot for participatory readers to add to and develop, using a wide range of multimedia—hence its subtitle, *A Networked Novel*.

Again, the way the three comparative digital fictions map onto the two strands of the L-L spectrum shows the great diversity with which digital writers approach (cognitive-ergodic) ludicity and literariness. In the following chapter, we shall move one step further and look at a set of digital fictions that do implement ludic-mechanic features to see how play with the reader can be combined with actual gameplay, or elements thereof.

6 "Your Innocence Drifts Away": Antiludicity and Ludic Mechanics in *The Princess Murderer*

6.1 Introduction

Moving further along the literary-ludic continuum, this chapter deals with a second type of ludic hypermedia literature as outlined in chapters 3 and 5: it examines texts that implement actual ludic mechanics, such as game interface elements or minigames. More specifically, I shall close-read a digital fiction that not only implements ludic mechanics but indeed thematizes and problematizes default lusory attitudes and gamer behavior. *The [somewhat disturbing but highly improbable] Princess Murderer* (TPM) by geniwate and Deena Larsen (2003) has a distinctly antiludic agenda that it implements through both the digital narrative it tells and its technological and semiotic design. Thematically and generically, *TPM* mixes elements of the Romantic fairytale, the crime mystery, pornographic magazines, and discursive-interactive elements of digital genres such as Flash fiction, fan fiction, hypertext, and point-and-click adventure game. Following a strongly feminist agenda, it applies the *unnatural narratological*[1] technique of *multiperson narration*, and particularly varieties of "textual *you*" (i.e., various narrative uses of the second-person pronoun), to expose misogynistic elements coded into blockbuster videogames (Ensslin and Bell 2012; Richardson 2006). Of particular analytical interest is the way in which the text integrates a common videogame interface device—a performance meter, or counting mechanism—for satirical and critical purposes. The princess census, which I shall look at in more detail in section 6.3, subverts (antiludically, as it were) mainstream game players' gullibility toward in-game sexism and violence, as well as their expectation of being able to win through mindless killing and other violent means.

I shall begin by introducing the idea of antiludicity as a creative agenda for avant-garde game designers and digital writers. This will then be followed by a ludostylistic analysis of *TPM* that focuses in particular on how antiludicity manifests itself ludologically, ludonarratologically, ludosemiotically, and textually. The chapter will close, as usual, with a discussion of where on the L-L spectrum *TPM* is situated.

6.2   Antiludicity as Subversive Design Practice

As Meades (2013, 73) argues in a recent essay on illicit game modifications, "[p]lay itself has an anti-ness (anti-form, anti-aesthetics, anti-philosophy, and anti-play) that is obscured or at least dismissed when discourses of legitimization prioritize some kinds of play other others." What he is referring to is play's inherent potential and tendency to subvert itself and/or the structures underlying it, particularly in gameplay. This becomes most evident in subversive player behavior, such as cheating, *hacking, modding*, or *griefing*, which is part and parcel of videogame culture yet subject to delegitimization discourses and practices on the part of manufacturers and various legal bodies protecting copyright and intellectual property. Thus, subversive practices among gamers are as ubiquitous as they are frowned on by lawmakers and industry stakeholders, and we could argue that the fact that their legitimacy is constantly questioned may partly be the reason for their popularity.

Another type of practical deconstructivism in videogame and related new media cultures is what I have called antiludicity, a metaphenomenon that occurs primarily in the independent and art game sectors but also in related, noncommercial practices such as digital creative writing. Antiludic design uses elements from videogame architectures such as interface items, rules and feedback mechanisms, or even complete minigames (puzzles, jigsaws, etc.) to critique structural, thematic, and cultural aspects of games and gaming. As pointed out in section 2.6, this quasi-iconoclastic experimentalism détours aspects of commercial game development and gamer culture by appropriating ludic structures and reassembling them playfully and subversively into new architectures and narratives. As we shall see in chapter 9, *slow games* are a radical example of antiludic game design, as they force players to proceed at an extremely slow pace, evoking a meditative mood that makes players reflect on their actions and other aspects of videogame culture.

Antiludicity in independent game design is often coupled with a tongue-in-cheek approach. After all, even the most medium-critical game designers tend to seek to create fun and/or entertaining experiences for their players. The PC-based *Progress Quest* (Fredricksen 2002), for example, is a so-called *zero-player game* parodying *EverQuest* (Sony Online Entertainment 1999) and other MMORPGs and CRPGs (offline Computer Role-Playing Games). Role-playing games in general are characterized, among other things, by their emphasis on players collecting repository items and Experience Points (XP). Therefore they usually exhibit a wide variety of named entities, which are in line with the logic of the respective gameworld. As a result, players tend to end up with vast quantities of items, such as armor, poisons, spells, and health potions, many of which they need to drop halfway through the game in order to make room for new, more useful or relevant objects.

Progress Quest targets players' often unreflected freedom to make almost infinite choices and the accompanying greed for more commodities. More specifically, it critiques the auto-attack mechanics of contemporary RPGs, which leave players as bystanders rather than active participants in combat situations. What players have to do in standard auto-attack situations is select an individual or group of enemies and trigger the auto-attack mechanism, after which the system executes the combat independently of any further player input. *Progress Quest* takes this player inactivity *ad absurdum*: the only thing the system allows players to do in terms of interface interaction is customize a player-character (from a humorous list of names, assets, and stats). Once the player presses the "Sold" button, the game goes into zero-player mode, which means all agency is removed and the game literally plays itself in front of the player's eyes. Along the bottom of the interface, text segments are displayed, changing every few seconds and updating the player on what is happening (i.e., what his or her avatar is doing, apparently) at any given moment—for instance, "Executing an Undernourished Stung Worm," "Heading to market to sell loot," and "Selling an orc snout." At the same time, the purely verbal interface shows how players' stats are changing, how their XP levels are developing, and which quests they are pursuing at any given point.

Another antigame is Armor Games's platform parody *Achievement Unlocked* (2008, again for PC). It features an abstract, 2D interface consisting of spikes, bars, walls, and empty spaces, through which the player has to navigate an infinite number of elephants, one by one, to save them from the spikes that are distributed and moving across the screen. There is no narrative meaning whatsoever attached to these elephant avatars, however, which seem to have been chosen as a random piece of interactive design. As a matter of fact, randomness is the principal semantic driver of this game. Players are literally flooded with "achievements," which are fed back to them by the system without their being aware of having achieved anything, or how. The number of elephant respawns does not seem to have any effect on player performance or progress, and the list of apparent achievements, labeled arbitrarily (e.g., "Get Off Your Seats," "Pit Hat Trick," and "Horizontal Confusion"), runs along the right hand side of the user interface, too fast to keep track of during gameplay. The impression that this arbitrary array of ludic elements and effects is there to play with the player, so to speak, is underscored by the game's soundtrack, which is a fast-paced blend of fairground tunes and circus flourishes.

Clearly, antigames such as *Progress Quest* and *Achievement Unlocked* don't appeal to players through high levels of playability. On the contrary: they are played by parodically minded users who don't mind sacrificing their usual gaming experiences for various degrees of humorous self-reflexivity and self-criticism. Still, as soon as the parodic intent of an antigame has been grasped and appreciated, the likelihood is that players lose interest and stop playing for good. After all, the point suggested by the procedural rhetoric of the game has been made and taken, and any further engagement with the game is bound to further reinforce its underlying message rather than provide novel narrative content or ludic challenges. In the remainder of this chapter, we shall look at an example of how antiludically minded digital fiction writers engage creatively with players' expectations of narrative games as well as players' tendency to lose interest as soon as a self-critical, rhetorical point has been grasped.

6.3   "Clicking" Damsels in Distress: *The Princess Murderer* and Its Antiludic Agenda

In what follows, I shall provide a ludostylistic reading of *The Princess Murderer* that serves to highlight in particular the text's antiludic agenda. Tapping once again into the four main compartments of the ludostylistic toolkit, my focal areas will include (1) elements of ludic mechanics in the text; (2) the ways in which multiperson narration and particularly textual *you* are used to create the illusion that the reader-player (RP) is complicit in the crimes against the fictional princesses rather than an innocent onlooker; (3) the multimodal interplay between language and other semiotic resources and how it is used to entangle readers into the *unnatural narrative* network at hand; and (4) the specific textual (intertextual, intermedial, and interdiscursive) elements at work in the text that underscore *TPM*'s parodic and critical outlook. As always, I shall deal with the above features in no particular order other than in terms of how they coalesce creatively.

The Princess Murderer is a Flash-based digital fiction that remediates Charles Perrault's Enlightenment fairytale "La Barbe bleue" ("Bluebeard" 1961/1697). In so doing, it places itself in a mythological canon and transforms elements of Perrault's source text ludically, diegetically, and multimodally. Bluebeard, whose major function in *TPM* involves raping and murdering princesses, is represented in terms of a stereotypical Manichean villain. A baddy par excellence, he conforms to the ludic convention of othering (i.e., constructing another being or person as something different from the playing self) any animate obstacle that comes in the way of the player-character.

By targeting the original story's patronizing patriarchal undertones and inherent misogyny, *TPM* satirizes what I have elsewhere called "subludic misogynist teleology" (Ensslin and Bell 2012, 59),[2] that is, the stereotypical melodramatic trajectory of adventure games wherein typically male heroes have to save typically female victims from typically male monsters (think of *Donkey Kong*, *The Legend of Zelda*, or the *Mario* series). More than this, however, the text satirizes preconceptions of interactivity itself (Picot 2003); it parodies the hyper-attentive, high-speed hardware and software interaction often observed in Generation M gamers (Hayles 2007). As Picot (2003) observes, despite its title, *TPM* is "not a murder mystery, because we already know that Bluebeard is the murderer. The real mystery, the real subject of the piece, is to do with the relationship between the cool blue text [a trope that recurs throughout the narrative] and us, its viewers/readers." This metafictional, self-reflexive, and media-critical trajectory is confirmed by the authors, who explain that

we want the readers to straddle both worlds—to be aware that this is a game, this is a screen, and yet to enter into the play and world view of the characters. . . . The Princess Murderer constrains readers as much as possible . . . We wanted to create this frustration of power and powerlessness as a response to early hypertext works that placed readers as co-author merely because readers must participate in creating meaning and story. (geniwate and Larsen, in Picot 2003)

Thus, *TPM* acts interdiscursively (in the sense of referring to a whole discourse rather than just a text) as a generic criticism of other forms of digital narrative and their accompanying critical theories, many of which have overemphasized the degree of readerly freedom and agency present in this type of narrative. This, again, underscores *TPM*'s place near the literary end of the spectrum.

Semiotically, *TPM* transcodes and remediates key symbolic elements of the original story: the interface is kept blue most of the time and the door leading to the infamous forbidden room features schematically on the entry page of the narrative as a pictographic link transporting users into the storyworld. The narrative employs such interactivity, however, in the service of a broader literary (or metanarrative) purpose. Thus, the framing of the interface itself foregrounds written text in small, blue print displayed in rhomboid-shaped windows, suggesting *TPM*'s critical, reflexive relation to the larger tradition of Bluebeard stories that it seeks to renarrate—and recontextualize—via user participation (see figure 6.1).

As mentioned previously, *TPM* contains ludic-mechanic elements that are strongly evocative of various blockbuster genres. As shown in figure 6.1, the interface displays a "princess census" across the lower left-hand side of the interface. It shows how many princesses are in the castle at any given time. It rises and falls bit by bit with every click performed by the reader-player, and each click symbolizes either the murder of a princess (with a downward click) or the addition (or "breeding") of a princess to the existing group (with an upward click). Yet the princess census only superficially serves as a performance meter or progress bar. As Picot (2003, n.p.) notes, "[r]esembling as it does the fuel-gauge in a conventional driving-and-shooting video-game, it introduces an element of game-play into the work: but it's a game which can't be won. There is no end-point. There are certain limits beyond which further text is unavailable." In other words, princesses serve as mere objects to be counted, or a commodity to be audited, and while it may seem, at first glance, that players can master the logic of

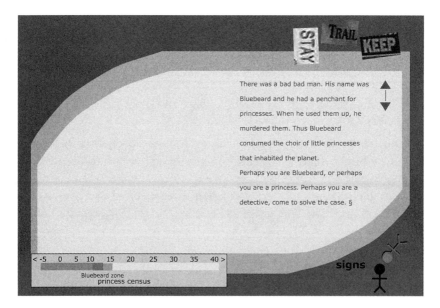

Figure 6.1
Screenshot of *The Princess Murderer*'s user interface.

killing and breeding damsels in distress, they are bound to lose themselves in what turns out to be an infinite tangle of places, characters, and actions. Importantly, the lexias displayed in each frame subtextually critique players' chauvinist lusory attitudes by alluding to their assumed pleasure in or nonchalance toward click-rape and click-murder.

Thus, while *TPM* superficially looks and feels like a computer game, the engaging reader-player will find that it intends to be quite the opposite: it uses its interactive and narrative elements to détourn standard videogame representations and gamer behavior. The phenomenological effect this has on players is that "the more [they] engage with its game-playing aspects— basically, clicking rapidly from one 'page' to another in order to change the scores displayed at the bottom of the screen—the more difficult it becomes to pay attention to its literary content" (Picot 2009). Hence, the text quite literally stages the clash between deep and hyper attention (see also chapter 8) and exposes the fact that onscreen readers are tempted to sacrifice close reading to the need for fast onscreen (inter)action, that is, clicking. This effect is closely related to the aforementioned tendency of antigame players to lose interest quickly, as soon as they've grasped the underlying procedural rhetoric.

Narratologically, *TPM* situates itself in a tradition of multiperson narration (Richardson 2006), which refers to the combination of first, second, and third-person narration. Richardson (2006) distinguishes between two major types of multiperson narration: centrifugal and centripetal trends. In centrifugal narration, a polyphony of voices occurs that never seems to converge into one but often becomes more diffuse in the course of a narrative. Conversely, centripetal narration sees multiple voices come together in one, central voice. *TPM* exemplifies centrifugality as first, second, and third-person narration remain distinct narrative strands throughout. Since it never becomes entirely clear who is referred to by individual instances of textual *you,* in particular (e.g., "Perhaps you are Bluebeard"; "As long as you keep clicking the outcome is inevitable"), readers must oscillate ontologically between the fictional and the actual world. After all, they are clicking from lexia to lexia to read the narrative, thereby killing or breeding princesses consecutively—are they therefore part of the storyworld, that is, Bluebeard himself?

The text features two different openings that are randomized to reduce reader agency: the first option features the villain as a homodiegetic narrator, who introduces himself as follows:

My name is Bluebeard. I sit in my castle like a spider in its lair. The minor female royals are drawn to me, despite their terror. Their little hearts jump when they hear my name, their soft little hands flutter pointlessly in the air, their flabby white arms burdened with lace and silk and innocence.

They come seeking their fortune, but instead they find their fate construed in a past present future tense constrained by my name: Bluebeard.

The alternative opening introduces a *heterodiegetic*, omniscient fairytale narrator who uses a range of oral, or conversational, storytelling conventions, such as the inevitable "There was a(n)" (albeit without the genre-typical temporal adverbial "once upon a time"), lexical reduplication ("bad bad"), simple syntax, simple past tense, and reader address:

There was a bad bad man. His name was Bluebeard and he had a penchant for princesses. When he used them up, he murdered them. Thus Bluebeard consumed the choir of little princesses that inhabited the planet.

Perhaps you are Bluebeard, or perhaps you are a princess. Perhaps you are a detective, come to solve the case.

Interestingly, a sense of guilt and responsibility is gradually built up and increasingly reinforced by the narrative, which pushes the reader-interactor into the position of the killer, Bluebeard himself, through the use of textual *you* (Herman 1994, 2002; Ensslin and Bell 2012). The second-person pronoun draws the reader into the diegesis by confronting him or her with the choice of adopting the perspective of one of the participants in the narrative: the villain (Bluebeard), the victim ("a princess"), or a character from a different genre, the crime mystery ("a detective, come to solve the case") (figure 6.1). But whereas in a game that choice would have to be actualized by selecting a character to play, *TPM* leaves it open, thus enabling a more speculative and reflexive mode of engagement with the text.

Textual *you* is embedded in most videogame interfaces (Ensslin 2011a), as well as those of related media, such as hypertext and interactive fictions. Both in-game instructions and manuals encode the reader-player verbally in terms of a strongly apostrophic and directive textual *you*, most typically through direct commands (e.g., "Press X to fight"). Equally common for digital narratives are statements about imaginary truths involving the player's alter ego in the game (e.g., "You are standing on top of a massive canyon"). Employed in literary contexts, textual *you* becomes a subtle tool for creating various other types of reader engagement. For instance, Stuart Moulthrop's hypertext fiction *Victory Garden* (1991) employs a plural form of textual *you* in the lexia "Our American Way of Life" to evoke a collective audience as a means of drawing readers' attention to their roles as interactors with the text as well as their extrafictional roles as politically informed, historical individuals (Bell 2010, Bell and Ensslin 2011).[3]

As this analysis will show, *TPM* exemplifies the ways in which digital fictions can employ textual *you* to debunk the standards and mechanisms of narratives distributed by purveyors of popular entertainment. Used in this parodic manner, it blurs the boundaries between game and fiction while simultaneously subverting the subjective, uncritical behavior and attitudes exhibited by users prone to hyper-attentive modes of engagement.

The lack of control over the multilinear reading path that *TPM* invites readers to pursue, coupled with changing narrative perspectives associated with varying uses of textual *you*, complicates the contextual anchoring necessary to understand the fiction's changing frames of reference. Similarly, the multitude of fictional genres, narrative styles, and registers evoked by the narrative, ranging from detective fiction to pornography, creates a polyphony of voices, thus underscoring the subversive stance of the text vis-à-vis other digital genres.

Once the reader-player has stepped through the infamous door on the index page into the narrative, a mostly pictorial display welcomes him or her. The center of the page depicts a signpost pointing in three directions representing the three main strands of the narrative. In the top right corner, three interactive image buttons contain the words "stay," "trail," and "signs," both indicating and obscuring the navigational options they seem to represent. In the bottom right corner, textual *you* documents the reader's action and suggests what he or she needs to do to navigate the text: "You are reading the signs / Scattered images contain clues" (figure 6.2). Much like a detective, readers are thus left to find out for themselves how to "read the signs" and the "clues" hidden in "scattered images." Clicking on one of the three image buttons at the top plunges the reader into the narrative proper.

The text following the introductory lexia is divided into three major narrative strands. The first strand is a narrative that sees the reader-player killing off more and more princesses, accompanied by a falling princess census. It thematizes the reader-player's sadistic tendencies, implied in the action of repeated clicking: each click, in effect, adds to the suffering of the girls. This strand of the story appeals to the reader's sympathy for the victims by documenting what he or she is doing, metaphorically speaking, by clicking. Simultaneously, RPs are critiqued by the text in regard to the brutality underlying their (click-)action, despite or, indeed, because of the fact that there is no other way of navigating and reading. Similarly, the reader's increasing guilt is reflected in the text at a moral or ethical level ("the conjunction between you and Bluebeard grows stronger. / Your innocence drifts away with each sign you select and starting again won't change that"); a criminological level ("Now there are only 5 [princesses]./ Their

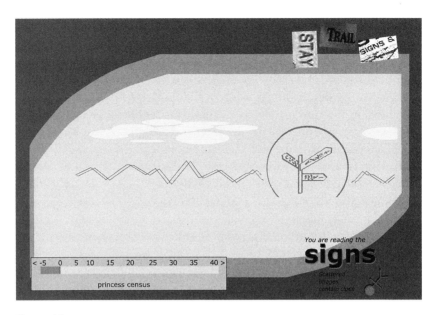

Figure 6.2
Stepping into the fictional world of *TPM*.

disappearance has been noted. You are a suspect"); a metamedial level ("the princesses you slaughter convert to data on your conscience"); a gender-critical, humanistic level ("Nor are the princesses unfeeling ciphers: they inherit emotions and even sensuality from your hotworld"); and a metafictional level ("just . . . one . . . final . . . chunk of text; text in the sky, under the bed, text to consume other texts, texts consume . . ."). On the whole, readers experiencing *TPM* are inadvertently confronted with the question of whether or not they should feel included in the group of addressees referred to by *you*, which leaves them wavering between different readings of *you* and therefore anchoring events, by turns, in contexts associated with the virtual and the actual world.

In the second narrative strand, the census rises to the point where too many princesses are in the castle. Instead of featuring any type of textual *you*, this strand is dominated by first-person narration instantiating the villainous voice of Bluebeard, who sets out to convey his sado-masochistic pornographic account thus: "My name is Bluebeard. I sit in my castle like a spider in its lair. The minor female royals are drawn to me, despite their terror. . . . After I have consumed their virginity, I consume their liver." Again, diegetic or world-creating statements are coupled with metadiscursive and metamedial statements ("I keep their vocabulary for my secret princess census"; "My cock my code. Killing princesses is a matter of changing their visibility setting. I will slaughter her with logic").

As readers reach "limbo," that is, some sort of final stalemate that suggests closure yet turns out to be an infinite loop, they are told that "[t]he crowd of princesses obscure[s] the text. Destroy some before venturing on." This is strongly reminiscent of adventure or role-playing games, in which a full repository of items sometimes forces players to replace individual objects strategically (see section 6.2).

An interim strand, sitting ontologically between the fictional and the actual world, is reached when the reader clicks "castle" in an attempt to escape the inevitable endings of either of the two first strands. In true deconstructivist fashion, however, this strand addresses the reader directly, thematizing the aporia of their navigational endeavors: "Where do you think you are going? What do you think you are doing? Why do you think you are doing it? You are lost in the castle." The reader has no other option than to leave this strand through the "escape" route, which brings them to the third major narrative strand—the police investigation.

This third strand transcends the ontological boundaries of the fairytale world without altogether leaving the level of diegesis. The ontological confusion is reinforced by quasi-critical header phrases opening each lexia that create seemingly random intertextual, metafictional, metamedial, spatial, and situational frames of reference, some of which refer to parts of the castle and its inhabitants ("Discarded letters in the castle vestibule disclose information about"; "Erstwhile castle virgins eating their own words eventually vomit this") while others are borrowed from other fictional narratives (e.g., "Tattooed onto Ophelia's stomach is the following") and nonfictional genres (e.g., "Insinuated subliminally by the TV advertising is"). These examples show that deliberate anachronisms and illogical pairings in the header phrases are used to evoke the idea of random story and text generators, adding to the ontological hesitation caused by different uses of textual *you* and the ontological transgression between different fictional worlds (the fairytale and the police interrogation room).

The narrative setting of this third strand of *TPM* is a police interrogation in which textual *you* appears in the form of fictional second-person narration (which traditionally refers to a character in the storyworld rather than the actual or *implied reader*): "The handcuffs chaff [*sic*] your wrists. In the interrogation room the police shove photos before you, mocking you with illusions of (cool, blue) freedom." There is also a (meta)fictionalized address between convict and police (convict: "Let me construct my own texts and you'll see"). The discourse of guilt suggested by the narrative frame (strand

1) renders the reader a metatextual accomplice in the alleged crime (of killing "the princess"). Hence the exposed reader is made to relate personally to the accusations directed at a seemingly *intradiegetic* or storyworld-internal *you*. Depending on the path chosen by the reader, his or her inscribed role will alternate between that of suspect, witness, and victim. The interrogation becomes increasingly abusive, with a hypertextual lack of closure projected onto the fiction through a suggestion of never-ending torture and imprisonment: "The psychologist inserts into your mind: *There is no escape; only (en)closure*" (italics in original). Again, this third strand can be left by clicking "escape" in the bottom right corner of the display, which returns the reader to the triadic signpost shown in figure 6.2.

In a select few instances of readerly enagement with *TPM*, a fourth, additional narrative strand emerges, which does not materialize with every rereading. This ghostly strand is narrated from the point of view of an Amazon queen who has come to take revenge on Bluebeard. The text is hidden in such a subtle way that it may be seen as a reference to hacking, modding, and other subversive practices in game culture, in which cheat codes are used, for example, to access user-generated gaming content or to facilitate or speed up progress. Such non-preinscribed narratives and mechanics are open only to the most adamant and creative modders and hackers, few of whom tend to be female and even fewer of whom are likely to be interested in seeing a woman take revenge on the phallocentric storyworld unless she is a scantily clad, hypersexualized Lara Croftian shero.

While popular digital media such as game manuals and walkthroughs profusely implement second-person apostrophe, the literary and subversive uses of textual *you* in *TPM* critically undermine the role of the second person in videogame texts and paratexts. As *TPM* never commits to any of its potential protagonists, it radicalizes what Richardson (2006, 21) describes as a "continuous dialectic of identification and distancing . . . , as the reader is alternately drawn closer to and further away from the protagonist." Readers of *TPM* enact a range of ontological and perspectival oscillations that ultimately expose the reader-player's role as an accomplice in many videogames' misogynist teleological trajectories.

Furthermore, by turning textual *you* upside down and making readers reflect on their willing commitment to popular media discourses, *TPM* problematizes neoliberalist subjection to commodity capitalism. Second-person apostrophe, coupled syntactically with present tense indicatives and imperatives, occurs ubiquitously in journalism, advertising and other PR materials, cookbooks, travel guides, and, of course, software and hardware manuals. It thus serves as a powerful, thought-provoking device in *TPM*, challenging the advertising industry's monopoly of *you* and the fact that most of their uses of the pronoun are gendered (Richardson 2006, 30). In the same way that cookbooks are written for an implicit female and fix-it manuals for an implicit male *you*, videogame manuals are often patronizingly "pinked up" if pitched at a young, female audience, or, indeed, pronominally male-gendered if directed at male players.

6.4   Discussion

Ludic mechanics in digital fictions can take a variety of shapes and forms, and the degree to which readers feel they are playing a game (or games) while reading a novel or short story varies accordingly. This section aims to compare and contrast *TPM* with two other contemporary digital fictions that embed ludic mechanics in very different ways without necessarily falling into the ludic half of the L-L spectrum generically: Kate Pullinger and Chris Joseph's *Inanimate Alice* (2005–2009) and Andy Campbell and Judi Alston's *Nightingale's Playground* (2010). Both texts gain their game-like quality largely through elements of conditionality, where continuous reading of the narrative text partly depends on readers' successful gameplay.

The online Flash fiction *Inanimate Alice* is an award-winning, multilingual work in progress. So far it comprises four episodes ("China," "Italy," "Russia," and "Hometown") that follow Alice, the protagonist, from childhood into adolescence. "Set in a technology-augmented near-future" (Pullinger and Joseph 2013), the first-person narrative takes the reader through various stages of Alice's development from a technology-savvy child to an experienced young videogame programmer. Accordingly, the language of the narrative changes from that of a child to that of a mature adult, as does the way Alice interacts with her changing social and geographic environments. Whereas in "China" (episode 1) she is still a young girl without much awareness of the political implications of her father's professional role in the oil industry, the two following episodes ("Italy" and "Russia") convey to the reader the affluent yet socially excluded situation of her parents, the domestic role of Arab women, and the personal risks involved in being foreigners in a socially and politically restrictive environment. During their stay in an Italian ski resort (episode 2), the narrative harks back to the family's actual residence in Saudi Arabia, where Alice has her own private tutor, Ayisha, with whom she communicates via her handheld Ba-Xi (a fictional brand name) device. Like an *idée fixe* or a *Dingsymbol*, the gadget recurs in each episode, taking on increasingly sophisticated shapes and functionalities. In its quasi-techno-utopian function, it works as an intermedial reference to the mobile technology boom, and Alice uses her gadget to create her own animations and to communicate with her imaginary friend, Brad—an animated character whom she herself has programmed. Episode 3 ("Russia") contains the first dramatic turning point in Alice's life, when her parents are expelled from Russia for political and economic reasons, the details of which are left to the reader's imagination and intertextual frame of reference. Episode 4 sees Alice and her parents settled into a murky, working-class home in suburban Middle England, where she goes to school for the first time and experiences the challenges and peer pressures of teenage life.[4]

Not only does this text feature a handheld device (the Ba-Xi) that metaphorically stands for mobile gaming, but readers have to play minigames in order to progress with the narrative. Episode 1 ("China"), for instance, contains a section in which eight-year-old Alice takes pictures of wild flowers as she passes by them in her mother's car. The flowers appear and disappear on screen and the cursor turns into a mini-Ba-Xi to represent, iconically, the way Alice holds her gadget to take photographs. Readers have to mouse over the flowers to enact this process and the narrative doesn't continue until all flowers have been captured in this way.

Episode 3 ("Russia") has two interactive modes: "read only" and "read and play the game." The former contains an animated representation of a Ba-Xi-based matryoshka (nesting dolls) catching game, created by Alice herself. The latter, however, has an actual matryoshka catching game superimposed onto the digital narrative, and readers have to catch one doll per scene in order to succeed in bribing the airport security guard in the final section: the guard will comply only if all dolls in the episode have been collected, and once the last doll has been captured, reader-players will receive a vividly animated reward interface flashing up numerous, multicolored instances of "You did it!" Read-and-play mode therefore affords a radically different interactive experience than read-only mode. It represents Alice's world and interests in a more immediate, multisensory, ludic, and immersive way, and readers are made to realize that experiencing a digital fiction involves far greater interactive versatility than reading the verbal narrative contained in it. In fact, the way the Russian dolls are hidden in unpredictable places around the interface makes readers scan the screen in a far more comprehensive, searching way than concentrating on words only or even words and images would require.

Campbell and Alston follow a slightly different approach to game-like conditionality in Nightingale's Playground, a tetralogy of digital fictions revolving around a male protagonist, Carl, who is in search of a semi-imaginary ex-fellow-student, Alex Nightingale. In the first part of the tetralogy, Consensus Trance I, Carl finds and opens an old suitcase filled with bric-a-brac, triggering memories of Alex. He follows these memories to Alex's house. *Consensus Trance II* starts as Carl reaches the door and enters the house, at which point the reading experience becomes an embodied, 3D narrative performance. Part three is Alex's science fieldwork book, which contains further clues about his semi-fictional identity, his relationship to Carl, and the mysterious Sentinel game around which their relationship seems to have revolved. Readers can turn the pages via mouse-over and drag-and-drop. Finally, part four is a paper-under-glass document, or e-book. Ludologically, of course, the first two parts are most relevant to this study. Nevertheless, the entire tetralogy may be seen as a narrative riddle in the tradition of the crime mystery and, hence, as a combination of traditional literary play (with the reader) and elements of literary gaming.

Consensus Trance I, the first segment, is an interactive Flash fiction that uses static background images for its interface design and requires readers to click, zoom, and pan across the interface to find narrative sequences. Only once they have read all of the hidden fragments are new narrative elements, or "levels," as we might call them, unlocked. Narrative progress therefore depends on the reader-player's successful interaction with the interface. A similar approach is taken in *Consensus Trance II*, a Coppercube 2.0-based[5] "work of digital fiction that presents a readable, written narrative within a 3D game-like environment" (Dreaming Methods 2010, 1). While it isn't a game per se, it uses the same navigation mechanics, or "control situation" (Dreaming Methods 2010, 1), as well-known, PC-based first-person shooters such as *Half Life* (Valve Corporation 1998) or *Quake* (id Software 1996): moving the mouse will pan the camera; pressing the arrow keys will move the first-person avatar; and pressing Escape will close the session. The 3D-enabled reader walks through the rooms of a house, picking up narrative fragments on the way that will "further the story" and unlock doors to more rooms and narrative chunks. Thus, game-like conditionality again features strongly but in slightly less obvious ways than in *Inanimate Alice*.

In the following schematic representation of where on the L-L spectrum the three digital fictions discussed in this chapter are located I shall treat both *Inanimate Alice* (*IA*) and *Nightingale's Playground* (*NP*) as conflated units rather than treating each episode or part of them individually. This is to reflect the idea that both narratives establish their ludic and narrative coherence holistically rather than episodically.

As shown in figure 6.3, the specific ludic mechanics of the three digital fictions bring them very close, generically, to actual games. This is most strongly the case with the playable version of *IA*: it embeds actual minigames that are conditionally linked to narrative progression. But the conceptual proximity to actual games also derives from the fact that the language used

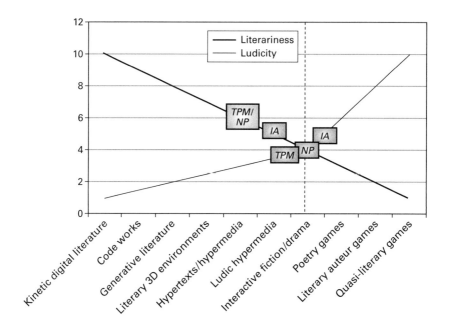

Figure 6.3
The Princess Murderer (*TPM*), *Inanimate Alice* (*IA*), and *Nightingale's Playground* (*NP*) distributed across the L-L spectrum.

is deliberately simple and child-like and therefore much more akin to the user-friendly, nonpoetic language used in commercial computer games. I have colocated *TPM* and *NP* on the literariness scale since they both follow a strong narrative poetics and require far more literary close reading than *IA* does. With regards to ludicity, *TPM* is less playable than the other two digital fictions as it doesn't rely on ludic conditionality for its narrative progression. Nor does it use game-like interface controls, such as panning and moving through 3D spaces in first-person mode using cursor keys (as in *NP*), or using mouse-over for catching 2D objects (as in *IA*). *TPM*'s main ludic device, the princess census, is ultimately a delusive device used to distract, confuse, and criticize rather than guide and reassure readers in their interactive endeavors. After all, of the three digital fictions discussed in this chapter, only *TPM* uses aspects of game design for an antiludic agenda (to expose readers as "clickoholics," which puts them on an equal footing with hyper-attentive gamers). Conversely, both *IA* and *NP* feature ludicity to enhance rather than impede or critique an immersive reading experience. We may conclude, therefore, that they are far less attached (if at all) to an avant-garde design agenda than *TPM* is.

7   Of Windsighs and Wayfaring: *Blue Lacuna,* an Epic Interactive Fiction

7.1   Introduction

In the previous chapter, we saw how ludic-mechanic elements can operate in digital fictions to a greater or lesser extent without diminishing their readerly agenda. Conversely, this chapter will venture further into ludic territory and focus on perhaps the most hybrid of all literary-ludic genres in the digital sphere. Interactive fictions consist almost exclusively of text in the sense of typescript, and they "must succeed as literature and as game at once to be effective" (Montfort and Moulthrop 2003, 1). In other words, they functionalize close reading in such a way as to make textual understanding a prerequisite of successful gameplay. Reading the text both literally and between the lines is important for lateral thinking and progress in IFs. By the same token, the reader-player's own linguistic and narrative creativity is required to crack the most difficult puzzles posed by the text.[1]

IFs are largely an independent sector phenomenon: they tend to be freely downloadable, often come with their source code attached, and are accompanied by a creative and receptive culture that consists mostly of aficionados, experimental writers, and indie game designers. IFs are descendents of the commercially traded 1980s Infocom text adventures in that they follow their basic format of a text window displaying chunks of narrative and ludic information, as well as having a prompt follow each chunk.[2] Players have to enter simple text commands after these prompts, such as "GO NORTH" (abbreviated "N" or "NORTH"), "OPEN LETTER," or "SAVE" (to save the game played up to a certain point). This will trigger narrative chunks conveying essential information about the avatar's situation and (possible) actions, such as "You can only return home from here." Interestingly, and to repeat a major concern of the previous chapter, here again we can see how deeply rooted textual *you* is in game culture, as the second-person pronoun and directive utterances are used extensively in IF to construct the storyworld via RP address and commands. While classic text adventures do not have any literary aspirations to speak of, however, most literarily minded IF writers place a strong emphasis on novelistic features such as impressionistic and emotive descriptions of situations, landscapes, and events; the relationship between the reader's avatar and other characters; and linguistic playfulness and other types of literary experimentalism.

This chapter will zoom in on perhaps the most extensive, lyrically ambitious, and narratologically complex IF currently in existence: Aaron A. Reed's sci-fi fantasy epic *Blue Lacuna: An Interactive Novel in Ten Chapters* (2008). Following a general introduction to IF as a digital verbal art genre, I will offer a ludostylistic reading of *Blue Lacuna* (*BL*). It will focus in particular on the IF's unique ways of developing character based on the RP's decisions; on ways in which it facilitates play-reading (an effect I refer to as reverse ergodicity); and on the way it functionalizes aspects of prose language to enable and structure gameplay. The final section will then provide a comparison between *BL* and other "literary" IFs and place the selected texts on the L-L spectrum.

7.2   IF as the Classic Hybrid between Adventure Game and Literary Narrative

According to electronic literature pioneers N. Katherine Hayles and Nick Montfort (2012, 452; see also Montfort 2003), interactive fiction tends to be defined as "a text-based narrative in which the user is offered navigational possibilities . . . , assets to pick up or refuse (such as a sword or key), virtual objects to view and manipulate, and a framework in which the user can win or lose." In other words, IFs share a core range of characteristics with computer and particularly adventure and role-playing games: an underlying story or gameworld that reader-players explore, navigate, and interact with as they respond to interface prompts; repository items that can be collected, dropped, and put to various ludic uses; props that are positioned in gameworld settings and may be interacted with in various ways; and, not least, a set of victory and/or termination conditions that adds a sense of closure to an otherwise multilinear, open-ended interactive experience. IFs can be won, or successfully completed; many of them allow reader-players to score points; they pose challenges that have to be overcome to enable narrative progress; and they offer narrative worlds that emerge through exploration, experimentation, and interaction rather than presenting fully formed stories.

That said, IFs are strongly indebted to literary culture, not least because they use linguistic information to cause RPs to activate their imaginative powers and construct, from textual material, narrative worlds and events. Due to the options given to RPs, IFs are "arborescent" (Ciccoricco 2012, 475): they follow a branching structure that is contingent for its development on readers' decisions and actual linguistic input at crucial points in the story. Thus, the verbally manifested text—displayed much like a dialogue between interactor and text machine (Aarseth 1997)—informs interactors' narrative understanding and mental images of the storyworld and story arc. The resulting imaginative constructs can therefore be quite different from reader to reader and depend very much on the individual choices made and commands entered.

Because IFs tend to assign roughly equal importance to literary narrative and adventure game (but see section 7.5 for a more refined view), they are often referred to as the most hybrid genre within the field of literary gaming. In an early essay, leading IF practitioner and theorist Nick Montfort (2004) explored an entire set of labels to approach a definition of IFs that paid tribute to its generic complexity and ambivalence: "story," "game," "storygame," "novel," "world," "literature," "puzzle," "problem," "riddle," and "machine." He found that while each covered aspects of IF as a narrative genre, none of them captured its essence comprehensively. "Story," for instance, relates to the observation that interacting with IFs results in sequentialized narratives that can be retold, although, of course, those sequences tend to differ from reader to reader. "Game" is too broad a concept to pay tribute to the technological and phenomenological specifics of IF. The term may best be understood in terms of "contest," which can refer to many aspects of competitive play—for instance, between author and reader, between readers, or even the internal competition of players trying to beat themselves in the sense of improving on their earlier scores. Furthermore, most IFs gain much of their game-ness from the "puzzles," "problems," and "riddles" that players have to solve in order to jigsaw together the storyworld and its narrative events. That said, there are IFs without any of these features, so they can't be used as defining criteria. "Storygame" is a term introduced by Buckles (1985; see Montfort 2004) to refer to the embeddedness of one or many games (or rather, as I would put it, elements of ludic mechanics) in the overarching story, yet again the term is too inclusive to apply to the specific characteristics of IF. The term "novel," as discussed by Montfort (2004), is useful only insofar as it alludes to the time it takes to complete an IF—"short story" might be used for works that tend to take significantly less time to read than an average novel. "World" is another slightly reductive term except, perhaps, for the fact that it describes the setting as the starting point of the reader's interactions, rather than there being a ready-made story. As pointed out elsewhere in this book, "literature," although not used as an evaluative term, simply cannot be applied to all IFs because not all of them purport to be verbal art in terms of linguistic foregrounding and self-reflexivity. For my comparative discussion in the final section of this chapter, I have therefore chosen four works that exemplify digital literariness in unique ways.

In relation to the term "machine," Montfort (2004, 315) stresses that IFs are ultimately programs, or executable codes, that operate via parsing input and rule-based output. They simulate narrative worlds on the basis of natural language parsing and generation. In addition to that, they may (yet are not required to) contain ludic-mechanic elements such as points scoring, riddles, and puzzles that are functionalized as prerequisites for narrative progress. By the same token, they may contain a particular literary, or poetic, aesthetic, which can include lyrical descriptions, character development and complexity, and various types of wordplay.

It is in the nature of some literary IFs to play or experiment with the conventions of their own genre. Emily Short's *Galatea* (2000a) and Ian Finley's *Exhibition* (1999), for example, do not keep score (Montfort 2004, 312). Instead, IFs may focus, for example, on characterization techniques and character complexity, multiple perspectives, or different endings and/ or storylines without victory conditions. Many offer rewards not (only) in the form of points or level-ups (we might rather clumsily call them *chapter-ups*) but rather in the shape of new and often surprising narrative material, metaphysical, psychological, or spiritual insights, or simply the literary reader's delight in wordplay and other traditional literary "games." The following introduction to *Blue Lacuna* will present further writing and design techniques that help to accentuate IF's readerly, literary potential without sacrificing its hyper attentive appeal.

7.3   *Blue Lacuna*—Epic, Novel, and Game

Reed's *Blue Lacuna* (2008) is an "interactive novel" of epic dimensions that blends novelistic and ludic-mechanic features into a coherent, emotive, and suspenseful reading/playing experience. According to its online blurb, it is "an explorable story in the *tradition* of interactive fiction and text adventures. It's a novel about discovery, loss, and choice. It's a game about words and emotions, not guns" (emphasis mine). Thus, its mission statement explicates the author's ambition to present the IF's interactors with a readerly experience inspired by that of conventional interactive fiction, but one that can indeed be likened to a novel. Readers can expect a complex narrative structure, a long and potentially multilayered series of plot events, a large number of more or less rounded characters, and the linguistic means used by novelists to project a detailed, nuanced image of the storyworld's setting(s) and the main characters' personalities, motivations, thoughts, and emotions. Similarly, readers can expect high levels of suspense and possibly even philosophical depth evoked by events, dialogues, and representations of thought. I would argue that *BL* achieves these novelistic aims without falling into the descriptive trap—a pitfall facing many IF writers with high literary ambitions who deliver an overabundance of repetitive and lengthy descriptive passages, thus running the risk of losing impatient, hyper attentive players prematurely.

Generically, *BL* mixes elements of science fiction and fantasy. The storyworld is set on the imaginative, sylvan island of Blue Lacuna, a tropical nature reserve surrounded by the sea. It includes both fantastic and (super)natural phenomena (such as a bewildering species of large trees called "windsighs" and a swarm of intelligent super-bees) and peculiar signs of human and alien technological interference (such as a treehouse and an egg-shaped alien spaceship). The windsighs appear "stunted or out of place," and while they seem of little or no ludic or narrative importance at the opening of the fiction, they turn out to be seminal symbolical and interactive elements in later chapters.

The player-character (P-C), who can be male or female, gay or straight, is described as an artist or "wayfarer."[3] Having left her lover, Rume (again either male or female), to follow her "Call," the P-C finds herself on Blue Lacuna, ready to explore its vast expanses and complex technological mechanisms.

Following the expository prologue and first chapter, chapters 2 to 6 of *BL* see the protagonist exploring the island step by step. She finds out how to operate a highly complex steam piping system in the island's defunct volcano, how to read a series of encrypted messages left in various places around the island, and how to unlock or engineer paths to previously hidden or inaccessible places, such as the pyramid on the mountain, the island off the seal beach, and the massive windsigh on the saddle above the water cave. Finally, she learns how to open the pyramid and operate its interiors via passwords to arrive in two external worlds, Forest and City, which form the settings of chapters 8 and 9, respectively.

During her ramblings around the forest and the beach, the protagonist meets Progue, the only other human being inhabiting the island. In their early dialogues Progue seems at least partly mad, yet throughout the interactive story the P-C receives an increasing amount of information about him, his family, and his biography that explains his madness and ultimately presents him as a fully-fledged, rounded, and plausible character. The protagonist learns that he lost both his wife, Rengin, and his daughters, Lethe and Phoebe, under mysterious circumstances while on the island. The P-C infers, mostly from her dreams and by decoding encrypted messages, that the girls somehow disappeared into the volcano and/or were possibly kidnapped by the aliens who invaded the island. She learns that Progue's mission on the island was the same as the one she faces toward the end of the narrative, but that he went insane rather than completing this mission. The final confrontation in chapter 10 involves the protagonist and Progue, and the communicative choices made by the P-C determine the resulting destiny of the island. Blue Lacuna may become either a colony of a vast technophilic, postapocalyptic galactic empire (if the P-C chooses to bestow it to the City world), or effectively a large plantation of carefully tended windsighs—symbols of a symbiotic human-nature relationship, where humans are subjects of natural powers (if the player opts for the Forest community). By the same token, the P-C's communicative selections determine Progue's destiny and whether or not he ultimately gets a happy ending in the form of a metaphysical reunion with his deceased wife.

The term "epic" is an appropriate attribute for *BL* for a number of reasons. First, *BL* offers a storyworld of vast dimensions. It comprises ten chapters that take readers through three different subworlds: the beautiful, almost deserted island of Blue Lacuna (chapters 2–7 and 10), and two additional utopian (or dystopian) worlds called Forest and City (chapters 8 and 9), the existence of which the RP does not even learn until more than halfway into the IF. Second, the P-C's experience with this world is accurately described as a "journey" by the game's blurb: it equals the experience of an epic fantasy hero (such as Frodo in *The Lord of the Rings*); it stretches over several fictional weeks (or more, depending on the actual time RPs require to complete the challenges set by the game);[4] and it involves an extensive explorative journey during which the RP gradually learns about the internal workings of the island and how they might unlock previously inaccessible regions. Finally, the philosophical, moral, and emotional implications of the P-C's interactions and choices have a sense of grandeur in that he or she has to choose between an artistic career ("art") and a life that favors strong human bonds ("love") both at the beginning and the end of the narrative. Not only does the storyline change according to these choices, but the full extent of the IF's narrative and interactive meanings may alter the P-C's mindset radically over the course of the narrative.

Due to its sheer textual expanses (approximately 375,000 words of Inform 7 code) and a multitude of playerly options shaping the storyline in various ways, a single playthrough is likely to take up to a week or more to complete (depending on the interactor's creativity, patience, experience, and lateral thinking abilities, as well as the occasional workings of pure chance). That said, it lies within authorial expectations that committed RPs attempt more than one playthrough to experiment with alternative avatars, behavioral or communicative choices, and pragmatic decisions at important junctures within the narrative, in order to see how these variations alter *BL*'s narrative and ludic meanings and the interactor's experience. Furthermore, there are two overarching interactive approaches programmed into the text: it offers a story mode and a puzzle mode (a similar agenda as that shown in *Inanimate Alice*, episode 3—see section 6.4 of this book), the latter containing the kind of ludic-mechanic elements one would expect from an adventure game, such as riddles and other cognitive challenges, and the former allowing readers to bypass such elements or simplify them to facilitate the flow of reading.

7.4   A Ludostylistic Approach to Analyzing *Blue Lacuna*

In this section, I offer an eclectic ludostylistic analysis of *BL*. It will include ludological and ludonarratological considerations based on my personal puzzle mode experience, focusing on how narrative and ludicity are interwoven to evoke a coherent game- and storyworld. In particular, I shall explore how the P-C's choices and interactions with other characters result in diverse story endings.[5] Another ludonarratological focus will be on external narrativity—here in the form of the author's online "Hints"—and how it is embedded in the IF's overall paratextual macrostructure. Ludosemiotically, I will examine how *BL*'s prose style is functionalized so as to foreground specific verbal structures (such as descriptive adjectives) that tie in with ludic elements (such as door codes that have to be cracked). In terms of mediality, my major concern will be the ways in which *BL* transcends the ergodic conventions of its genre, for instance, by offering linguistic shortcuts and other simplifying mechanisms. Intertextual and intermedial links will be considered as part of this exploration because they constitute what we may call "imaginative shortcuts" to help readers create highly complex mental representations of the gameworld(s) and the events happening within.

The puzzle-mode experience of *BL* contains a range of ludic-mechanic features that give readers the impression that they are playing some kind of game, or rather a series of consecutive minigames. More precisely, RPs realize they have to meet certain challenges, or carry out a certain number of explorative moves, in order to progress with the narrative. In other words, narrative development is inextricably connected with and contingent on playerly performance and the extent to which RPs master the heuristic ergodicity (see chapter 5) offered by the text. For example, the P-C can reach the top of the mountain only once she has figured out how to send enough power into the ropeway system leading to the summit, and realized that she has to climb into the crate and handle the lever described by the narrative in order to activate the mechanism. This process is complicated by the fact that the pipe powering the ropeway system receives enough steam only if the other two pipes connected to the boiler in the volcano's caldera are completely deactivated. This complex learning process involves a considerable amount of trial and error as well as patience on the part of the RP.

BL isn't exactly a game that can be won. After all, it offers various different narrative versions, openings, and endings, and there isn't a "right" or "wrong" conclusion. There are equivalent alternatives rather than more or less preferable outcomes or even targets that have to be met in order to succeed. However, the sense of achievement and relief resulting from chaptering up and/or reaching the end of the narrative—after days or even weeks of hyper attentive immersion—can be likened to that of leveling up, winning a tricky battle, or reaching the end of a game. It can feel more earned than reaching the last page of a 500-page novel, which is, of course, also associated with a sense of relief and achievement, but in a way that is less dependent on the reader's own intelligence, creativity, and lateral thinking abilities.

A particularly pertinent aspect of *BL*'s ludonarrativity is the way in which character complexity and development are interlinked with the P-C's choices and progress. Progue, for example, initially appears mostly like a madman who has decided to spend the rest of his life on the island, ranting and creating idiosyncratic sculptures. In the course of the P-C's interactions with him, however, he turns out to be a highly complex character and his actions and behavior increasingly seem more coherent, motivated, and logical.

Character development occurs in a variety of ways. For example, the P-C is bound to undergo moral and emotional transformations during her adventures and interactions on the island and the two other worlds, and the motivations of her actions and choices are likely to transform as a result. My own character chose art over love at the opening of the IF. Having learned about Progue's tragic family history, however, she changed her mind in chapter 10, choosing the humane over the career-focused route. Furthermore, the number of conversational turns dedicated to a specific character is stored by the system as a score, determining which particular character is going to be foregrounded at the end of the narrative. According to the author, "one of the major differences [between different versions of the story] is that there are three different epilogue sequences based on whether the system thinks your choices have made the story more about 1) Progue, 2) Rume, or 3) yourself. For instance, spending more time with Progue makes his epilogue more likely, and performing selfish acts makes the self-centered epilogue more likely" (Personal correspondence, March 8, 2013).[6]

BL follows an important trend associated with game culture: it presents itself not as a singular textual object but rather as the nucleus of a wider textual ecology (see Ensslin 2011, 42) designed around it. It downloads from a website that also contains *BL*'s full source code; a prelude (or rather stump thereof, as the full "blueful" text has ceased to exist online[7]); an "About" page listing awards, acknowledgments, and special features; a Java-based excerpt playable online (rather than on a Glulx interpreter, which is needed for the full text); the download page; reactions, quotes, and endorsements; a contact page; and a section where RPs can make donations. Importantly, a further menu item is "Hints," which comprises the author's tips for solving the most difficult challenges and includes his own contact details for RPs who are stuck despite the hints. The Hints page also offers links to labeled and unlabelled pictographic maps of the island to help RPs "find their bearings." The main part of its text, however, is structured in terms of written questions and answers, grouped by some geographic sections of *BL* (e.g., subtitled "The Volcano" and "The Mountain") and some numbered chapters. Seen as a whole, it forms some kind of *proleptic*, dialogic re- or rather pretelling of the narrative as a whole. Based on the RP's assumed questions and the author's suggestive clues and direct answers, a considerable amount of narrative information is revealed simply by reading this page. Furthermore, RPs cannot guess at any given point during their interaction with *BL* how long its chapters are (or will turn out to be in their individual cases), and how much progress there still is to make to reach the end of each, and, indeed, the whole, narrative. The Hints page fills this knowledge gap to a considerable degree, thereby creating a strong sense of anticipation, suspense, and closure. RPs who ignore the Hints page are put at a considerable disadvantage compared to their initiated counterparts and are therefore far more likely to either give up before completing the IF or at least spend considerably more time meandering the island.

Ludosemiotically, most IFs are limited to black typescript on a white background. Some rare exceptions (such as Jim Munroe's *Everybody Dies*— see section 7.5) contain occasional illustrations, but the core appeal of this digital genre is the imaginative demands it makes on the reader, who has to construct and memorize from the text not only mental representations of entire storyworlds but, indeed, the complex mechanisms underlying the IF's ludic structure. *BL* does not supply any illustrations. However, it aids its readers by color-coding key words in the text that can be entered after a prompt without any accompanying syntax. Words in blue are object keywords that, when entered, allow readers to progress with the story or receive more or less important descriptive information about the marked word. Words in green are exit points that take RPs from one location to the next (such as "doorway" or "down"). They are saved on the player's inventory as so-called landmarks, which can be accessed later via shortcuts. This particular feature contributes significantly to *BL*'s smooth flow of interaction because it prevents unnecessarily lengthy navigation via the conventional directional command system.

More generally, *BL* features a number of ludic-mechanic mechanisms that render it more fluid and accessible than most other IFs I am aware of. The landmark shortcuts, the keyword navigation system, the random input parser in the dream sequences, and carefully embedded tutorials and hints are all instances of what I would refer to as reverse ergodicity: where program code is used in such a way as to facilitate rather than disrupt or complicate the reading process in nontrivial (ergodic) interactive systems. These aspects increase the readerly potential of the puzzle-mode version without sacrificing the text's ludicity. The latter is ensured by the sheer complexities of the remaining challenges, for which no hints or clues are offered.

The way intertextuality and intermediality feature in *BL* can be seen as another element of reverse ergodicity—an element that operates on an imaginative rather than ludic-mechanic level. The text is full of allusions to dystopian and/or science-fiction novels and movies (*1984*, *Blade Runner*, *Avatar*), books on digital media culture (Sherry Turkle's *Alone Together*, 2011),[8] and earlier adventure games and text adventures such as *Myst* and *Zork*. These cognitive links are stored in the experienced RP's memory and activated on reading passages such as "Alone Yet Together" (the title of a human Möbius strip sculpture in "City," chapter 9). Having created an associative intertextual link to a world like that of *Myst*, for example (an early 3D graphic adventure videogame; Cyan 1993), aids RPs in imagining the physical setting of *BL*, as well as its interior workings.

BL differs from most other literarily ambitious IFs in that it uses a profusely impressionistic if not lyrical prose style designed to produce a strong emotive effect on the reader and to lend the narrative an almost meditative atmosphere. The following passage is a description of the "Beach, Near the Abandoned Cabin": "The sun sinks slowly towards the waves, which sparkle in brilliant reflections of gold and silver, sending dancing patterns of light over the black lava flow behind the cabin. White sand flecked with bits of seaweed and debris stretches in a great arc around the lagoon." The frequent occurrence of color adjectives ("gold," "silver," "white"), coupled with action verbs used as predicates of inanimate objects ("dancing patterns"), lends *BL*'s prose style a vivid, sensuous tone, thus projecting a storyworld that is both rich in emotions and actions.

Color adjectives also have an important ludic-mechanic function in *BL*. They form part of riddles that have to be solved to gain access to locked locations. The door in the beach cabin's backroom, for example, can be unlocked only by using a complex color code: "six small bands" in different colors that are evocative of items the player may or may not have encountered previously. The description of the red band, for example, is "A deep, rich crimson," a synonym of red that also appears in the description of some fruits near the treehouse: "The berries are plump, the ripest ones a deep crimson." Hence, the code word to be entered here is "berry."

To have literary ambitions, an IF does not need a sophisticated lyrical-poetic approach to novelistic language. More important for literary IFs is the ways in which they functionalize language, using it not only as a means of narrative communication and input parsing but as a self-reflexive, creative ludic-mechanic tool. As we have seen in this section, *BL* functionalizes descriptive adjectives, for example, so that a poetic tool gains a secondary, ludic-mechanic function. The following section will show how other literary IFs approach functionalized novelistic prose as a ludostylistic instrument.

7.5 Discussion

There is no doubt that the IF genre lends itself to linguistic-stylistic exploration and experimentation. After all, of all genres of electronic literature (with the exception of hypertext) and digital games, it is the most linguistically driven, with an interface that uses almost exclusively written language rather than an assembly of multimodal codes. A rare exception to this language-only approach in IF is Jim Munroe's (2008) "Interactive Fantasy" *Everybody Dies* (*ED*). Listed in the *Electronic Literature Collection, Volume Two* (Borràs et al. 2011), it features "well-developed characters, lively writing," and numerous "stylish illustrations" by Michael Cho.[9]

ED's literary ambitions go beyond "lively writing" and rounded characters, however. Unusually for an IF, it uses first- (rather than second-) person narration, and the perspective changes between different characters, making it a multiperson narrative. The initial protagonist is Graham, "your standard variety skid, rocker, or metalhead depending on which suburb you grew up in." He works at a Cost Cutters supermarket. His adolescent thoughts are represented in a slangy, interior-monologue style, fraught with expletives. However, in the course of the narrative the first-person avatar's perspective switches between characters, for instance, from Graham's to Ranni's, a toilet cleaner at Cost Cutters, and then to that of his line manager, Lisa. These perspectival shifts co-occur with stylistic changes, for example, from Graham's youthful slang to the colloquial Standard English spoken by Ranni: "It's my ceremonial dagger. I'm a Sikh, OK? It's my religion." This particular quote is an example of another unnatural narrative technique followed by *ED*: the characters occasionally respond to the RP directly, temporarily transgressing the boundary between the intradiegetic world of the characters and the reader's extradiegetic world. Ranni's slightly irritated reply to the reader's command, "x kirpan," represented above, can thus be seen as a brief but poignant instance of metalepsis.

The entire narrative discourse is interspersed with the intrusive voices of the four main characters. As Lisa takes over as first-person narrator, for instance, Ranni breaks into her interior monologue: "Dream? interrupts Ranni from somewhere in the back part of my head. No." The overall impression this multivocality evokes is that the RP's avatar cannot only change between embodied characters but is also open to infiltration from other, physically separate entities. This perspectival openness, paired with the first-person point of view throughout, makes for a highly dynamic, unconventional IF reading experience.

Hence, *ED*'s main literary appeal lies in the way it uses narrative language and perspective. However, ludologically it follows a creative approach as well. Clearly, unlike *BL*, it does not use a sophisticated parsing system. The commands available to the reader are mostly default IF verbs and nouns such as "LOOK," "EXAMINE," "INVENTORY," and "NORTH." What is more important from a ludological perspective is the way in which *ED* parodies the significance of death and respawning that is characteristic of videogames. The P-C inevitably dies many times throughout the IF, in the roles of various characters. However, rather than taking players back to the beginning for a fresh start, the deaths turn out to be dreams, and the ends of the dreams coalesce with perspectival shifts between characters. For example, it is possible for P-Cs to "die" after just a few turns, "[a]nd yet, somehow, the game continues" from the point of view of another character.

The 2D illustrations inserted in the text following the protagonist's apparent death(s), or rather dreams, operate complementarily to the written text. Whenever the P-C enters a dream sequence, the IF begins to replace text with evocative images. For example, after plunging into the river, RPs are shown memory fragments of what the protagonist saw immediately before dying: images of an approaching fish containing a smaller fish inside its stomach. Thus, illustrations in *ED* add an element of pictographic mimesis to the otherwise purely verbal diegesis. Rather than representing what the written text says iconically, in a different semiotic mode, the images offer additional narrative information, the exact explication of which RPs have to construct from the images alone.

As IF writer Emily Short (2008) puts it, the ludostylistic tools used in *ED* exemplify how literarily ambitious IF writers "explore ways to change registers in order to achieve [IF's] full potential as a medium." "Register" here may have at least two meanings: linguistic styles, as exemplified by Ranni's and Lisa's language, discussed earlier, and different semiotic modes, such as written language and image. Clearly, using images not only as a substitute for verbal language but also as an independent, spiritual, or dreamlike mode of narration isn't a novelty in itself in the history of narrative arts. Comics and graphic novels, for instance, draw on this method profusely and effectively. However, the way *ED* embeds its illustrations in the RP's interactive experience, interspersing commands such as "LOOK" with pictorial information, shows a large degree of literary, ludic, and semiotic creativity.

The main playerly objective of *ED* is to find seven shopping carts altogether and return them to the supermarket parking lot. However, accomplishing this task does not constitute the victory or termination condition of the IF. Nor does the player score any points. Indeed, what turns out to be more important in *ED* is the multivocal narrative discourse between the four main characters, Ranni, Lisa, Graham, and Patrick, and the way in which they seem to try to take over the narrative lead from each other, as if it were a competition between *intradiegetic* "players" rather than a competition between the extradiegetic player and the text (or the implied author). Thus, *ED* gains its ludicity through a highly unconventional approach to agonistic literary play. Consequently, although it places a strong emphasis on narrative experimentation, its ludic feel comes close to that of *BL*.

Montfort (2000) takes a different approach to literary IF in *Ad Verbum* (*AV*). Inspired by Oulipian linguistic and literary self-reflexivity, this work operates largely on verbal puns, synonymy, alliterations, and other conventional language "games." The narrative revolves around the pending demolition of the Wizard of Wordplay's mansion, which the RP has to prepare for by removing from the building any "worthless" remains that prevent a narrative plot from unfolding. And, indeed, this IF does not aim to project a vast and complex storyworld as *BL* does. On the contrary, its creative focus lies in the micro- rather than macrostructures of narrative language. RPs are tested on their alliterative and lexical abilities. Ironically, avatars can pick up a "verbosifier" early in the game to boost their linguistic abilities. However, the bulky tool turns out to be an obstacle when attempting to enter rooms on the first floor—a humorous allusion to the uselessness of verbose language when it comes to a tightly organized narrative plot.

Much to the linguistically minded reader's comic relief, *AV* satirizes the descriptive conventions of its own genre by parodying IF's emphasis on spatial exploration and navigational prowess. It does so, for instance, by means of lexical reduplication ("the difficult difficult difficult door"), nonsensical neoclassical compounds ("antepenultimate lobby"), and alliterative noun phrases used for place names and objects ("Ebony Eatery"; "stainless steel stapler"). Furthermore, rather than finding it difficult to access rooms, readers of *AV* have to find creative ways to exit them, mostly by means of alliterative wordplay. The Neat Nursery, for instance, is described as a "[n]ice, nondescript nursery, noticeably neat. Normally, nurslings nestle noisily. Now, none. No needful, naive newborns." Once inside, the reader is presented with matching alliterative passages from literary history, such as "Non nonny, nonny . . . nonny . . ." from Shakespeare's *Hamlet* (act 4, scene 5, "Ophelia's Song"). The item to be collected in the nursery is a "nifty nappy." However, using the standard commands "TAKE" or "GET [NAPPY]" leads to alliterative error messages such as "No! No! Negative, novice. Nasty notation." Conversely, entering the quasi-synonym "NIP" leads to success: an extra three credit points and the tongue-in-cheek admonition, "Naughty, naughty! Nibbling nappies not normal." Following the successful collection of the target item, the player can exit the nursery only by entering a previously memorized alliterative cue word, provided by some earlier text—in this case "New."

As shown in the previous paragraph, feedback on the player's performance is a constitutive element of *AV*. Similarly, completing the game will trigger the system message, "You have won," suggesting a playerly scenario. However, the game label isn't appropriate merely because of *AV*'s performance-drivenness. The main objective of the IF isn't the evocation of a complex storyworld with rounded characters and a diversity of narrative styles and atmospheres. Instead, *AV*'s main objective is to collect all required items from the mansion and put them in the dumpster—a simple, run-of-the-mill adventure game scenario. Achieving this aim is the sole victory and termination condition facing RPs. Importantly, the main accompanying challenge for RPs is to exploit their verbal (rather than, say, exploratory, directional, or even martial) capacities as well as other linguistic aids (such as thesauri and dictionaries) to navigate and interact with the gameworld. Thus, it is a humorous metalinguistic agenda, implemented in a highly sophisticated and elaborate writerly manner, that lends *AV* its distinctive literary appeal.[10]

The final literary IF I wish to consider, albeit briefly, in this section is Emily Short's *Galatea* (2000a). Rather than exhibiting a rich narrative world, this "interactive fiction piece" accentuates dialogue-driven characterization. Its focus is on the eponymous NPC Galatea, a live statue created by the legendary Pygmalion of Cyprus, with whom RPs converse via their avatars at an artificial intelligence exhibition. Central commands that have to be entered to talk to her are imperative forms of *verba dicendi*, such as "ASK [person] ABOUT [topic]" and "TELL [person] ABOUT [topic]." No shortcuts or other reversely ergodic means are offered, but since the average duration of reading the IF is a mere ten minutes, readers are unlikely to lose patience over typing extensive or repetitive commands.

In the course of the conversation, readers learn about their avatars' and Galatea's biography and background. The RP's avatar, represented textually by IF's characteristic *you*, is a "famous critic" of "artificial intelligence pieces" who is "writing a review of the exhibition." The conversation between the two characters gradually reveals the nuances of Galatea's complex character, her hopes and worries, and the difficult relationship she had with her late "artist." Methods of direct characterization include, for instance, descriptive adjectives ("anxious, chilly, visceral"; "natural, and yet somehow studied") and generic affirmative clauses ("Animates are notoriously poor at processing uncontextualized personal information"). Somewhat more subtle and revealing are the indirect and suggestive ways in which characterizations and character relationships are evoked: for instance, via ellipses ("While he was carving me, there was no strangeness, but afterward . . ."); direct speech (So I'm a machine. According to you."); interior monologue ("And why, exactly, did you need to get that out in the open?"); and behavioral observations ("she studies the effect [of her toenails] whenever she isn't looking at you").

Like *BL*, *Galatea* isn't an IF that can be won. It is a multilinear conversational narrative that offers a variety of different pathways and endings, many of which strike the reader as unexpected or abrupt. Not only is Galatea's mood different according to the choices made by the RP, but she may also come across as more or less independent, clever, and creative. One rather disappointing ending occurs just as Galatea decides to talk in more detail about her experiences with the human world: suddenly the exhibition closes for the day and the P-C doesn't even get an opportunity to say good-bye to her. In another, somewhat more interesting, ending, Galatea challenges her interlocutor—"Maybe we're both machines; maybe neither of us is"—thus lending the narrative a posthuman touch. Yet another ending sees Galatea returning to an inanimate state, a highly emotive move symbolizing suicide. However, it is not the aim of *Galatea* for RPs to explore all possible narratives embedded in it, or to find one particular, "correct" ending, but rather to reflect on the stories and endings "dispensed" to them individually (Short 2000b).

Having examined four interactive fictions that follow different yet equally powerful literary agendas, we can now attempt to map them along the L-L spectrum. This is a trickier undertaking than is the case with other instances of literary gaming because in literary IF both narrative and ludic-mechanic elements are rendered in terms of writing and both are inextricably interconnected. Therefore, the juxtaposition displayed in figure 7.1 should be seen mainly as a representation of how different the four IFs are in terms of their relative degrees of ludicity and literariness.

The graph also shows that literary IFs by no means sit comfortably and unambiguously halfway between the ludic and the literary ends of the spectrum. *Galatea*, for instance, is located in the literary half with respect to both literariness and ludicity. Due to its emphasis on diverse narrative pathways and possible endings, it reads much like a hypertext fiction. *AV*, by contrast, affords a mostly playerly experience. Not only does it exhibit a number of key ludic features, such as victory and termination conditions, points scoring, challenges, riddles, and feedback, but it plays with language in highly capricious ways that transcend the standard poetic foregrounding of language and the kind of verbal ilinx associated with concrete and Oulipian poetry. The comic effects evoked by this approach cater to the fun and entertainment dictates of mainstream game culture, and hence the overall "feel" of *AV* is probably the most ludic of all four IFs discussed in this chapter.

BL, which has been the main focus of this chapter, has in its full phenomenological scope a slightly more literary than ludic character—even

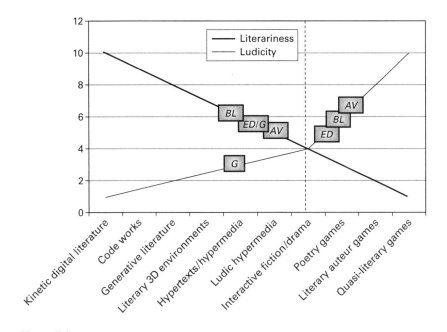

Figure 7.1
Blue Lacuna (*BL*), *Everybody Dies* (*ED*), *Ad Verbum* (*AV*), and *Galatea* (*G*) mapped along the L-L spectrum.

when "played" in puzzle mode. Clearly, the challenges facing the RP in the form of riddles are such that many playerly attempts are necessary to complete its ten chapters. Yet it is an IF that can't and doesn't want to be won. Like *Galatea,* it offers many possible, equivalent pathways and endings, and it is the reading experience itself that is emphasized by the text as much as or even more than the experience of playing an extensive adventure game. *BL*'s carefully crafted, emotive prose style runs through the narrative and begs for close reading. Furthermore, the way in which literary means (such as descriptive adjectives and keyword shortcuts) are married with ludic challenges augments the readerly appeal of this IF.

Like *Galatea, ED* experiments with narrative discourse and is therefore roughly colocated with the former on the literary scale. Though it starts out with a strong ludic appeal (collecting shopping carts as challenge and target), later on in the narrative it turns out that the authorial intent is far more inclined toward unnatural narrative techniques, such as multiperson narration and the use of competing voices as an intradiegetic game, so to speak. Its overall phenomenological effects are therefore slightly more skewed toward the literary than the ludic end of the spectrum.

It should not come as a surprise that this chapter is the longest of all the analytical chapters in this book—IF is among the oldest and most prolific forms of literary gaming. Along with literary hypertext, it is most strongly indebted to print culture and demands high levels of deep and hyper attention from its interactors. It makes extensive use of the traditional means of written narrative art (rather than creative multimodality). Still more important, it experiments with new forms of literary creativity insofar as they are enabled by the digital medium in general and the executable code of, say, an Inform 7 program more specifically. Literary IF combines the arts of verbal narrative, poeticity, and digital ludicity and this creative interplay generates highly complex linguistic artifacts that require careful and detailed analytical attention.

8   The Paradox of Poetic Gaming: *evidence of everything exploding*

8.1   Introduction

So far in this book we have dealt with instances of literary gaming that were either primarily readerly in design or—as we have seen in the case of IF—difficult to define as either game or narrative fiction. This chapter, by contrast, examines digital media that are made and referred to as games, but whose playable material is linguistic or rather poetic in nature: poetic (or poetry) games are a type of computer game that has an explicit or implicit poetic agenda without sacrificing or diminishing the phenomenological gameness that lies at its core. "Poetic" here has to be seen as a rather broad concept that emphasizes creative and artistic engagement with linguistic and poetic units (e.g., letter, syllable, word, phrase, line, verse) as opposed to the creation of fictional worlds through verbal narrative—although, of course, this distinction has blurry boundaries. Poetry games replace core elements that we know from standard videogames (e.g., avatars, enemies, weapons, settings, props, backgrounds) with linguistic material. In so doing, they foreground the verbal art idea underlying their design. Equally important, they critique and challenge players' hyper attention by confronting them with textual material that requires deep attention for in-depth understanding and intertextual referencing.

Put another way, what we are looking at here are (mostly browser-based) digital games that RPs interact with in a primarily game-like way even though their semantic content is linguistic or poetic in nature. Players have to perform ludic actions such as shooting or catching words, jumping along lines of poetic verse, and maneuvering across navigable text documents, and they score points (or similar success evidence) as they go along. In order to level up or win, they have to meet a number of challenges set by the rules of the game, and the game is completed if and when its victory and/or termination conditions have been met.

Discursively, poetry games are referred to as games in their title and/ or front matter (e.g., the index page of the host website). Marko Niemi's *Stud Poetry* (2006), for example, is a digital "poker game played with words instead of cards. Your goal is to build as strong a poetry hand as you can and, of course, to win as much money as you can. Stud Poetry is a game of courage and faith, and a bit of luck too." Thus, Niemi explicitly characterizes his work in terms of a number of core ludic-mechanic features, the most important of which are "game," "goal," and "win." Similarly, version 3.1 of Jim Andrews's *Arteroids* (2006) is subtitled "[a] literary machine and computer game that explores the relations between games, art, play and poetry" and contains, as its core shell menus, "How to Play," "Game Mode," and "Play Mode." Furthermore, its title is a pun on *Asteroids* (Atari 1979), one of the first and most popular arcade games on the market. Another explicitly labeled poetry game is Gregory Weir's *Silent Conversation* (2009). Its start page suggests that players "[p]lay *more* games at [the] Armor Games [website]" (emphasis mine), implying that this artifact is primarily playerly in design despite its strong emphasis on literary material functioning as setting. Hence, although poetry games have a very clear literary agenda, the basic interactive mode they presuppose is gameplay.

The discursive framing assigned to poetry games is corroborated by the ludic mechanics underlying them. They contain, in various forms and manifestations, the core ludic mechanisms outlined in the early chapters of this book: risks, challenges, progress measurement, game action (e.g., shooting, running, jumping, hitting), rewards, and success and failure mechanisms. Technologically, poetry games run on the basis of specific game engines, algorithms, or animation software that enables game-like interaction—for example, Flash (*Silent Conversation*) or Shockwave (*Arteroids*).

The particular combination of deep-attentive close reading and hyper-attentive gaming afforded or, indeed, required by poetry games creates a phenomenological paradox—a receptive and interactive clash that game designers deliberately build into their designs to make players reflect on their own expectations and habits of gameplay. Aesthetically, this results in unique reading/gaming strategies, which in turn prioritize ludic-kinetic and cognitive-ergodic interaction. To arrive at a profound understanding of any literary game text, then, players have to find ways of focusing on both efficient gameplay, resulting in progress and ultimately completion, and thoughtful, analytical readings of written language in combination with other semiotic modes. It is, of course, possible that multitasking Generation N gamers can efficiently employ both strategies at the same time (a hypothesis to be corroborated by further empirical research). Nevertheless, it is almost impossible to imagine that the textual and ergodic complexity of poetry games would allow interactors to form a comprehensive mental model of the text without experimenting with both hyper-attentive and deep-attentive cognitive styles in multiple revisitations and interactive variations (Ensslin 2007; Ciccoricco 2007a). Thus, like most other artifacts analyzed in this book, poetry games have to be replayed multiple times in order to be grasped as complex multimedia artifacts. Yet the way in which this iterative comprehension process operates in poetry games differs from how it works in primarily readerly texts, where cognitive-ergodic ludicity or ludic mechanics are embedded rather than forming the macrotextual foundation of the user's interaction.[1]

In what follows, I shall first explore some theoretical and aesthetic considerations underlying poetry games. They are a prime example of how contemporary digital media, and particularly art games, détourn elements of commercial games and other elements of popular capitalist culture to amuse, entertain, and critique gamers' uncritical stance toward mainstream game culture (see also chapter 6).[2] Second, I shall provide a close ludo-stylistic analysis of Jason Nelson's poetic browser game *evidence of everything exploding* (2009) to demonstrate the metaludic and neo-avant-garde aesthetics typically underlying art games, and the phenomenological clash between deep and hyper attention that the game evokes. The chapter will close, once again, with a discussion of Nelson's game in relation to its place on the L-L spectrum and in comparison with other poetry games.

8.2   Digital Détournement in Game Art and Art Games

We are bored with the suburbs, the stale imperialist sexist engineering biased corporate game industry, and with new academic ludology that reifies existing superstructures. We are ready to play reality TV off camera. We are frustrated with our governments and the military superstructures that control gamespace. We don't want to play by rules we never agreed upon in the first place. Anyways, even if we had fun playing those games to begin with, it is now more entertaining to mess them up, or to invent new unsanctioned games inside gamespace. If big players are intervening in gamespace, then it is time for Situationist gaming. (Schleiner 2011, 157)

As mentioned in chapter 2, art games, including literary art games, typically détourn elements of mainstream gamer culture. In so doing, they follow a more or less explicit, radical, and/or demagogic philosophy. Perhaps the most agonistic and eloquent approach to explicating anticommercialism and anti-institutionalism in relation to game art and art games is taken by artist, writer, and curator Anne-Marie Schleiner (2011, see opening quote).

In a manifesto-like style, she accuses the gaming industry of sexism, imperialism, and negligence toward player needs as far as rules are concerned. She demands an artistic upheaval that undermines and sets out to play with the rules (and repetitive game structures) imposed by the gaming industry as well as its alleged accomplices: academic ludologists who study and thereby reconfirm mainstream phenomena and governments that support if not promote the use of violent videogames for military training purposes.

Schleiner, as well as the practitioners implementing her manifesto, follows the avant-garde traditions of anticonformist, revolutionary movements such as Dadaism, Surrealism, Fluxus, and Situationism, whose artists "used play as a means to provoke, reverse and reveal structures and to offer new readings and ways of understanding" (Dragona 2010, 27). The Dadaists implemented in their works a playful attitude toward conventional, institutionalized forms of art, which is perhaps best represented by Marcel Duchamp's *Fountain* (1917)—a urinal signed "R. Mutt." This work détourns capitalist mass production by taking the object out of its usual environment, turning it upside down, and giving it an atmosphere of uniqueness and artistic intent through signature and repositioning.

The Surrealists (e.g., André Breton and Salvador Dalí) played with the boundaries of human imagination and realism by producing dreamlike representations that evoked the arbitrary, aleatorical workings of the subconscious mind.

Strongly influenced by the Dadaists, the Fluxus movement produced mixed-media artifacts (*intermedia*) and unplayable games involving social interaction and humor. Robert Filliou's *Optimistic Box 3*, for example, is a wooden chess box containing no pawns but instead two labels saying "So much the better if you can't play chess" on the outside and "You won't imitate Marcel Duchamp" on the inside.

Finally, the Situationists demanded that play should permeate all areas of life by blending playfulness and creativity and by appropriating and subverting "not only . . . game features, assigning to them new properties, but also . . . concepts and ideas, assigning to them new meanings" (Dragona 2010, 27; Vaneigem 1967). Situationist (inspired) art challenges institutionalized art that follows the conventions and political constraints of the museum and other official, public exhibition spaces. Christo and Jeanne-Claude's wrappings, for instance, of Pont Neuf (1984) and the German Reichstag (1995), exemplify this agenda poignantly.

Spearheaded by Schleiner's online show "Cracking the Maze: Game Plug-ins and Patches as Hacker Art" (1999), recent years have seen a growing number of game art exhibitions. Bearing in mind the anti-institutionalist philosophy underlying these alternative, subversive forms of art, this seems somewhat surprising if not hypocritical. Clearly, exhibitions provide an ideal platform for the dissemination of non- and antimainstream game culture that would otherwise go unnoticed by the wider public. Further, if the exhibition is held in a physical location like a museum, for example, the logistic advantages of indoor spaces for computer game technologies and all their technological requirements are obvious. However, one cannot deny the somewhat schizophrenic character underlying the idea of public exhibition—online or off—when it comes to neo-avant-garde ludic artifacts. After all, for these sorts of events objects are selected and put together following a specific curatorial agenda. Therefore, I would argue that (literary) art games pose a welcome alternative to Game Art: they tend to be produced for private, home-based consumption; they are typically listed on indie game databases and freely accessible digital art and literature collections; and because they don't have to subject themselves to any curatorial philosophies or ideologies, it is up to players themselves to pick and choose whichever artifacts appeal to them most.

Art game developers use games as a reflective, critical tool to challenge "the normative and expected" (Morgana 2010, 7). They adopt Situationist and other avant-garde mindsets and strategies to détourn and subvert mainstream game structures and culture, whereby détournement comes to be understood as "an overturning of the established order; an unforeseen activity within the institution, utilizing its tools and imagery that overthrows conventions to create new meaning by appropriating and juxtaposing" (7–8). In this respect, they belong to the same subversive league as hackers, cheaters, and modders, who aim to disrupt videogame consumerism by modifying and evading commercially imposed rules and structures, as well as mainstream game culture's most dominant (and often stereotypical) memes and tropes. As Morgana (2010, 10) puts it, "an artgame may employ novel interfaces, non-mainstream narratives, retro visual language, experimental gameplay and other strategies. An artgame may be any interactive experience that draws on game tropes. Artgames are rapidly détourning mainstream game expectations, although whether designers specifically use the term whilst producing transgressive and novel independent games is a moot point." Thus, avant-garde agendas are often left implicit by art game designers, which may suggest that they're less politically interested than their twentieth-century forerunners and would rather focus on the creative processes at work than on the cultural and/or political implications of their activities and products.

Since art game designers operate outside the commercial dictates of the mainstream game industry, their innovative and experimental remit is virtually boundless aside from the limitations imposed by the technological tools they (can afford to) use. Financially, they tend to rely on their own private budgets, player donations, and/or arts council funding. Hence, their products tend to be considerably less sophisticated technologically and require far shorter play times than average blockbuster titles. The entertainment, artistic, and critical appeal of these games, however, can be infinitely greater, especially as far as scholarly and analytical engagement is concerned. Some art games are so short that players (and critics) may wonder what their point is, but, as is the case with most deconstructivist, avant-garde art, art-ness itself is ultimately contingent on a combination of authorial intent and playerly acceptance.

Ultimately, art game design is motivated by two major factors. First, experimental game designers seek to develop and implement *auteurship* (see also chapter 9). Their aim is to express their specific identities and artistic agendas in unique, idiosyncratic ways, which they would not be able to do in a larger, commercialist production environment. And second, art game designers aim to broaden the horizons of game culture and to help develop videogames into an established art form with manifold theoretical and practical approaches, technologies, genres, and expressive styles, thus extending the range of artifacts and creative and interactive practices available to players. Literary gaming is evolving rapidly as a subform of art game development at the interface of creative writing, visual arts, and game design.

Metagames, that is, games that are about games and gaming, are among the most salient and poignant forms of art games.[2] They use metaludic design strategies, such as borrowing or emulating interface items from other games; intertextuality; and intermediality, often in a tongue-in-cheek manner. Anti-games, a subform of metagames, are even more specific and/or political in their artistic remit in that they use antiludic design to question, challenge, and/or ridicule aspects of commercial game culture.[3] The remainder of this chapter will now zoom in on a poetry game that merges metaludicity and metalanguage. It is concerned with the ways in which poetry games make players reflect on the relationships between language, play, and game and the extent to which the clash between deep and hyper attention, between close reading and successful gameplay, may or may not be overcome.

8.3 Pop-Surrealism and Poetry Gaming: Jason Nelson's *evidence of everything exploding*

In what follows, I offer a ludostylistic analysis of Jason Nelson's (2009) poetry game *evidence of everything exploding* (*EEE*). In particular, my reading will focus on questions of mediality (hardware, software, ergodicity, and textuality); the ludonarratological setup of the game in terms of themes, characters, backstory, cut scenes, and textual clues; ludological principles of genre, gameplay, rules, strategies, victory and termination conditions, and types of play; and ludosemiotic effects caused by multimodal overlays and poetic language play. Once again, it is in the nature of the task that these elements have to be interwoven with each other in the analysis, and that some require more detailed attention than others to bring out the self-reflexive, metaludic character of the game.

EEE is the third installment of Nelson's Flash-platform poetry game tetralogy *ArcticAcre: Oddities and Curious Lands* (www.arcticacre.com). The collection's subtitle suggests that players are in for a fantastical archipelago of humorous, "pop-surrealist" (Destructoid.com 2007) artifacts, all of which have self-reflexive titles: *game, game, game and again game* (2007b, labeled "land 1.435"); *i made this. you play this. we are enemies* (2008, labeled "land-m 2.7-b"); *evidence of everything exploding* (2009, labeled "land e: 3.6+"); and *alarmingly these are not lovesick zombies* (2007a, labeled "land z: 4.-9"). A link in the bottom right-hand corner of the index page labeled "bonus land 5.4-0" refers players to one of Nelson's best-known works, *this is how you will die* (2005), an aleatoric gambling machine predicting the cause, nature, and aftermath of the player's death.

Like the other pieces in the tetralogy, *EEE* is framed as a game that has to be played, first and foremost. The index page contains "instructions to play this game" and tells players where to click to "explore and play." However, it also reflects the hybridity, generic evasiveness, and aesthetic autonomy of the artifact by labeling it "an art game creature/digital poem," thus preparing players for an unusual, complex gaming experience with a unique, neo-Frankensteinian textual monster.

The game itself intertextualizes and appropriates elements of platform gaming, Dadaist collage, and *palimpsestic* writing. Its backstory explains that in 2004, "ten sheets of paper from various sources, coated in an unknown chemical solution," were discovered in the Arctic. These pages contained "word groupings or phrases . . . highlighted with accompanying drawings, images and strange texts and stories." Edited in this multimodal, annotated format, the documents provide the visual backdrop to each of the game's ten levels, featuring, as the index page mysteriously indicates, "NASA, BILL GATES, THE SPANISH FLU, DADAISM, JAMES JOYCE, FIDEL CASTRO and other strange and wonderous [*sic*] evidence." More specifically, they include the first page of an early print version of the *Dictionarium Britannicum* (level 1); the musical program of the 1920 Festival Dada in Paris (level 2); the NASA flight plan for the 1969 Apollo 11 lunar mission (level 3); Bill

Gates's 1976 "Open Letter to Hobbyists" (level 4); a public health statement issued by the city of Washington D.C.'s division of sanitation in September 1918 about the hazards of the then-spreading influenza epidemic (level 5); a 2006 threat letter from the law firm Branfman & Associates to writer Neil Gaiman about an allegedly illegal link on his Tomatoes Are Evil website (level 6); the first page of James Joyce's "The Delivery of the Letter" section from *Finnegans Wake* (level 7); a 1956 rejection letter from the Museum of Modern Art to Andy Warhol (level 8); a letter from Fidel Castro to the U.S. President (level 9), and the U.S. patent for the pizza box (level 10). In their totality, the documents manifest in idiosyncratic and Dadaistically random ways[4] the game's thematic agenda, which is displayed on the cover page:

Our entertainment industry is obsessed with doomsday and conspiracy, with creating/forcing/hoaxing connections between ideas/documents. Films/books/games convince us secret tales/stories are hidden in each spaceward journey, old books, and law offices, there are secret codes in our computers, our dictators and our artworks. Evidence of Everything Exploding creates it's [sic] own prophecies and conspiracies, building poetic/secret connections within semi-historical documents. Explore and play and be prophesized.

We're thus dealing with a game that aims to aestheticize and subvert the effects of hypermediation, which include fragmentation, the constructed nature of cohesion, and the conflation of disparate meanings and its concomitant semantic simplification. These ruptures and loss of meaning permeate the mediated and mediatized worlds of politics, medicine, commerce, and the information society. They multiply to give rise to a preapocalyptic scenario, dominated by doomsday prophecies and other discourses of conspiracy and global destruction.

To the uninitiated player, the ten documents don't seem to share any thematic or structural features other than an overarching sense of explosiveness: for instance, biological (the Spanish Flu), commercial (Gates's "Letter to Hobbyists"), semantic (the all-inclusive *Dictionarium Britannicum*), and scientific (NASA's flight plan). So rather than introducing and following a coherent, immersive gameworld, the game introduces a seemingly disjointed repository of so-called characters (NASA, Bill Gates, etc.) and themes. What they share, however, is a procedural rhetoric (Bogost 2007) that aims to depict "our current entertainment industry['s] obsession with doomsday and conspiracy" in our hypermediated society and its apocalyptic, fragmenting, and fragmented aura. Against this backdrop, the game introduces its own prophecies of explosive things to come (like plagues, wars, and computer viruses) that have to be unlocked level by level, much like pseudo-rewarding cut scenes in narrative blockbusters.

The game has a simplistic rule set consisting of the four instructions outlined on its start page: "1. use arrow keys to move" (for navigation); "2. avoid and unlock things" (for strategy and actions); "3. reach the reach/ reach" (for victory and termination conditions); and "4. win for matchbook tales" (for rewards). Whereas the first and second rules are straightforward, run-of-the-mill instructions found in many PC-based games, the third and fourth ones deviate from players' normal expectations. "Reach the reach/ reach" is a modification of requests such as reaching the goal (e.g., of a racing game), center, exit (of a maze), top, or bottom (of a conventional Snakes-and-Ladders-type platformer). Its double reduplication of "reach" has a self-referential function reminding players that games tend to super-ficially project fictional worlds in order to make players believe in what are essentially metaphorical meanings and objectives. The aim of a game, however, ultimately lies in its own game-ness, and we mainly play games for their own sake rather than for the narrative worlds they conjure up.

Rule number 4, "win for matchbook tales," is even more cryptic than number 3 as players are made to wonder what a matchbook tale is and why they would be motivated to perform well in the game in order to be rewarded with them rather than credits or other countable units. The function of the matchbook tales is akin to cut scenes interspersed between levels in commercial videogames to bridge the loading gap, move the nar-rative forward, and reward players with a brief period of lean-back, filmic entertainment. Ironically, many players, and particularly hardcore gamers, don't appreciate these kinds of rewards. On the contrary, they skip cut scenes if possible in order to continue their hyper attentive gameplay as quickly as they can. Considering the rather controversial nature of reward cut scenes, it comes as no surprise that Nelson implements interlevel cut scenes parodically to "reward" or, rather, ironically penalize players of *EEE*. The cut scenes are short video clips featuring a nonsensical, overdrama-tized tale about matchbook logos and labels, filmed and orally narrated by the author himself. The narrations appear entirely spontaneous and unscripted, prompted ekphrastically by the images on the matchboxes shown in the clips. Level 3, for instance, rewards players with the follow-ing nonsense tale: "Perhaps King Edward's reign was too tight-fisted, those little cigars he made, and Kelly, Mr Kelly was the only one that would feed him. Of course, his light was too dim to actually see the fact that he was pointing to the muscles on his forearm; and the runner, well, the run-ner just kept running, just kept moving until he opened up in his yellow shoes, his annoying smile." The thus-narrativized everyday objects show the interplay of the physically explosive potential of matchboxes and their semiotic refashioning as symbols of the late capitalist entertainment industry's merchandize mania.

Playing *EEE* happens via cursor keys and mouse, and it feels much like walking through the maze of an interactive avant-garde exhibition. Players navigate their avatar-cursor-arrow from landmark item to landmark item, activating interactive elements (often by chance rather than design) and avoiding enemies (mostly abstract, animated units) that will set them back in their trajectory to each level's "reach/reach" destination.

The game can only be "won" (or rather "completed") when the player manages to decode the logic of its multilayered, multimodal interface. Superimposed on each background page are navigational, multimodal, and linguistic/discursive elements that are partly animated, partly still, partly hidden and unlockable through avatar roll-over, and partly permanent. The outlines of the navigable mazes are palimpsestically layered on top of the background texts, and successful gameplay can happen only if and when the player invests time to study and close-read each interface to identify how the individual layers work together.

EEE's interface gives players clues through numbered highlights in the text as to how to navigate each level's maze. Rolling over these landmarks triggers a visible explosion that releases multimodal overlays comprising explanatory and/or poetic text boxes, but it also activates palimpsestic interface modifications like playful doodles, for example, over the first syllable of "Da-da" in Level 8 ("A. Warhol Judged"), and other multimodal features such as a self-ironical, multimodally enhanced, or tagged, photograph of the author-designer himself in Level 9 ("Young Fidel Castro"). The functions of these superimpositions are diverse: they may serve an explanatory purpose to RPs in deep-attentive mode, enhancing deep attention by making them pause and reflect on what they have read (there is no stopwatch to beat in this game). Alternatively, players in hyper attentive mode are likely to find the superimpositions distractive and annoying because they impede fast-paced, successful gameplay. Overall, they create a playful tension between logical reasoning and creative thinking about the possible meanings of the incoherent elements and the urge to play on and win the game.

Some clues are less obvious than others (as in every game): in level 9 ("Young Fidel Castro"), for example, the avatar can reach its destination only when it literally stops moving to allow the inimical, camouflaged arrow squadrons to move past it. On hitting one of the level's landmark interface items, the following text is projected onto the interface: "stop n' read cause yer cool like that." So if the player hasn't figured out the stop-n-let-pass mechanic of the level by then, the verbal clue (if read functionally rather than expressively) may help him or her complete it. This particular clue also alerts players to the importance of combining hyper attention with deep attention, of pausing game-play in order to start close-reading the text on screen. After all, the fact that this explicit operational advice appears in the penultimate level of *EEE*—just before its satirical showdown: the pizza-box patent—indicates its conceptual significance for *EEE*: that it is the aforementioned phenomenological clash between close reading and hyper-attentive gaming that forms the aesthetic core of this literary game.

In the higher levels of *EEE*, the player's expectations are subverted through unexpected shortcuts and built-in cheats. For example, in level 8 ("A. Warhol Judged") the cubistic maze can be skipped simply by moving straight to the "open" point, which then opens a direct path, or shortcut, to the level's exit point (see figure 8.1). Similarly, the fact that level 10 ("American Invention") is unplayable and, instead, instantly moves on to the closing feedback, "you have reached your final proof," is evocative of the fact that various commercial games are based on a "culture of cheating"

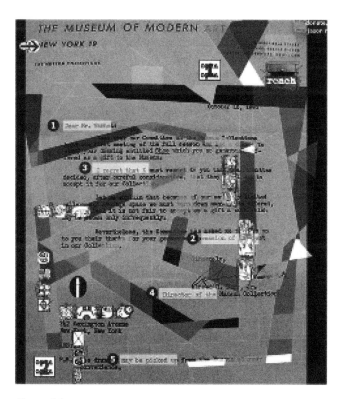

Figure 8.1
Screenshot of *EEE*, level ("evidence") 8: "A. Warhol Judged."

and allow players to score highly or win only if they develop effective subversive strategies (Dumitrica 2011).

EEE is not only unique in its ludic mechanics but also in the terminology it uses for standard game components. It refers to "levels" as "evidence" (of everything exploding), and the feedback given to players after each level replaces the monotonous "You've won" with a range of transitive, nonsynonymous verbs, such as "you crushed (won) level one," "you rocked (won) level three," and "you spucked (won) level nine." The verbs either denote or connote (sexual) aggression, thus alluding to and critiquing the attitudes of chauvinist gamers, who happily subject themselves to mindless killing sprees and misogynist behavior (see chapter 6).

Finally, Nelson's game challenges players to reflect on the aesthetic tension between hyper and deep attention. They see themselves forced to close-read the multiple codes and layers of the interface in order to work out new navigational and ludic strategies for each level, and less so in a purely functional way (because that's how ludic interfaces are normally read) but instead with a focus on the metaludic, poetic, and sociocritical meanings that the game seeks to convey through its overall procedural rhetoric. In challenging players to combine deep and hyper attention in unprecedented ways, *EEE* demands and aestheticizes replay, suggesting that repetition not only improves gameplay but furthers semiotic understanding and reflection. Through elements like the carnivalesque cut-scene reward system, we can see that Nelson plays with the reader-player in a Dionysian, paidiac way, causing effects of vertigo while maintaining the rhythmos of rule-based gameplay. We're thus dealing with a full-fledged literary meta- and antigame that blends a wide variety of ludostylistic elements to afford a worthwhile gaming experience while at the same time celebrating neo-avant-garde détournement and an aggressive critique of the destructive, institutionalized effects of contemporary creative industries.

8.4   Discussion

In its ludic-poetic design, *EEE* does justice to its authorially assigned generic label of "an art game creature/digital poem." Rather than simply being a game that plays with poetry, it implements the phenomenological clash between deep and hyper attention in far more pronounced ways than can be observed in other specimens of the poetry computer game genre. In this section, I shall therefore compare and contrast *EEE* with two other previously mentioned poetry games, Andrews's *Arteroids* and Weir's *Silent Conversation*, as well as with some other literary-ludic texts and genres to explain where *EEE* sits on the L-L spectrum and why I have placed it there.

Arteroids is described on its main menu page as "[a] literary machine and computer game that explores the relations between games, art, play and poetry." Having said that, operating this "literary machine" feels mostly like playing a game, despite the fact that the material substance of its component units is verbal (words and phrases). *Arteroids* is a Shockwave-based, poetic transmediation of the 1979 Atari arcade game *Asteroids*, in which players have to shoot asteroids while avoiding collisions with them. *Arteroids* is provocatively subtitled "[a] literary shoot-em-up computer game—the battle of poetry against itself and the forces of dullness." Its designer, Jim Andrews, advises reader-players to "throw away [their] preconceptions about poetry" (2006). The aim of the game is to shoot as many words and phrases traversing the screen as possible from a nodal point labeled "poetry," using the cursor keys to move and the "x" key to fire. Therefore, the subversive trajectory of this game seems to lie less in an antiludic than an antipoetic stance, as it uses détournement to overturn a conventionally pacifist genre by means of "safe" galactic warfare (Crawford 1984). Interestingly, the game features both a play and a game mode:

In "game mode" you play with what you are given and scores are saved. In "play mode," you can compose/save/edit the texts you encounter when playing; and you can adjust all the parameters of the app: textual density, velocity, fictive friction, whether the texts can "kill" you, etc. "Play mode" is more a Do-It-Yourself combination of odd poem editor and videogame adjuster so that you can mash poetry and game together in a way that permits you to think about both without worrying about being killed. "Game mode" is a videogame, though there, also, you can read the text at low velocities. The velocity increases as you progress through levels. (Andrews 2007, 58)

Put differently, Andrews has built cognitive-ergodic ludicity and ludic mechanics proper, in the sense of two different play options, into the macrostructure of this game, thus drawing readers' attention—albeit implicitly—to the phenomenological differences between deep- and hyperattentive media consumption.

Game mode focuses players' attention on navigating and shooting, and even though they are likely to read (or rather skim) the words they are aiming at, their priority can hardly be to create a mental image of the possible linguistic or poetic meanings of the exploding text, or to read any deep meanings into what they perceive as written text. Play mode allows players to create their own shoot-'em-up text units with the aim of turning players into wreaders. Players can skip between levels and have an infinite lifeline, yet the actual gameplay differs little from game mode. According to Andrews (2005), *Arteroids* is "about cracking language open . . . in the sense that the fundamental symbols of writing are no longer simply the letters in the alphabet and other typographical marks. Writing is now a larger thing." Through the game's procedural rhetoric, Andrews seeks to show that the "end of language" as we know it is nigh and that the age of new media heralds a completely new, more fluid and ergodic relationship between signs, meanings, and meaning-making processes. This procedural rhetoric, however, is not accompanied by long stretches of poetic text and other multimodal elements that need to be close-read in combination for a complex mental image of the text. In fact, gameplay is not disrupted by intrusive text as is the case in *FFF*, and as a result, playerly hyper attention goes largely undisturbed by deep-attentive readerly interpretation.

In his poetic-intertextual Flash-platform game *Silent Conversation* (2009), Gregory Weir takes the player on a journey along a line of words and other formal arrangements of text, explicitly requesting them to "read the stories and the poems in this game thoroughly by touching as many words [with the cursor and space keys] as [they] can" (Weir 2009). With jumping and running moves reminiscent of *Super Mario Bros.* and other platform games, players need to increase their score by ensuring they have touched, and hence read, every single word in the line—an allusion to the necessity of close-reading literary, and particularly poetic, texts. The procedural rhetoric of the game suggests that some words are literally harder to grasp, reach, or touch than others, and the fact that at times several attempts are required to "hit" a word or group of words serves as a metaphorical reference to the hermeneutic efforts required when aiming to understand the deep and multilayered meaning of poetic texts (figure 8.2).

The player's achievements at hitting as many words as possible are captured in a score between A and F, thus evoking high-school testing mechanisms. That said, the game's pedagogy is conciliatory and generous: it teaches players that there will be a learning curve before they play the game well, which, on a figurative level, translates into the perceived difficulties facing novice readers of stylistically demanding literary texts. Every level-up unlocks another creative text by an eminent author, such as William Carlos Williams ("XXII") and H.P. Lovecraft ("The Nameless City, Part I"). In their thus-remediated form, the poems and stories transform into abstract game settings without losing their own semantic and symbolical meanings. Indeed, the fact that some words are harder to hit than others adds another, medium-specific layer of poetic meaning.

Silent Conversation is located near *Arteroids* on the literariness scale, yet its readerliness is slightly more pronounced. Unlike the latter, it does not allow wreaderly contributions to the text. Instead, it uses existing poems

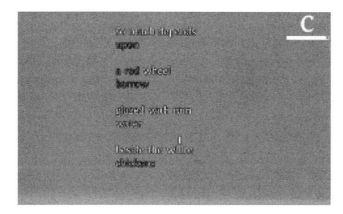

Figure 8.2
Screenshot from *Silent Conversation*. The highlighted words have been hit. The cursor/avatar is just above the word "white."

and fictions as settings for its levels, and players have to move their avatar (a simple cursor line) along two-dimensional, horizontally scrolling landscapes comprising lines and towers of texts. Navigation happens at a fairly slow speed, which allows players with advanced gaming skills to read the text while playing the game. However, as difficulty levels rise, the player's concentration is bound to be directed solely at efficient navigation and scoring, and longer texts especially, such as "The Nameless City," are likely to be played hyper-attentively rather than read in deep-attentive mode. Paradoxically or not, the game's website advises players to "[r]ead carefully. Run and jump through the text of stories and poems, from the horror of Lovecraft's 'The Nameless City' to the simple beauty of Bashou's frog haiku. Go for completion or race through the pieces you've mastered!" Therefore, although the context in which the game can be accessed (the Armor Games website) clearly suggests that we are dealing with a playerly artifact, the actual instructions emphasize its readerly nature, and RPs are given a choice between completing a deep-attentive play-reading with a high score or concentrating on hyper-attentive, fast-paced gameplay, regardless of its exact outcome.

EEE places far greater emphasis on readerliness than *Arteroids* or *Silent Conversation* do. It uses ludic mechanics as well as the Dadaist technique of text collage at various levels of interface design. Its levels are set on written documents (rather than pictographic backgrounds). These documents are increasingly superscribed and annotated quasi-palimpsestically during the course of playing, and the amount of close and rereading required to piece together the textual jigsaw brings its degree of literariness close to its ludicity level. In fact, the amount of close reading required to begin to understand the game (no matter how surreal its content) is similar to that of a standard nonlinear hypertext or hypermedia narrative (such as *Firefly* or *Figurski*). Therefore, as shown in figure 8.3, its place on the L-L spectrum is a lot more ambiguous than that of *Arteroids* and *Silent Conversation*, both of which emphasize a playerly rather than readerly agenda much more clearly. While *EEE*'s degree of ludicity is roughly equal to that of the other two games, its emphasis on literariness is far more pronounced—so much so that it features in the same region as most literary hypertexts and (ludic) hypermedia.

To conclude, this chapter has offered a ludostylistic reading of *EEE* with the aim of demonstrating how profound the rupture between deep and hyper attention can be in poetry games if readerly and playerly elements are employed to almost the same degree of phenomenological intensity. *EEE* is clearly driven by ludic mechanics and playerly moves and, in terms of ludicity, sits comfortably in the ludic half of the L-L spectrum. However, if we take into account its strong focus on linguistic and multimodal

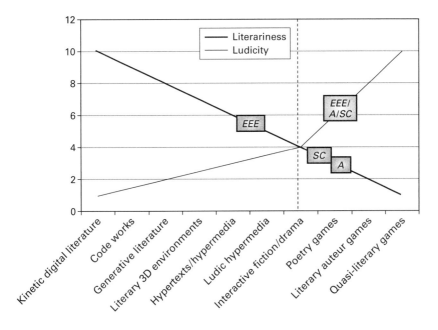

Figure 8.3
The three poetry games as located on the L-L spectrum. *EEE* stands for *evidence of everything exploding*, *A* for *Arteroids*, and *SC* for *Silent Conversation*.

foregrounding and the sheer amount of text (both written by Nelson and copied and pastiched) to be close-read by players (in several revisitations), the actual location of *EEE* on the L-L spectrum is ambivalent. In terms of ludicity, it is comparable to other poetry games like *Arteroids* and *Silent Conversation*. In terms of literariness, however, it is more akin to ludic digital literature such as hypertext poetry and fiction—especially if they share a surrealistic thematic focus such as that seen in *Figurski at Findhorn on Acid* (see chapter 4).

9 From Paidia to Ludus: *The Path*, a Literary Auteur Game

9.1 Introduction

With my analysis of poetry games in the previous chapter, we have firmly entered videogame territory and started moving toward the ludic end of the literary-ludic spectrum. As I mentioned previously, this area is far less abundantly populated with artifacts than the literary half of the spectrum. Arguably, this is related to the fact that there are currently far more examples of literary play than of literary games, both in print and electronically. My archival research for this book has found a rather limited number of literary e-games that truly merit the label and haven't already been mentioned in this book.[1] However, as art game designers and digital writers are beginning to reach out for new creative collaborations and cross-media applications, we can expect to see literary e-games proliferate in the years to come.

This final analytical chapter deals with what I have called literary auteur games. Like poetry games, these are artifacts that have to be played, or at the very least their interactive make-up and graphical user interface (GUI) design suggest that they do. Their formal literary elements tend to be far less pronounced and possibly more controversial than in poetry games, and their main conceptual and aesthetic focuses lie on the designers' very personal auteur style, a unique artistic "stamp" that may be most visible in the game's graphical or audiovisual design and/or its unique form of gameplay. Hence, the game's literariness may not stand out *prima facie* as it does in poetry games and ludic digital literature. Yet on closer examination—and I shall demonstrate what such an investigation might look like—it becomes clear that language is foregrounded as verbal art rather than used as a purely functional tool, for example, for background storytelling, playing instructions, and character dialogue.

In the second half of this chapter, I offer a ludostylistic analysis of the literary-artistic auteur game *The Path* (Tale of Tales 2009a). It is a transmediation of "Little Red Riding Hood" and follows a strong antiludic agenda (see chapters 6 and 8). Its subversive conceit goes as far as to give many of its players the feeling that it isn't really a game at all. Rather than catering to their needs for fast action and progress, it makes them reflect critically on their actions and lusory attitudes and also on the philosophical message(s) suggested by its procedural rhetoric. With this in mind, in the following section I will introduce three antiludic design elements that are at work in *The Path*: slowness, dérive, and allusive fallacy. I shall then move on to a detailed ludostylistic analysis of *The Path,* showing how its antiludic elements combine with a range of other ludonarratological and medial features to evoke the image of a literary art game. Of major importance here are the ways in which this game inspires literary reading in the sense of metaleptic oscillation, interior monologue, and analeptic and proleptic ambiguity.

9.2   To Game or Not to Game: Slowness, Dérive, and Allusive Fallacy

In chapters 6 and 8, we looked at a range of design elements used to express both meta- and antiludic agendas. I discussed how antiludicity follows principles of détournement in that it appropriates ludic structures from commercialist game culture and reassembles them playfully, subversively, and often humorously into new architectures and narratives. This section introduces three further forms of antiludicity that are at work in *The Path* and have caused many a critic to question the game's essential game-ness (e.g., Rose 2009; Samyn and Harvey 2012): slowness, dérive, and allusive fallacy. In a nutshell, the terms refer to the slow pace of movement demanded by a game; the aimless yet psychogeograpically conscious meandering rather than purposeful navigation associated with this kind of movement; and the misleading use of interface items that support the impression of blundering rather than systematic, logical reasoning.

Slow games are exactly what their label implies: games that cannot be played at the high speed normally expected by players. They force players to proceed at an extremely slow pace, thus evoking a meditative mood. The main purpose of this design feature is to give players breathing space and further exploratory options, to make them reflect on their actions and other aspects of videogame culture, and to force their attention to elements of the gameworld they would normally ignore and therefore fail to appreciate. As Corcoran (2010, 20) puts it,

in opposition to the trend of fast-paced games that tempt the user to win faster and shoot more, Slow Gaming has become an almost movement comprised of developers and gamers alike. It has filtered to mainstream titles—the seemingly endless "open" worlds seen in games like Grand Theft Auto, for example, give players countless hours of non-linear game time in addition to the main story objectives. Slow Gamers espouse the virtues of exploring absolutely everything because Slow Gaming is about appreciating the environment, and taking the time to reflect on it.

Despite the fact that the commercial game industry uses "safe" aspects of slow gaming (such as seemingly infinite, explorable spaces) to increase the pleasures of mainstream gameplay, there is no doubt that independent game developers have been the ones to explore this design feature in the most creative and pioneering ways. Game artist Cory Archangel, for example, launched the projection *Super Slow Tetris* in 2004 "to test rather than reward the player" (Corcoran 2010, 21) with an extreme slow-motion version of the original Nintendo game. Based on a "reprogrammed Nintendo paddle" (Migros Museum für Gegenwartskunst [Migros Museum of Contemporary Art] 2005), this "endurance piece" shows the artist's subversive take on the digital media industries' "calculated boredom" (Chaffee 2007). thatgamecompany's *Flower* (2009) has a less humorous and more meditative purpose. It foregrounds backgrounds, which are often sidelined by commercial game developers. The player slowly follows a flower dancing in the wind at a speed that augments the importance and beauty of the surrounding pastoral scenery—so much so that the latter becomes a "character" in its own right (thatgamecompany 2013).

One of the most productive designers in the area of slow gaming has been the American video artist Bill Viola. His PlayStation3-based *The Night Journey* (2009) uses the perspective of a first-person shooter (FPS), but without offering players the "ubiquitous 'gun hand'" (Corcoran 2010, 23) they would normally expect to come with it. Instead, players are supposed to become meditative explorers, to move slowly and pause to look around and reflect on what they see in the gameworld. "Here, the heart of the interaction is to slow down and to see past the surface in a process of raw discovery. Looking deeply into things is rewarded" (24). The slowness requirement is further reinforced by the chosen technology, a "low light surveillance camera" from the 1970s that renders images blurred if players navigate too quickly: "[i]f the player races through it, they might have an interesting experience visually and enjoy some cool smearing effects, but they will not see below the surface" (25).

The effects of slow gaming are, to a certain extent, akin to the Situationist principle of dérive. According to Debord (1958/1981, 51), this principle refers to "a mode of experimental behaviour linked to the conditions of urban society: a technique of transient passage through varied ambiences."

Drifting through space without any intention of following a certain direction or path opens up possibilities of free exploration and experimentation, of spatial and temporal free play, as it were. Applied to videogame play, dérive can be considered an antiludic concept because in mainstream game culture even exploration tends to be purpose- and progress-driven, whereas in subversive indie projects this utilitarianism is suspended.

Strictly speaking, the Situationist concept of dérive relates to "a technique of *rapid* [rather than slow] passage through varied ambiences" (Debord 1958/1981, 62, emphasis mine). Furthermore, to Debord the term was associated primarily with city expericnccs (rathcr than experiences with rural and/or natural environments) and the close connections between cities' architectural and social morphologies. Nevertheless, there are a number of qualities of the dérive that are related to slow gaming, as I will show in my analysis of *The Path*: other than the nineteenth-century bourgeois, chauvinist flaneur or the sexually interested voyeur, the person on dérive is both genderless and classless, and the controlling gaze associated with flaneurism and voyeurism is replaced by a focus on the constructedness of the subjective image (McDonough 2002, 255–257). Furthermore, the dérive involves "playful-constructive behavior and awareness of psychogeographical effects . . . quite different from the classic notions of journey or stroll" (Debord 1958/1981, 62). In other words, it describes a conscious, reflected type of spatial behavior that takes into account and muses on spaces and their inhabitants. Translated into the setting of a sociocritical art game, playful constructivism and psychogeographical awareness can adopt an entirely new range of hermeneutic meanings.

Bearing in mind the contextual implications and historical contingencies of the original Situationist concept, it is no doubt a risky undertaking to map the dérive directly onto experiencing a gameworld that is mostly sylvan and therefore independent of the specific social and physical architectures of the postmodern city (although, of course, the woods in *The Path* are populated with animate creatures and furnished, so to speak, with objects of everyday life). Therefore, I suggest a method that adopts the playful, exploratory yet simultaneously sociocritical stance characteristic of the dérive. This method uses spatial hermeneutics to read psychogeographic meanings into places, props, and settings, as well as the ways in which they form elements of a coherent whole.

Finally, the ludosemiotic term *allusive fallacy* (Ensslin 2014b, 77) refers to design features that use semiotic devices such as intertextuality, *pro-*, and *analepsis* as "disconcerting rather than cohesive narrative and navigational devices." Generally speaking, interface elements tend to be designed in such a way as to aid players via clues by helping them form associative links to other texts, both fictional and factual (intertexts), and by providing flashforwards (prolepsis) and flashbacks (analepsis) to what has/might have happened or what is/may be about to happen. In a mainstream narrative videogame, these associative links and allusions are there to help players find solutions to problems, fill narrative gaps, and gain a more comprehensive picture of the backstory or gameworld. Conversely, allusive fallacy happens when this idea of *alluding* (Latin for "to play at," or "to refer to something via wordplay") to other texts or past or future events turns out to be a purposeful deception. Players who are subjected to allusive fallacy are deliberately misled in a game, for instance, by deceptive semiotic clues leading them in the wrong direction or suggesting false interpretations more generally. The effects of this technique vary from game to game, depending on the game's genre, tone, and procedural rhetoric. In a comical game, allusive fallacy may make us laugh about our own inability to read the signs properly, whereas in a game like *The Path* this technique is likely to enhance feelings of horror and apprehension.

9.3   *The Path*—Transmediation, Tragedy, Trauma

The Path is a ludic transmediation of Charles Perrault's (1961/1697) "Little Red Riding Hood" ("Le Petit Chaperon Rouge"). This means that not only does the game remediate the original fairytale in the sense of refashioning it in a different medium (Bolter and Grusin 1999), but it also continues the story by expanding the storyworld, adding new characters, and developing the narrative further (Jenkins 2006). We can therefore say that *The Path* is— much like *The Princess Murderer* in relation to "Bluebeard"—firmly situated in an intertextual, mythological canon. It is a fictional game that requires, for its subludic meanings, multisensory receptive processes and therefore deep attention on the player's part, thus evoking a critical-reflective stance.

 The Path replaces the linear plot of the original folk narrative with a gameworld located in a contemporary gothic setting, and increases the original character repository by introducing six female protagonists at different stages of adolescence. For their player-characters, reader-players can choose from six sisters aged nine through nineteen whose names are all quasi-synonyms of the color red (Robin, Rose, Ginger, Ruby, Carmen, and Scarlet) and who are dressed in various hues of saturated red and black. They all have their own age-appropriate personalities and ways of expressing themselves. Robin, the youngest, is a lively child dressed in the famous Grimmsian red cap who loves playing in the woods. Wolves are "her favorite kind of animal" (Tale of Tales 2013). Rose is a precocious eleven-year-old who enjoys and enthusiastically protects the beauty and innocence of Mother Nature. She wears a black dress with a red hemline and bright red stockings. Thirteen-year-old Ginger is a tomboy and full of wild ideas. Determined never to grow up, she tends to become completely absorbed in gameplay. She wears black Native American feathers in her red hair, and the two red, studded belts wrapped loosely around her short black pantsuit give her the appearance of a bandit. Ruby, the "goth," is a pessimist and nihilist. Her black leg brace suggests an injury, but we do not learn why the enigmatic fifteen-year-old is actually wearing it. The only color she allows in her appearance is in the black and red stripes of her shirt. Seventeen-year-old Carmen is aware of her beautiful body and the effect it has on the male gaze. She enjoys flirting and dreams of a man who will hold and protect her. Her tight black and red shirt and leggings, as well as her swinging gait, underscore her sexual appeal. Scarlet, finally, is the oldest in a family "with an invisible mother" (Tale of Tales 2013). Being responsible for her younger sisters takes its toll, and she longs for a calmer life and the company of a like-minded individual. Her outfit (long black trousers and red turtleneck top) and orderly hairstyle display a level of formality that reflects maturity and seriousness.

Each sister's version of "Little Red Riding Hood" represents one level of the game and starts in exactly the same way: by leaving the big city to pay a visit to grandmother, who lives in a dark forest. The only instruction the P-C obtains at the beginning of each level is to "go to grandmother's house" and to "stay on the path." The path that unfolds in front of the P-C leads through the woods straight to grandmother's house, and getting there without straying into the forest is not a challenge at all. On entering the building without having explored the woods, however, players are confronted with an unsatisfactory situation: they are told by the final scoreboard that they haven't collected any items or opened any doors, but what seems most disturbing is that they haven't encountered the wolf, for which reason they have failed. The game's feedback communicates to players that it is desirable if not mandatory to confront the wolf, and quite clearly there is no other way of succeeding than to stray from the path into the woods to collect items, experience places, and interact with objects and characters, no matter how seriously such behavior breaks the minimalistic rule set of the game.

Each character's story and destiny are thus unconditionally reliant on encounters with the mythological wolf, which manifests itself in various physical and abstract shapes and forms. Robin is killed by a literal wolf while attempting to play with it in the graveyard. Rose drowns in the misty lake, the dangers of which she underestimates. Tomboy Ginger's wolf is a female peer (the Girl in Red), who confronts her with her own femininity (Samyn and Harvey 2012), an internal conflict that is mirrored symbolically in the wire fencing and electric pylons strewn across the field of flowers. Ruby is tempted by a young man in the playground who offers her a joint and possibly seduces and rapes her, although only the smoking is shown in the game.[2] Similarly, Carmen is seduced by a sturdy forester, with whom she consumes alcohol at the campsite and who later rapes and kills her. Scarlet's temptation, finally, is perhaps the most subtle and mysterious one, as she is caught up in playing the piano in the ruined theater.

As Ryan and Costello (2012, 112) point out, the inevitability of meeting the wolf is due to the game's tragic element of *hamartia*: an Aristotelian concept referring to "a fatal mistake made in ignorance by the protagonist." Hamartia doesn't typically occur in videogames and other interactive narratives because it "requires a separation between the audience who is aware of the mistake and the protagonist who is not. In contrast, a game requires the player to take on the role of the protagonist and optimize his or her choices in order to win. Thus, a rational player, the argument goes [according to Bernstein and Greco 2004], would never choose to procrastinate like Hamlet or blind himself like Oedipus and this refusal makes interactive tragedy unachievable" (Ryan and Costello 2012, 112). Having a set of tragic game characters therefore requires players to adopt double roles: that of the sympathetic yet powerless onlooker, and that of the proactive player-interactor who takes responsibility for his or her actions and is theoretically able to avert a tragic ending. As in classical drama, the sense of disempowerment caused by the inevitability of the girls' deaths and/or traumas is likely to produce feelings of catharsis (emotional cleansing through suffering with the hero) in players of *The Path*, and I would argue that this emotional effect is greatly heightened by the fact that players have no choice other than to actively send the girls in the wolf's direction in order to succeed in the game.

Thematically, the game emphasizes adolescent girls' vulnerability and victimization. The stories of the individual characters constitute the six levels of the game, which can be played in any order. "The path" symbolizes the trials and tribulations of young females—the joys, dangers, and traumatic experiences involved in their journey to adulthood. The wolf appears in various shapes and forms, symbolizing whatever the greatest temptations and dangers are at any given age: sexual curiosity, lack of experience with natural and man-made forces (water and electricity), drugs, wild animals, and even artistic endeavor. The game thus situates itself firmly in the creative and critical canon surrounding its urtext, and in particular the much-debated sexual connotations, psychoanalytical interpretations, and feminist concerns associated with "Little Red Riding Hood" (Dundes 1989; Zipes 1993) while offering a new, contemporary answer to the question of what to make of female curiosity, disobedience, and developmental needs.

The transmediation of "Little Red Riding Hood" offered by *The Path* has a distinct cognitive-developmental trajectory. It exploits the educational potential of immersive gameworlds to trigger in players reflections on human cognitive, physical, and emotional development and the significance of trauma for human emotions and comprehension. The six characters symbolize the process of adolescent maturation, which is full of temptations, failures, and disappointments. By enacting a series of traumatic experiences that no one wishes to have for themselves or their children, the game enables players to empathize with the characters and to draw conclusions for their own lives.[3] Likewise, the game itself shows how the human brain deals with post-traumatic stress. After each girl's symbolical or metaphorical death, she finds herself lying outside grandmother's house in the rain and, having dragged herself into the house, or rather a surrealist rendering of it, a similarly surrealist, dark, and threatening cut scene is triggered that provides further hints as to what actually happened to the girl and the psychological and physical trauma to which she has been exposed.

A pedagogical yet not entirely uncontroversial reading of *The Path* thus relates to the therapeutic and educational effects of childhood trauma that may "encourage or compel the child to move toward or attain maturation" (Tribunella 2010, xiv). Such a reading would subvert if not reverse the message of the original Enlightenment and Romantic fairytales that preach obedience and the necessity to avoid traumatic events at all costs, especially when one is a young girl. Simultaneously, of course, it would raise the questions of what types and degrees of traumatic experience might indeed be beneficial, and how necessity would be balanced with precaution and education.

9.4   A Ludostylistic Analysis of *The Path*

This section offers a ludostylistic analysis of *The Path* that will focus on the following elements: it will discuss the particular design features that evoke a readerly impression among players—more specifically, superimposed, written interior monologues on the one hand and metaleptic oscillation between the game text and some of its paratexts on the other; how the game exhibits a strong self-reflexive, metaludological agenda; and, finally, how it implements slow gaming, dérive, and allusive fallacy to achieve a procedural rhetoric that subverts if not reverses the traditional moral and educational messages associated with "Little Red Riding Hood" (see the previous section).

The Path is rendered fully in 3D using a Quest3D engine and downloads for PC and Mac from its official website. It is subtitled "a short horror game" (Tale of Tales 2009a) and thus is discursively framed in a way that promotes it as primarily playerly rather than readerly. However, *The Path* also features a multitude of aesthetic, auteur-like elements that approximate a piece of literary art.[4]

First, the game's macrostructure is labeled with fictional and dramatic terms. It consists of three "acts": act 1, "The Red Apartment," forms the opening of each level and features the characters that the player can choose from at any stage of the game. It demonstrates how many lives, or sisters, the player has left, thereby underscoring the gothic feel of the storyworld. Act 2, "The Forest," represents the main site of gameplay as the P-C meanders through the woods in search of collectible items and adventures, and is where she meets her instantiation of the wolf. Whenever the P-C comes near an interactive item, a short cut scene is triggered that details what happens in the interaction, such as picking up a skull from the graveyard or climbing a tree. Act 3, "Grandmother's House," starts as soon as the P-C has reached the front door of the building. It is a semi-interactive cut scene in which the player can only move forward by repeatedly pressing any key or button. It takes the P-C through a nightmarishly enlarged and refurbished version of the house, with seemingly endless corridors and countless doors and stairways. The journey inevitably ends in grandmother's disfigured bedroom and is followed by the enigmatic scoreboard.

The Path's three-act structure is overlaid with chapter labels for each level. Each final scoreboard says "End of chapter [x]," thus suggesting the player has performed a readerly rather than playerly activity. Clearly, chapter labels are fairly common even in commercial (narrative) games. However, the player's avatar changes with each chapter, and *The Path* does not involve any "real" point scoring leading to level-ups and character development over time, as is the case, for instance, in computer role-playing games. Its level architecture is thus horizontal and nonhierarchical rather than vertical,[5] bringing it closer to a collection of short stories or chapters in a novel than a standard videogame. Finally, the gameplay experience resembles the close, or deep, attention often given to the details of a fictional, autobiographical narrative far more than the achievement-oriented hyper attention afforded and demanded by most videogames.

Curiously, despite its narrative trajectory, the game does not feature any spoken or written dialogue between characters or between P-Cs and NPCs. Likewise, the player isn't guided by any voice-over or written instructions. Apart from the sparse instructions at the beginning, the name labels for characters in act 1, and the written scoreboard at the end of each level, hardly any verbal language is used. This augments the importance of a very unusual device occurring in multiple places throughout act 2: little snippets of interior monologue that are worded so as to match each character's stage of cognitive and emotional development and to act as a mimetic device for their unique personalities. On entering the ruined theater, for instance, Scarlet muses philosophically, "[a]rt is where the nobility of humanity is expressed. I could not live in a world without it." By contrast, Robin's interior monologues are linguistically and intellectually less sophisticated. In the graveyard, she monologizes, "People die. It's hard to imagine for a kid like me. They die and we put them in the ground. Like flowers." Hence, no matter how short and abrupt, interior monologues serve an important lyrical and characterization purpose, thus corroborating the literary feel of the game.

Finally, the *epitextual* environment surrounding the game reinforces its literary atmosphere. The game's official website (www.tale-of-tales.com/ThePath) features blogs for each sister and a number of fictional entries they have written, as well as comments from various fictional and actual visitors (see figure 9.1). Again, the style of writing has been adapted to match the age of each character, and the entries convey additional personal, emotional, and anecdotal information about their fictional authors. Eerily, every LiveJournal, as the blogs are called, ends around the same date—between January and April 2009—coinciding with the run-up to the release of the game. The mixture of actual and virtual narrative—between fictional entries and (seemingly) actual responses from readers—causes the effect of metaleptic oscillation, which means an "ontological hesitation" (McHale 1999, 184) between players' actual world and the fictional world of the game. Readers seem to be drawn into the gameworld by interacting with the fictional characters via their blogs, an effect that further supplements the immersion evoked when RPs are represented by an avatar in the gameworld.

In addition to its literary features, *The Path* thematizes a self-reflexive, *metaludological* concern: the adolescent development from paidia (free play) to ludus (rule-governed play) (Carter 2010; Caillois 1958/2001; see chapter 2, this book). The six adolescent stages represented by the girls show the

Figure 9.1
Excerpt from *The Path*: Scarlet's LiveJournal with reader comments.

dangers of both paidiac and ludic play, as well as of the various interim stages between these two poles. The procedural rhetoric of the game tells players that childlike curiosity can lead to traumatic events just as easily as can calculated, rule-governed adult behavior like the "serious" competitive games of sexual attraction and artistic activity. It is therefore hardly surprising that, despite the fairytale theme, the game is deemed "unsuitable for children" and "decidedly a game for the mature mind" (Tale of Tales 2009b, 3).

The Path foregrounds certain aspects of computer game mechanics and aesthetics for critical purposes and détournement. It takes several days to complete, which is mostly because this slow game (Tale of Tales 2013, Westecott 2010) almost exclusively allows walking (rather than running or flying). The slow pace of character movement helps maintain deep rather than hyper attention in players and enables them to reflect on thematic issues surrounding sexual violence and lost childhood. Cut scenes, of which there are many, cannot be skipped or paused and therefore must be watched from beginning to end. They occur whenever the player approaches an interactive feature, be it as harmless as the flowers the girls can pick (for no apparent ludic-mechanic reason, incidentally) or as frightening as the various wolf encounters. Collectively, the scenes add to the tardiness of narrative progression and to the meditative atmosphere the game sets out to communicate.

The second ludonarratological principle I would like to explore is the dérive. While playing the game, players increasingly comprehend the psychogeographic meanings inherent in the props and settings they encounter in the gameworld. They come to realize that their aimless meanderings serve a philosophical, moral, and spiritual purpose. They find that every successfully played chapter ends in the same, tragic way: it shows the "played" girl lying outside grandmother's house in the rain—broken, violated, and physically and emotionally damaged. Similarly, spatial exploration becomes some kind of sociocritical engagement and every object and character encountered inevitably adopts a foreboding or lamenting function, alluding to the traumas that have already been experienced and/or are due to occur in the near future.

The Path adopts a trajectory of minimum constraint, at least as far as navigational agency is concerned. The destinations chosen by P-Cs invariably direct them away from the beaten track. In fact, the gameworld is designed to encourage aimless wanderings in the nightly forest, thus causing players to roam rather than navigate. Put differently, once in the woods, the P-C is left to her own devices and the scarcity and delusive nature of apparent semiotic indicators (such as steam rising up from the ground, rays of sunlight breaking through the trees, path-like patches of sand, and specks of light appearing and disappearing like glowworms) serve to misguide her. Elsewhere (Ensslin 2012a), I refer to this type of (non)navigation as inductive rather than deductive because it creates paths in a bottom-up manner from player exploration rather than a top-down fashion from precoded navigational aids. The resultant aesthetic of disorientation ties in with the overall impression of spatial infinity, which suggests illusory agency (see chapter 5) and raises the question of whether "real" agency is indeed a desirable quality in videogames.

Finally, let me examine allusive fallacy in the sense of semiotic devices deployed as misleading clues in *The Path*. Of particular importance for this undertaking is the game's interface. During the first playthrough, the interface in act 2 shows only the confusing scenery of the nightly forest. From the second playthrough onward, however, the interface margins depict superimposed visual, iconic clues pointing to sites that can be visited (indexed by the lake and field of flowers icons in the left-hand margin of figure 9.2), and information about the location of the wolf (represented by a paw in the bottom right-hand corner) relative to the avatar's position. Somewhat less clear-cut are symbolical devices such as the white twirls all around the margins. The steadily moving Girl in White (a dynamic navigation aid) is symbolized by the sharp-white twirl immediately to the left of the paw but, without consulting the manual, players are unlikely to easily understand how to read the somewhat cryptic symbols. Indeed, the larger, blurred twirls are likely to remain a mystery throughout, thus contributing to the allusive fallacy of the game.

Most strikingly, whenever the P-C approaches an item that is allocated to another sister, a close-up of that sister is projected on the interface (figure

Figure 9.2
Visual "clues" in *The Path*'s interface margins (Ruby's chapter).

9.3). That said, this allocation may also not be obvious to players who haven't read the manual. Indeed, to the close reader/player on the dérive, this device doesn't just operate as an intertextual hint of another chapter of the game and/or a ludic pointer toward inoperability but, indeed, as a proleptic or analeptic device alluding eerily to another sister's past or forthcoming suffering and death.

In their entirety, the allusive devices deployed in the game have a strangely disconcerting effect on players, especially if they have embarked on the game without consulting the manual. They cannot help feeling that they are aimlessly meandering through the woods and that their trajectory increasingly directs them to the frightful but inevitable encounter with the wolf. This sense of inevitability and, figuratively speaking, educational necessity lies, I would argue, at the core of *The Path*'s procedural rhetoric.

9.5   Discussion

In this final section I shall draw a comparison between *The Path* and three other digital narratives, only two of which (*To the Moon* and *Braid*) are what

Figure 9.3
Superimposed image of Carmen as Ruby finds the wire fence in *The Path*.

we may call literary auteur games, albeit for different reasons than *The Path*. The third comparative work is Donna Leishman's Flash- and Javascript-based interactive narrative *RedRidingHood* (2001/2006). I have chosen to include it in this discussion because it is described as a "*playful* retelling of the Little Red Riding Hood fairy tale" in the blurb of its entry in the *Electronic Literature Collection, Volume One* (Hayles et al. 2006, emphasis mine). However, the word *playful* isn't explained at any length and therefore begs investigation in contrast with *The Path*.

At first glance, it may come as quite a surprise to see *RedRidingHood* (*RRH*) listed in a collection of electronic literature. After all, the text hardly seems to display any verbal language, with the exception of a small number of text snippets and Red's diary. The most important text fragment is arguably the clipped fairytale introductory phrase "Once upon a not so far away," modified for the purposes of appropriation and satire. The rest of the narrative is a mixture of crudely drawn, audiovisual 2D animation and interactive image links, such as flower petals that fly up into the air on mouse-over. The book displayed graphically on the first interactive page of the narrative only alludes to the literary culture that inspired this remediation.

Mouse interaction mostly triggers animated sequences in a consecutive fashion. Nevertheless, with repeated interaction the reader notices that during Red's journey through the forest some clickable links open her diary, in which she keeps secret notes of her personal concerns, fears, and desires. These fantasies are closely linked with contemporary representations of the mythological wolf, such as a handsome skateboarder or a man dressed in black (much like a burglar) approaching Red as she sleeps in her bed in the final scene.

The word *playful* may at best relate to the satirical ways in which the fairytale has been adapted, or, indeed, to the cognitive-ergodic ways in which reader-viewers can interact with the interface. Cognitive-ergodic interactivity is meaningfully integrated into the interface, for instance, as Red follows her mother's request to go to grandmother's house. The request is represented nonverbally by showing the mother's moving mouth, which can subsequently be clicked to activate another animated scene. This next scene shows Red following her mother's spoken (yet inaudible) request and leaving her contemporary, council-estate, high-rise flat to make her way through the woods to grandmother's house. Cognitive-ergodic interactivity reaches its peak when Red has fallen asleep among the flowers and the interactor can choose between letting her dream and waking her up. Letting her dream activates various sequences of interactive animations that show Red's subconscious dreams, which involve angels planting dreams in her head, embryos that can be made to grow, toys in her bedroom that come to life (supervised by the heads of herself and her friends), and many other surrealist ideas.

On the whole, *RRH*'s ludicity is almost exclusively cognitive-ergodic. The only potentially ludic-mechanic aspect is the choice the interactor has between letting her dream and waking her up, and this choice leads to an experience that is more akin to reading a multilinear hypertext or hypermedia fiction than to playing a game. Similarly, *RRH*'s literariness is largely limited to a very small number of textual snippets, some of which are copied and modified from fairytale and comic strip intertexts, as well as from her diary entries. These entries operate largely as a conscious counterpart to her subconscious sexual and violent dreams. Seen as a multimodal whole, these details represent her as a complex, twenty-first-century female character—a young girl with strong sexual and emotional needs and fears who is, therefore, juxtaposed to the dependent, seemingly mindless, and flat character we know from the Perrauldian and Grimmsian fairytales. In terms of literariness, however, *RRH* is situated in the region of quasi-literary games such as *Myst* and *Syberia* (see section 3.4) that typically use in-game literary technologies such as books and/or re- or transmediate canonical literary texts.

Due to its underemphasis of both literary and ludic-mechanic features, I have placed *RRH* below the other texts discussed in this section on both measures of the L-L spectrum (figure 9.4). *RRH* can be seen as "a story for adults that blurs the line between an adolescent girl's conscious and unconscious fantasies" (Jacobus 2010), rendered as a hybrid piece of interactive animation. Playable in the true sense of the word, however, it is not.

The first literary auteur game that I'd like to bring into this comparative discussion is Freebird Games's (2011) *To the Moon* (*TTM*). Rendered in 16-bit pixelated design, this nostalgia-evoking, point-and-click adventure game strongly features its main auteur's (Kan Gao) graphical imprint. The game's main characters are two scientists, Dr. Rosalene and Dr. Watts, who are hired by the aged Johnny Wiles on his deathbed to reconstruct his memories so that he might remember the reason for his final wish—to go to the moon. The player, alias Dr. Rosalene and Dr. Watts, embarks on a ludic-mechanic, biographic journey to bring back Johnny's memories of his deceased wife, River, how they met, how they lived their life together, and the tragic events that ultimately caused Johnny's amnesia.

Unlike most blockbuster titles but in line with many serious and art games, *TTM* "dares to tackle themes about life, death and the importance of living with the memories of the best and worst of times" (Gallegos 2011).

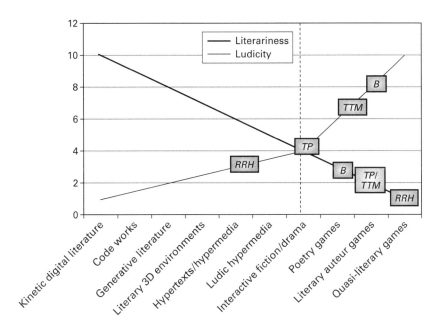

Figure 9.4
The Path (*TP*), *RedRidingHood* (*RRH*), *To the Moon* (*TTM*), and *Braid* (*B*) mapped onto the L-L spectrum.

Level by level, layer by layer, players unveil elements of Johnny's past, jig-sawing together his complex biography. This is done by means of mne-monic objects that have to be retrieved from Johnny's house and other places where he spent parts of his life.

The gameplay of *TTM* is largely predictable, straightforward explora-tion and puzzle-solving. Its main focus lies on its narrative complexities and the carefully crafted dialogues between its characters. It is this focus mainly that makes *TTM* a literary game. It involves a lot of reading—more than would be necessary for a purely functional representation of informa-tion. While written dialogues are a well-known aspect of point-and-click adventures, the language used in *TTM* has clearly literary functions, such as indirect characterization (as in *The Path*) and the creation of a specific nar-rative atmosphere. Its overall effect on the RP is one of deep sympathy with Johnny and his wife. Indeed, the game communicates emotions that are so intense that they may well be described as "cathartic" (Gallegos 2011), hav-ing an effect on RP's actual lives rather than simply creating an entertaining experience.

Despite its straightforward ludic-mechanic design, *TTM* features higher up on the ludic scale than *The Path* (figure 9.4). It is a game that moves through levels, that follows and instrumentalizes rules and challenges, that can be won, and that uses its ludic mechanics to communicate its procedural rhetoric. Rather than following a largely antiludic philosophy, it embraces proactive gameplay, even though the latter mostly serves a narrative and moralizing function. On the literary scale, *TTM* is roughly colocated with *The Path*. On the one hand, the sheer amount of written text by far exceeds that of *The Path*, and players have to make a serious effort to close-read innumerable communicative turns to work out both ludic and narrative meanings. On the other hand, *The Path*'s literary elements are more diverse in style and character, extending beyond the confines of the game itself to its auteured paratexts. So we might say that while *The Path* uses a wider range of narratological techniques, *TTM* has a more pronounced readerly agenda and cannot be played successfully unless its dialogic structure is willfully embraced.

The final literary game we will discuss in this chapter is Jonathan Blow's platform game *Braid* (2009). Although at first glance its graphical design doesn't seem to exhibit many literary features, actual gameplay reveals a number of elements that render it a piece of verbal as well as ludic-mechanic art. In level 1, the following text is displayed on screen: "Tim is off on a search to rescue the Princess. She has been snatched by a horrible and evil monster. This happened because Tim made a mistake." Clearly, this brief backstory doesn't appear particularly literary. Yet it gives a glimpse of the hamartia—the tragic essence—underlying the game's narrative: a crucial error made by the protagonist that underlies the game's narrative makeup.

Playing *Braid* resembles playing almost any platform game in the vein of *Super Mario* or *Donkey Kong*, and its main objective is almost too common: rescuing the princess from the monster (see also chapter 6). However, toward the end, the actual message of the game turns out to be radically feminist in nature. Just as Tim is about to save the princess, having gone through a long series of fiendish challenges, he learns that the princess doesn't want to be saved. Indeed, she is grateful that she was taken away by the monster, who will save her from the burden of marriage. This thematically antiludic message is communicated to the player through long passages of verbal narrative, displayed on screen whenever the avatar opens one of the green and red books in the epilogue. These passages are a series of literary texts that reveal the true meaning of the game—a critique of mainstream adventure games' stereotypical, subludic misogynist teleology (see section 6.3): "His arm weighed upon her shoulders, felt constrictive around her neck. 'You're burdening me with your ridiculous need,' she said. Or, she said: 'You're going the wrong way and you're pulling me with you.' In another time, another place, she said: 'Stop yanking on my arm; you're hurting me!'" Her dismay at his insistence on saving her and the multiple versions of their relationship going awry suggested by the previous quotation is complemented by the following passage: "He worked his ruler and his compass. He inferred. He deduced. He scrutinized the fall of an apple, the twisting of metal orbs hanging from a thread. He was searching for the Princess, and he would not stop until he found her, for he was hungry. He cut rats into pieces to examine their brains, implanted tungsten posts into the skulls of water-starved monkeys." This passage characterizes Tim (embodying chauvinist masculinity) as a Faustian character—a man obsessed with amoral scientific power and prefeminist gender values.

The excerpts quoted in the previous paragraph display carefully a crafted narrative discourse that contains a wide range of registers and literary vocabulary. Hyper-attentive gamers, who may decide to skip these passages, will not understand the deeper meaning of the game and will wonder, instead, what the point of their efforts has been. Thus, the game has a strong readerly agenda, and so I position it even higher on the literary scale than *The Path* and *TTM*—indeed, in the region of poetry games (figure 9.4). After all, without reading the essential narrative information provided by the in-game books and appreciating its lyrical, expressive style of writing, the game's complex and difficult ludic mechanic is largely meaningless. Likewise, *Braid*'s ludicity features far higher on the ludic scale than that of the three other artifacts discussed in this chapter, and it gains its full literary and ludic significance only in the final epilogue, as an ultimate reward for the full-fledged literary gamer.

10   Conclusion

This book has introduced literary gaming as a new object of digital media study, one that is relevant to ludologists and literary scholars alike, and one that might cause the disciplines of literary and game studies to enter into a more synergetic and collaborative relationship than has been possible so far. The body of texts that fall under literary gaming is growing rapidly and becoming increasingly diverse. It now ranges from literary texts driven mostly by cognitive and ergodic ludicity to literary games proper, which exhibit various forms of ludic mechanics. A principal aim of this book was to show that these artifacts can be analyzed systematically and comprehensively using a new, synthetic methodology called functional ludostylistics. This toolkit comprises four main compartments: ludology, ludonarratology, ludosemiotics, and mediality. Though its individual elements can be used eclectically to analyze almost any ludic or literary text in digital media and beyond, we can only speak of literary gaming if all four compartments are used.

To showcase literary gaming and its analysis in action, I took a cross-section of genres from the full literary-ludic spectrum as presented in chapter 3. What became quite clear in these analyses is the fact that individual exemplars of each media genre do not necessarily map onto the L-L spectrum (as outlined in figure 3.2) in a straightforward way. *Clues*, for instance, is roughly colocated with other literary hypertexts in terms of literariness or emphasis on readerliness, yet it deviates radically from the others in terms of ludicity. Thus, the genre concept isn't necessarily helpful when it comes to combining close reading and close play.

Throughout my analyses, I adopted existing theoretical and analytical approaches, such as Caillois's (2001) typology of play, Bogost's (2007) procedural rhetoric, and Ryan's (2006) functional ludonarrativism. Perhaps more important, however, I expanded the existing analytical frameworks by introducing new concepts particularly suited for instances of literary gaming: for example, aleatoric fallacy, which happens when randomized text generation is feigned and readers can't control it (*Loss of Grasp*); heuristic ergodicity, which applies to RPs as they learn how to navigate and interact with nonstandard textual interface designs (*Loss of Grasp*); antiludic design and unnatural narrative techniques such as textual *you*, which are used to expose readers as accomplices in crimes against in-game female characters and thereby subvert the misogynist ideologies underlying mainstream blockbusters (*The Princess Murderer*); external narrativity and paratexts, which become part of a player's wider mental image of a game's or IF's textual ecology (*Blue Lacuna*; *The Path*); the ludic functionalization of specific lexical categories, such as color adjectives (*Blue Lacuna*); reverse ergodicity as a means of facilitating reading in highly complex and challenging gameworlds (*Blue Lacuna*); and other forms of fallaciousness (e.g., dynamic lexias in *Loss of Grasp* and allusive fallacy in the interface design of *The Path*) that are implemented to mislead and surprise readers.

I revisited the Situationist concepts of détournement and dérive and applied them to poetic and literary auteur games (*evidence of everything exploding* and *The Path*). Though both concepts, and especially the dérive, do not map precisely onto the games under investigation, they can be adapted from their historical uses to show how literary games play with, rather than by, rules (Dragona 2010, 27); how they appropriate and thereby critique elements of mainstream commercial and popular culture; and how they highlight the importance of exploration and critical reflection, most adamantly through slow gaming.

At the heart of this study was a demonstration that the art, interactive practices, and discipline of literary gaming have come of age. I believe I have achieved this by fleshing out the intricacies of functional ludostylistics and by illustrating, through various close readings/playings, how it produces systematic and replicable analyses. That said, the tools mentioned and showcased in this book are to be seen as a starting point rather than an exhaustive list. As new literary games and ludoliterary artifacts are released, the toolkit will need to be expanded and adjusted.

I have emphasized in various places that full ludostylistic analyses (in the sense of using all four compartments of the toolkit) can only be applied to digital literature that exhibits ludic mechanics, and also to literary art games. However, my readings of the hypertexts in chapter 4 and *Loss of Grasp* in chapter 5 have shown that even texts governed mostly by cognitive-ergodic ludicity afford and merit ludostylistic examination, albeit to a limited extent. Since the methodology marries analytical concepts from a wide range of disciplines, I consider it sufficiently malleable to apply to instances of literary gaming that weren't considered in this book. This includes literary gaming in analog, nondigital media, no matter how patchy its documentation may be at present.

Clearly, the number of things this book has not managed to do is considerable. Arguably, the most obvious shortcoming is its failure to capture the creative field of literary gaming comprehensively. In fact, my future research into literary gaming will no doubt cause me to expand and change the L-L spectrum, and I look forward to the discussions with like-minded scholars that will help me do so. Likewise, the theoretical foundation and range of examples supplied in this book will hopefully trigger a lively debate among scholars and practitioners and inspire further creative and critical work in this area.

Second, due to spatial constraints, I had to select a cross-section of the L-L spectrum for my case studies rather than being able to present a broader view, one which would have included more marginal genres of literary gaming such as quasi-literary games and literary 3D environments. Similarly, with very few exceptions I had to exclude examples of nondigital literary (rather than language) games, not least because the body of such games known to me is still too small to merit a book-length study. However, I believe that the points I wanted to make about the distinctions between and most salient manifestations of literary play and gaming have come across more poignantly through this eclectic approach than they would have with a more far-reaching study.

Finally, despite the replicability and systematicity mentioned with regard to analytical methodology, there is no denying that the L-L spectrum as schematized in figure 3.2 is an introspective representation of the field under investigation. Neither the 0–10 scale nor the literariness and ludicity lines are based on empirical or mathematical principles. They schematize the mental image resulting from my very own hermeneutic activities and are therefore duly prone to attract criticisms of various kinds. I believe, however, that a more arithmetically inclined approach would have been inadequately positivistic. After all, hermeneutic activity simply isn't measurable to the same degree as, for instance, aspects of authorial language use (e.g., lexical frequencies and dominant grammatical patterns).

To further develop literary gaming as a field of research within ludology, creative, literary, and media studies, a range of projects comes to mind. An important one would be to examine literary gaming from the user's perspective, applying methods of empirical reader-response, audience, and player research. It would go far beyond the phenomenological observations made in this book and investigate systematically RPs' reading and playing strategies, their ways of coping with the clash between deep and hyper attention, and the psychological and physiological implications of combining close reading and gaming. Another possible project might look at the margins of literary gaming and investigate, in particular, games that reference print culture metamedially, such as *Myst* and *Syberia*, as well as those that use literary intertextuality to locate themselves in an inter- or transmedia storytelling canon (e.g., *Tradewinds Odyssey*, *The Path*, and the *Fable* series). Finally, it will be worth looking at the creators of literary-ludic artifacts and studying their creative agendas and processes. This may well result in book-length studies of individual author-designers (or teams) and their oeuvre, which I would see as a welcome indicator that digital literary culture is finally drawing level with print.

Notes

Chapter 1

1. Strictly speaking, it is misleading to refer to the reception of digital literature as *reading*. It involves many other sensory, interactive processes as well, including visual, aural, and haptic interaction. A more suitable term would therefore be *experiencing* (Bell et al. 2010). However, in this book my aim is to focus on the phenomenological distinctions between playerly and readerly texts. I shall therefore assume my readers' awareness of the broad multimodal array of receptive and interactive processes involved in reading digital media.

2. Conveniently or not, the German language does not distinguish lexically between play and game. It uses *Spiel* for both concepts.

3. Many of these studies are contributions to Guinness and Hurley's (1986) *Auctor Ludens: Essays on Play in Literature*. This volume marked another important step toward the recognition of play as a core element of writing and reading literature more generally. It takes a bottom-up approach by offering analyses of playful literature rather than purely theoretical essays, thus proving that ludoliterary scholarship had matured. The book is an attempt to root literature firmly in the cultural context of play. To the editors, play "has an incalculable importance for our understanding of literature in general and of individual works in particular" (vii), and they justify this view by defining literary play as "anything from surface ornamentation to the essential component of any creative activity whatsoever, or as integral to the as if [*sic*] presumption of all imaginative constructions" (vii–viii). Somewhat unfortunately, their emphasis is on *auctor* rather than *lector ludens*, on the playful/playing *author* rather than the playful/playing *reader*, which is somewhat paradoxical in a book that takes a primarily analytical approach.

Chapter 2

1. Kant expressed his main thoughts on play in *Critique of Pure Reason* (*Kritik der reinen Vernunft*, 1781), "Reflections on Anthropology" ("Reflexionen zur Anthropologie," 1798), and *Critique of Judgment* (*Kritik der Urteilskraft*, 1790).

2. Further philosophical thinkers that, due to spatial constraints, I cannot discuss at any length, include, for example, Spencer (*Principles of Psychology*, 1872) and Axelos (*Le Jeu du Monde*, 1969).

3. See also the work of Ehrmann, Spariosu, and Suits. Their work is referenced in several places throughout this book.

4. This binary division between virtual gameworld and outside reality has been critiqued by a number of scholars. Ehrmann (1968, 32), for instance, argues that Huizinga's idea "delimit[s] too categorically the sphere of play by opposing it to the real, to work, and so forth." More recently, the (semi-) permeability of the membrane surrounding the magic circle has been highlighted by scholars such as Klabbers (2009) and Myers (2012), and Consalvo (2009) queries the relevance of the very concept to contemporary games studies.

5. Strictly speaking, Bakhtin cannot be considered a poststructuralist as his writings predated the poststructuralist movement proper by several decades. Yet Western poststructuralist thinkers from the late 1960s onward greatly embraced and drew upon his work, especially because of its playfully subversive aspects. Likewise, the idea of the carnivalesque has been highly influential in twentieth- and twenty-first-century artistic practice.

6. Hutchinson's title alludes to Eric Berne's *Games People Play* (1964), a psychotherapeutic study that particularly stresses the importance of unconscious game- and role-playing in interpersonal relations.

7. In an appeal to current game developers, Adams (2007) lays down some ground rules for future art games. He demands, for instance: that such games should have a more complex objective than simply providing fun and entertainment—they should challenge players aesthetically and philosophically; that developers should experiment with the digital medium and take artistic risks; that prizes and awards should recognize artistic merit; that games should warrant genuine criticism and scholarship, which goes far beyond simple reviews and makes art games objects of study, discussion, and analysis; and that developers should consider themselves and each other as auteur-artists with their own individual styles, skills, and aesthetic agendas.

8. According to Bogost (2007, 2–3), "[p]rocedurality refers to a way of creating, explaining, or understanding processes. And Processes define the way things work: the methods, techniques, and logics that drive the operation of systems from mechanical systems like engines to organizational systems like high schools to conceptual systems like religious faith. Rhetoric refers to the effective and persuasive expression. Procedural rhetoric, then, is a practice of using processes persuasively," and in particular the ludic processes afforded by videogames' underlying algorithms.

Chapter 3

1. This list should be considered tentative and eclectic rather than ultimate and comprehensive. First, it cannot and does not aim to cover the entirety of literary-ludic artifacts, which would go beyond the confines of this study. Second, individual examples of each genre may deviate in various ways from the general textual and ludic tendencies exhibited by that genre. Finally, there are a host of individual literary ludic texts that defy subsumption under any genre umbrella. In fact, most of the works cited here have, in the past, been given a variety of generic labels and/or can easily be subsumed under more than one at the same time.

2. *Firefly* is italicized deliberately because on the whole it is more like a poetry cycle, or collection, than a single poem.

3. Historically, interactive fictions evolved from text adventures, which did not have any claim to literariness attached to them. Rather they were (and still are) games played solely through textual input and output. From this ludic genre has evolved a growing body of poetically sophisticated IFs that place an emphasis on close reading and poetic ambiguity, as well as other self-reflexive techniques.

4. Like *Arteroids*, *Façade* has been theorized and analyzed extensively, for instance, by Mateas (2004), Ryan (2006), and Schäfer (2009).

5. Juul's (2005) concept of games of progression refers to games that are structured much like a flowchart, "where players follow a fixed, predominantly linear narrative script that takes them through discrete levels" (Ryan 2006, 201). Narratives of emergence (Salen and Zimmerman 2004) happen in more open, sandbox-style architectures, "where players choose their own goals and actions in a world teeming with narrative possibilities" (Ryan 2006, 201). Jenkins (2004, 128) uses the term emergent narrative more broadly to refer to the personal stories that develop through gameplay.

6. As indicated in table 3.1, external narrativity refers to paratextual narratives, that is, narratives that emerge outside the gameworld. They include, for instance, narratives composed by players, such as playthroughs and walkthroughs; metaleptic narratives such as fictional blogs apparently written by game characters but accessible via a game's website; and transmediations of a game plot, such as fan fiction and other types of fan culture that develop a game's storyworld further outside the boundaries of the actual game (series).

7. I admit that textuality would fit just as well under text and discourse as a ludosemiotic element, and that this is one of numerous overlaps in the toolkit. For example, strictly speaking, verbal language should come under the inclusive term multimodality, yet I've listed it separately to stress the importance of verbal language for stylistic analysis. My decision to put textuality under mediality is motivated by the fact that ludoliterary texts tend to display complex self-referential and

extratextual meanings, which can be best understood when seeing the text as part of a sophisticated, networked media ecology.

8. I have chosen hypertext fiction as my entry point into the close analysis of literary gaming because it involves cases of both cognitive-ergodic ludicity and ludic mechanics, which can be read metaludologically (see chapter 9).

Chapter 4

1. According to Landow (1992), hypertext readers are empowered in that the text gives them the opportunity to become coauthors—hence the coinage *wreader*, a blend of writer and reader. For an overview of Landow's theory and the debate it triggered among first-wave hypertext theorists, see Ensslin (2007).

2. Hutchinson (1983, 13) argues rather sweepingly that all literature or, indeed, all texts contain play in some respect in that "they tease, frustrate, deny information, make suggestions [and], above all, . . . challenge the reader." Similarly, he contends that Caillois's classification is "not ideally suited to literary games" (6). This may well be true in the context of Hutchinson's own theory, which—somewhat misleadingly—limits *games with the reader* to the triad of enigma (puzzles or mysteries), parallel (allusions, subplots, allegories, etc.), and "certain narrative devices," such as self-conscious or unreliable narration (23). However, in a study such as the present one, which takes games as its starting point, this classification is both insufficient and ludologically undertheorized.

3. To follow the multimodal details of this analysis, readers are encouraged to look at the online poem itself, available at http://www.poemsthatgo.com/gallery/fall2002/firefly (September 18, 2013).

4. Slocombe (2006, 108) refers to this postmodern type of text as an "absurd situation novel" as its "narrative action revolves around an irrational series of events."

5. Findhorn likely refers to the actual Scottish ecovillage of Findhorn (near Moray), home of the Findhorn Foundation, an educational charity and spiritual community registered in 1972. Due to its New Age character, it has often been associated with drug abuse.

6. The references in square brackets refer to specific, named lexias.

Chapter 5

1. For more inclusive views of videogames as digital fictions, see Punday (2014) and Tosca (2014).

2. Rustad's (2012) concept refers to "literature that is created and read in social media environments, such as Facebook poetry and Twitter fiction . . . , where the

platform is a significant part of the aesthetic expression and the meaning potential" (Bell, Ensslin, and Rustad 2014, 10).

3. Ryan (2006, 201–203) further suggests examining: the various functions and manifestations of narrative in games; the types of structures game narratives can assume (e.g., narratives of progression, emergence, or discovery); the ways in which players learn about the game's underlying backstory and storyworld; the ways in which fictional world and game rules interrelate and whether there might be any alternatives in design and execution; and whether the ludic structures of a game are consistent vis-à-vis the storyworld in which they are embedded.

4. Clearly, different kinds of players will have different heuristic experiences and different learning curves. Someone who is used to playing games will be far more familiar with the strategies and tasks that players often have to undertake in games than someone who has never played one before.

5. The slashes refer to lexia changes, that is, each segment between slashes is displayed individually on screen.

6. For an insightful reading of this scene in terms of media-specific metalepsis, see Bell (2014).

7. "Contemporary" here refers to the five years previous to the time of writing. As digital technologies develop at positively breakneck speed, they tend to become obsolescent within a few years, and creative possibilities evolve almost exponentially alongside new software and hardware. Consequently, it is sometimes within a few years that digital media adopt the label "historical," as is the case with most Storyspace hyperfictions and a large number of online literary hypermedia that are purely based on hyperlink interactivity.

Chapter 6

1. According to the *Dictionary of Unnatural Narratology* (Alber et al. 2011), unnatural narratives are "fictional narratives that transcend or violate the boundaries of conventional realism." Typical forms of unnatural narratives include multilinear narratives (such as hypertext fictions), narrative unreliability, narrative points of view other than third- and first-person narration, and metalepsis (see chapter 9 of this book).

2. Much like its counterpart term *subtextual*, *subludic* refers to meanings suggested implicitly by a game's ludic mechanisms without being overtly expressed as such.

3. Unlike most interactive fictions and videogames, hypertext fiction foregrounds the importance of the authored text and limits reader agency to varying degrees of navigational freedom rather than allowing readers to enter into the coproductive, dialogic text construction characteristic of IF. The reader must move a mouse and

click a button or type a response on a keyboard in order to learn more about the fictional world and its inhabitants, whereas in IFs they enter commands in a text window to trigger new chunks of narrative. For an in-depth discussion of textual *you* and its uses in digital fiction, see Bell and Ensslin (2011) and Ensslin and Bell (2012).

4. The *Inanimate Alice* website contains a host of educational materials and references, especially for primary school children. The novel itself is conceptualized as a participatory narrative, inviting readers to continue writing the story and fill the narrative gaps left by the authors.

5. Coppercube 2.0 is "an exceptional program by Ambiera that can export 3D for PC, Mac, Flash and WebGL" (Dreaming Methods 2010, 3).

Chapter 7

1. With IFs in general it is impossible to put a nonambivalent label on the person experiencing them. There are elements that make the interactor feel like a reader; others are more playerly in character. Therefore I am using "reader-player" in this chapter whenever referring to the IF experience as a whole. Readerly and playerly elements are referred to as being experienced by "readers" and "players" respectively.

2. Strictly speaking, the very first text adventures (Will Crowther's *Adventure,* 1975) were noncommercial experiments as well.

3. In what follows, I shall refer to a female heterosexual protagonist, representing my own preferred setting. Any further references to the storyline are based on my individual choices, which are fully replicable through the transcript yet likely to differ significantly from other players' experiences and textual manifestations.

4. *BL* has a dynamic time system embedded in it. The number of commands entered is synchronized with the progress of diegetic time. Hence, during nighttime, for instance, certain mechanisms aren't functional because the P-C can't see them in the dark.

5. At this point I would like to thank Aaron Reed for his advice, assistance, and explanations relating to the conceptualization of *BL* as well as its trickiest riddles.

6. Incidentally, the Progue epilogue is the one described in the previous section, in which he is finally reunited with his wife.

7. This observation was made on March 18, 2013.

8. The intertextual references to *Avatar* and Turkle's *Alone Together* work only prospectively (although this is a paradoxical and hence controversial thing to say). *Avatar* was launched late in 2009, that is, months after *BL* was published, and

Turkle's TED talk and book appeared in 2011. Hence, we might argue that *BL* antici-pated a number of core ideas permeating the discourse of digital culture.

9. Illustrations per se aren't a novelty in text adventures and interactive fictions. For a detailed discussion of *ED's* forerunners, see Short (2008).

10. For a more detailed close reading of *AV*, see Chang (2004).

Chapter 8

1. It would exceed the scope of this book to go further into actual reader response or player research at this point, not least because the audience research producing empirical insights into literary gaming is still forthcoming.

2. I have decided to place an in-depth discussion of art games and their rootedness in the historical avant-gardes here rather than in a previous chapter because this chapter is the first to deal with "games" proper rather than ludic digital literature or the peculiar hybrid that is literary IF.

2. So-called serious games such as these are related to art games in that they seek to use ludic mechanics and procedural rhetoric as a critical or educational tool. Typical objects of these critiques are economic or cultural issues, such as McDonaldization (*McDonald's Videogame*), the global financial crisis (*Layoff*), and the wars in Iraq and Afghanistan (*September 12th*).

3. Yet, as we saw in chapter 6, antiludicity does not feature in games only. My dis-cussion of *The Princess Murderer* showed how it occurs in the design of an otherwise readerly digital fiction.

4. Strictly speaking, the documents aren't entirely random, although they may seem to be *prima facie*. According to Nelson himself (original grammar and spelling retained),

the levels arent as unrelated as you might think. There is a line between them. In some says, in many ways these are pivotal moments in history, albeit some more hidden than others. They are all represent moments of changing thought, of subverting how we understand the world. Maybe a description would help: 1. new ways of organizing language 2. the dadaist movement clearly had implications on how we understand art and lit. 3. a collective movement towards space, expanding our universal view 4. a shift from what could have been free and open technology and code to commercialisation 5. lawsuits gone insane . . . shift from an over litigation. 6. ok . . . this one is just about love and the notion of creating something both appealing and impenetrable. 7. evidence of how institutions are largely random places with the air of authority without the vision. 8. it's all about the money . . . global politics as random acts. ie . . . if the president had sent ten year old Fidel money. . . . no Cuban missile crisis etc. . 9. pizza box . . . the contemporary pandemic . . . over packaging, over eating, over everything oh and the 1918 flu . . . because that event changed the way we perceived each other and social spaces . . . in terms of the invisible threat and paranoia of viruses. (personal correspondence, April 7, 2013)

Chapter 9

1. Excluded from my discussion have been so-called poetic games that don't actually feature any language at all, such as Jason Rohrer's *Passage* (2007), or feature it to such a small degree that they figure rather as pieces of minimalist concrete poetry or conceptual art, such as Neil Hennessy's *Basho's Frogger and Jabber* (2000).

2. An alternative or even complementary interpretation would be that, after taking the drugs, Ruby is involved in a car accident, which is suggested by imagery used in the final cut scene showing her nightmarish journey through grandmother's house.

3. Although the game only alludes to violence and sexuality, "the overall melancholy mood of the game and the potentially unsettling course of events" may upset preadolescent players (Tale of Tales 2009b, 3).

4. That being said, I would not go so far as to agree with Martin's (2009) sweeping comparison that experiencing *The Path* is much like "an Angela Carter story, as siphoned through *The Sims*."

5. Horizontal structures (of difficulty) mean that each level, or chapter, is equally challenging. Therefore no level-ups are integrated into the game. This aspect of *The Path*'s architecture further supports its readerly nature because the organization of its chapters resembles that of a *Bildungsroman*.

References

Primary Sources

Andrews, Jim. 2006. *Arteroids*, 3.1. Accessed July 31, 2012. http://www.vispo.com/arteroids/arteroids311.htm.

Armor Games. 2008. *Achievement Unlocked*. Accessed August 21, 2012. http://jmtb02.com/achievementunlocked.

Atari. 1979. *Asteroids*. Sunnyvale, CA: Atari, Inc.

Barthelme, Donald. 1970. The Glass Mountain. In *City Life*. New York: Farrar, Straus and Giroux.

Beiguelman, Giselle. 2004/2006. *Code Movie 1*. In *Electronic Literature Collection Volume One*, edited by N. Katherine Hayles, Nick Montfort, Scott Rettberg, and Stephanie Strickland. Accessed August 1, 2012. http://collection.eliterature.org/1/works/beiguelman__code_movie_1.html.

Blow, Jonathan. 2009. *Braid*. Accessed August 2, 2012. http://braid-game.com.

Borràs, Laura, Talan Memmott, Rita Raley, and Brian Stefans. 2011. *Electronic Literature Collection Volume Two*. Accessed March 18, 2013. http://collection.eliterature.org/2.

Bouchardon, Serge, and Volckaert, Vincent. 2010. *Loss of Grasp*. Accessed July 30, 2012. lossofgrasp.com.

Brautigan, Richard. 1971. *The Abortion: An Historical Romance*. New York: Simon and Schuster.

Campbell, Andy, and Judi Alston. 2010. *Nightingale's Playground*. Accessed February 8, 2013. http://www.nightingalesplayground.com.

Cayley, John. 2001. *Windsound*. Accessed August 1, 2012. http://programmatology.shadoof.net/index.php?p=works/wsqt/windsound.html.

Cortazar, Julio. 1956/2013. "Axolotl." *Southern Cross Review*. Accessed September 2, 2013. http://southerncrossreview.org/73/axolotl.html.

Cyan. 1993. *Myst*. San Rafael, CA: Brøderbund.

Evans, Malcolm. 1982. *3D Monster Maze*. UK: J.K. Greye Software.

Dvorský, Jakub. 2003. *Samorost*. Brno, CZ: Amanita Design. Accessed September 2, 2013. http://amanita-design.net/samorost-1.

Dvorský, Jakub. 2005. *Samorost 2*. Brno, CZ: Amanita Design. Accessed September 2, 2013. http://amanita-design.net/samorost-2.

Fredricksen, Eric. 2002. *Progress Quest*. Accessed August 21, 2012. http://progressquest.com/dl.php.

Freebird Games. 2011. *To the Moon*. Accessed August 2, 2012. http://freebirdgames.com/to_the_moon.

geniwate. 2006. Concatenation. In *Electronic Literature Collection Volume One*, edited by N. Katherine Hayles, Nick Montfort, Scott Rettberg, and Stephanie Strickland. Accessed August 1, 2012. http://collection.eliterature.org/1/works/geniwate__generative_poetry.html.

geniwate, and Deena Larsen. 2003. *The Princess Murderer*. Accessed August 2, 2012. http://www.deenalarsen.net/princess/prin_murd.swf.

Hayles, N. Katherine, Nick Montfort, Scott Rettberg, and Stephanie Strickland. 2006. *Electronic Literature Collection Volume One*. Accessed April 3, 2013. http://collection.eliterature.org/1/index.html.

Hennessy, Neil. 2000. *Basho's Frogger and Jabber*. In *Electronic Literature Collection Volume Two*, edited by Laura Borràs, Talan Memmott, Rita Raley, and Brian Stefans. Accessed September 2, 2013. http://collection.eliterature.org/2/works/00_hennessy.html.

Holeton, Richard. 2001. *Figurski at Findhorn on Acid*. Watertown, MA: Eastgate Systems.

id Software. 1992. *Wolfenstein 3D*. Garland, TX: Apogee Software.

id Software. 1996. *Quake*. New York: GT Interactive Software.

Jackson, Shelley. 1995. *Patchwork Girl*. Watertown, MA: Eastgate Systems.

Kendall, Robert. 2001–2008. *Clues*. Accessed April 25, 2013. http://www.wordcircuits.com/clues.

Larsen, Deena. 2002. *Firefly*. In *Deena Larsen's Hypertext/New Media/ Electronic Lit/Possibilities Addicts Attic*. Accessed August 2, 2012. http://www.deenalarsen.net/firefly.swf.

Leishman, Donna. 2001/2006. *RedRidingHood*. In *Electronic Literature Collection Volume One*, edited by N. Katherine Hayles, Nick Montfort, Scott Rettberg, and Stephanie Strickland. Accessed April 3, 2013. http://collection.eliterature.org/1/works/leishman__redridinghood.html.

Lionhead Studios. 2004–2010. *Fable*. Redwood City, CA: Electronic Arts.

Loyer, Erik. 2001. *Chroma*. In *Electronic Literature Collection Volume One*, edited by N. Katherine Hayles, Nick Montfort, Scott Rettberg, and Stephanie Strickland. Accessed April 19, 2013. http://collection.eliterature.org/2/works/loyer_chroma.html.

Marsh, Bill. 2002. *Landscapes*. In *Electronic Literature Collection Volume One*, edited by N. Katherine Hayles, Nick Montfort, Scott Rettberg, and Stephanie Strickland. Accessed August 1, 2012. http://collection.eliterature.org/1/works/marsh__landscapes/index.html.

Miller, Robyn, and Rand Miller. 1993. *Myst*. Eugene, OR: Brøderbund.

Montfort, Nick. 2000. *Ad Verbum*. Accessed August 2, 2012. http://nickm.com/if/adverbum.html.

Montfort, Nick. 2008/2011. *ppg256*. In *Electronic Literature Collection Volume Two*, edited by Laura Borràs, Talan Memmott, Rita Raley, and Brian Stefans. Accessed August 1, 2012. http://collection.eliterature.org/2/works/montfort_ppg256.html.

Moulthrop, Stuart. 1991. *Victory Garden*. Watertown, MA: Eastgate Systems.

Munroe, Jim. 2008. *Everybody Dies*. In *Electronic Literature Collection Volume Two*, edited by Laura Borràs, Talan Memmott, Rita Raley, and Brian Stefans. Accessed September 2, 2013. http://collection.eliterature.org/2/works/00_munroe.html.

Nelson, Jason. 2005. *this is how you will die*. Accessed August 23, 2012. http://www.secrettechnology.com/death/deathspin.htm.

Nelson, Jason. 2007a. *alarmingly these are not lovesick zombies*. Accessed September 18, 2013. http://www.secrettechnology.com/zombie/lovesickzombie6.html.

Nelson, Jason. 2007b. *game, game, game and again game*. Accessed August 23, 2012. http://www.secrettechnology.com/gamegame/gamegame6.html.

Nelson, Jason. 2008. *i made this. you play this. we are enemies*. Accessed August 23, 2012. http://www.secrettechnology.com/madethis/enemy6.html.

Nelson, Jason. 2009. *evidence of everything exploding*. Accessed August 2, 2012. http://www.secrettechnology.com/explode/evidence.html.

Niemi, Marko. 2006. *Stud Poetry*. In *Electronic Literature Collection Volume One*, edited by N. Katherine Hayles, Nick Montfort, Scott Rettberg, and Stephanie Strickland. Accessed March 28, 2013. http://collection.eliterature.org/1/works/niemi__stud_poetry.html.

Perrault, Charles. 1697/1961. *Perrault's Complete Fairy Tales*. Translated by A. E. Johnson, et al. London: Penguin.

Pinto, Regina Célia. 2004. *Viewing Axolotls*. Accessed July 30, 2012. http://arteonline .arq.br/viewing_axolotls/#.

Pullinger, Kate, and Chris Joseph. 2005–2009. *Inanimate Alice*. Accessed August 2, 2012. http://www.inanimatealice.com.

Pullinger, Kate, and Chris Joseph. 2010. *Flight Paths: A Networked Novel*. Accessed January 14, 2013. www.flightpaths.net.

Pullinger, Kate, Stefan Schemat, and babel. 2004. *The Breathing Wall*. London: Sayle Literary Agency.

Queneau, Raymond. 1961. *Cent mille milliards de poèmes*. Paris: Gallimard.

Reed, Aaron A. 2008. *Blue Lacuna: An Interactive Novel in Ten Chapters*. Accessed August 2, 2012. http://www.lacunastory.com/.

Rohrer, Jason. 2007. *Passage*. Accessed March 28, 2013. http://hcsoftware .sourceforge.net/passage.

Sandlot Games. 2009. *Tradewinds Odyssey*. Accessed August 2, 2012. http://www .bigfishgames.com/download-games/5632/tradewinds-odyssey/index.html.

Shelley, Mary. 1818/1998. *Frankenstein; or, The Modern Prometheus*. Oxford: Oxford University Press.

Short, Emily. 2000a. *Galatea*. In *Electronic Literature Collection Volume One*, edited by N. Katherine Hayles, Nick Montfort, Scott Rettberg, and Stephanie Strickland. Accessed March 20, 2013. http://collection.eliterature.org/1/works/short_galatea .html.

Sokal, Benoît, and Microïds. 2002. *Syberia*. Toronto: The Adventure Company.

Sony Online Entertainment. 1999. *EverQuest*. San Diego, CA: Sony Online Entertainment.

Stern, Andrew, and Michael Mateas. 2005. *Façade*. Accessed August 2, 2012. http:// www.interactivestory.net/.

Tale of Tales. 2009a. *The Path*. Accessed August 2, 2012. http://tale-of-tales.com/ ThePath/downloads.html.

thatgamecompany. 2009. *Flower*. Tokyo: Sony Computer Entertainment.

Valve Corporation. 1998. *Half-Life*. Bellevue, WA: Valve Corporation.

Viola, Bill. 2009. *The Night Journey*. Accessed August 21, 2012. http://www .thenightjourney.com/statement.htm.

Waber, Dan, and Jason Pimble. 2005/2006. I, You, We. In *Electronic Literature Collection Volume One*, edited by N. Katherine Hayles, Nick Montfort, Scott Rettberg, and Stephanie Strickland. Accessed August 2, 2012. http://collection.eliterature.org/1/works/waber_pimble__i_you_we.html.

Wardrip-Fruin, Noah, Josh Carroll, Robert Coover, Shawn Greenlee, Andrew McClain, and Ben Shine. 2003. *Screen*. First shown at the Boston Cyberarts Festival 2003. Documentation available at *Noah Wardrip-Fruin*. Accessed August 2, 2012. http://www.noahwf.com/screen/.

Weir, Gregory. 2009. *Silent Conversation*. Accessed August 2, 2012. https://armorgames.com/play/4287/silent-conversation.

Wilks, Christine. 2008. *Fitting the Pattern*. In *Electronic Literature Collection Volume Two*, edited by Laura Borràs, Talan Memmott, Rita Raley, and Brian Stefans. Accessed September 2, 2013. http://collection.eliterature.org/2/works/wilks_fitting_the_pattern/FittingThePattern.html.

Wylde, Nanette. 2004/2006. *Storyland*. In *Electronic Literature Collection Volume One*, edited by N. Katherine Hayles, Nick Montfort, Scott Rettberg, and Stephanie Strickland. Accessed August 1, 2012. http://collection.eliterature.org/1/works/wylde__storyland.html.

Young-Hae Chang Heavy Industries. 2002. *Dakota*. Accessed August 1, 2012. http://www.yhchang.com/DAKOTA.html.

Secondary Sources

Aarseth, Espen. 1997. *Cybertext: Perspectives on Ergodic Literature*. Baltimore: Johns Hopkins University Press.

Adams, Ernest. 1999. "The Designer's Notebook: Three Problems for Interactive Storytelling," *Gamasutra*, December 29. Accessed July 11, 2012. http://www.gamasutra.com/view/feature/3414/the_designers_notebook_three_.php.

Adams, Ernest. 2007. Will Computer Games Ever Be a Legitimate Art Form? In *Videogames and Art*, edited by Andy Clarke and Grethe Mitchell, 255–264. Bristol, UK: Intellect.

Adams, Ernest. 2010. *Fundamentals of Game Design*. 2nd ed. Berkeley, CA: New Riders.

Alber, Jan, Henrik Skov Nielsen, Brian Richardson, and Stefan Iversen. 2011. *Dictionary of Unnatural Narratology*. Aarhus, Denmark: University of Aarhus. Accessed February 12, 2013. http://nordisk.au.dk/forskning/forskningscentre/nrl/undictionary.

Andrews, Jim. 2005. "The Battle of Poetry against Itself and the Forces of Dullness." *Games, Po, Art, Play, & Arteroids 2.03*. Accessed August 24, 2012. http://vispo.com/arteroids/onarteroids.htm.

Andrews, Jim. 2007. Videogames as Literary Devices. In *Videogames and Art*, edited by Andy Clarke and Grethe Mitchell, 54–58. Bristol, UK: Intellect.

Bakhtin, Mikhail M. 1984. *Rabelais and His World*. Bloomington, IN: Indiana University Press.

Beiguelman, Giselle. 2010. The Reader, the Player and the Executable Poetics: Towards a Literature Beyond the Book. In *Beyond the Screen: Transformations of Literary Structures, Interfaces and Genres*, edited by Jörgen Schäfer and Peter Gendolla, 403–426. Bielefeld, Germany: Transcript.

Bell, Alice. 2010. *The Possible Worlds of Hypertext Fiction*. Basingstoke, UK: Palgrave-Macmillan.

Bell, Alice. 2014. Media-specific metalepsis in *10:01*. In *Reading Digital Fiction*, edited by Alice Bell, Astrid Ensslin, and Hans K. Rustad, 21-38. New York: Routledge.

Bell, Alice, and Astrid Ensslin. 2011. "I Know What It Was. You Know What It Was": Second Person Narration in Hypertext Fiction. *Narrative* 19 (3):311–329.

Bell, Alice, Astrid Ensslin, and Hans K. Rustad, eds. 2014. *Reading Digital Fiction*. New York: Routledge.

Bell, Alice, Astrid Ensslin, Dave Ciccoricco, Jess Laccetti, Jessica Pressman, and Hans Rustad. 2010. "A [S]creed for Digital Fiction." *The Electronic Book Review*, March. Accessed July 16, 2012. http://www.electronicbookreview.com/thread/electropoetics/DFINative.

Bernstein, Mark, and Diane Greco. 2004. *Card Shark* and *Thespis*: Exotic Tools for Hypertext Narrative. In *First Person: New Media as Story, Performance and Game*, edited by Noah Wardrip-Fruin and Pat Harrigan, 167–182. Cambridge, MA: MIT Press.

Bernstein, Mark, and Diane Greco. 2009. *Reading Hypertext*. Watertown, MA: Eastgate Systems.

Bittanti, Matteo, and Domenico Quaranta. 2006. *Gamescenes: Art in the Age of Videogames*. Milan: Johan & Levi Editore.

Blake, Kathleen. 1974. *Play, Games, and Sport: The Literary Works of Lewis Carroll*. Ithaca, NY: Cornell University Press.

Block, Friedrich W., Christiane Heibach, and Karin Wenz. 2004. *pOes1s. Ästhetik digitaler Poesie/The Aesthetics of Digital Poetry*. Ostfildern-Ruit, Germany: Hatje Cantz.

Bogost, Ian. 2007. *Persuasive Games: The Expressive Power of Videogames*. Cambridge, MA: MIT Press.

Bogost, Ian, Simon Ferrari, and Bobby Schweizer. 2010. *Newsgames: Journalism at Play*. Cambridge, MA: MIT Press.

Bolter, Jay David. 1991. *Writing Space: Computers, Hypertext and the Remediation of Print.* 2nd ed. Mahwah, NJ: Lawrence Erlbaum Associates.

Bolter, Jay David, and Richard Grusin. 1999. *Remediation: Understanding New Media.* Cambridge, MA: MIT Press.

Booth, Wayne. 1983. *The Rhetoric of Fiction.* 2nd ed. Chicago: University of Chicago Press.

Bouchardon, Serge. 2014. Figures of Gestural Manipulation in Digital Fictions. In *Analyzing Digital Fiction*, edited by Alice Bell, Astrid Ensslin, and Hans C. Rustad. New York: Routledge.

Braun, Carol-Ann, and Annie Gentès. 2005. "Between Representation and Social Interaction: Fluxus Intermedia and Dialogic Form on the Internet." *Post Identity.* Accessed April 25, 2013. http://hdl.handle.net/2027/spo.pid9999.0004.201.

Bruss, Elizabeth. 1977. The Game of Literature and Some Literary Games. *New Literary History* 9 (1):153–172.

Buckles, Mary Ann. 1985. "Interactive Fiction: The Computer Storygame *Adventure.*" PhD dissertation, University of California, San Diego.

Bürger, Peter. 1984. *Theory of the Avant-Garde.* Minneapolis: University of Minnesota Press.

Butler, Judith. 1990. *Gender Trouble: Feminism and the Subversion of Identity.* New York: Routledge.

Caillois, Roger. 1958/2001. *Man, Play and Games.* Chicago: University of Illinois Press.

Cannon, Rebecca. 2003. "Introduction to Artistic Computer Game Modification." Paper presented at the PlayThing conference, Sydney, Australia, October 10–12.

Carter, Roxanne. 2010. "Robert Coover and the Tale of Tales: Insistence and the Iteration of Red." Paper presented at Electronic Literature—Archive and Innovate, Brown University, Providence, RI, June 3–6.

Catlow, Ruth, Marc Garrett, and Corrado Morgana. 2010. *Artists Re:thinking Games.* Liverpool: FACT.

Chaffee, Cathleen. 2007. "Profile: Cory Archangel." Accessed April 1, 2013. http://www.moma.org/interactives/exhibitions/2007/automatic_update/subs_wrapper.php?section=arcangel_interview.html.

Chang, Edmond. 2004. "Words Matter: Nick Montfort's *Ad Verbum.*" Accessed March 18, 2013. http://web.archive.org/web/20040616211115/http://www.edmondchang.com:80/668k/wordsmatter.html.

Ciccoricco, David. 2007a. *Reading Network Fiction*. Tuscaloosa: University of Alabama Press.

Ciccoricco, David. 2007b. "'Play, Memory:' *Shadow of the Colossus* and Cognitive Workouts." *dichtung-digital* 37. Accessed July 24, 2012. http://www.dichtung-digital .org/2007/ciccoricco.htm.

Ciccoricco, David. 2012. Digital Fiction: Networked Narratives. In *The Routledge Companion to Experimental Literature*, edited by Joe Bray, Alison Gibbons, and Brian McHale, 469–482. New York: Routledge.

Clarke, Andy, and Grethe Mitchell. 2007. *Videogames and Art*. Bristol, UK: Intellect.

Compton, Shanna. 2004. *Gamers: Writers, Artists & Programmers on the Pleasures of Pixels*. Brooklyn: Soft Skull Press.

Conklin, Jeff. 1987. Hypertext: An Introduction and Survey. *IEEE Computer* 20 (9):17–41.

Consalvo, Mia. 2009. There Is No Magic Circle. *Games and Culture* 4 (4):408–417.

Consalvo, Mia, and Nathan Dutton. 2006. "Game Analysis: Developing a Methodological Toolkit for the Qualitative Study of Games." *Game Studies* 6 (1) (December). Accessed July 24, 2012. http://gamestudies.org/0601/articles/consalvo_dutton.

Conway, Steven. 2010. A Circular Wall? Reformulating the Fourth Wall for Videogames. *Journal of Gaming and Virtual Worlds* 2 (2):145–155.

Corcoran, Heather. 2010. About the Journey, Not the Destination: Slow Gaming and an Interview with Bill Viola. In *Artists Re:thinking Games*, edited by Ruth Catlow, Marc Garrett, and Corrado Morgana, 20–25. Liverpool: FACT.

Corneliussen, Hilde G., and Jill Walker Rettberg.2008. *Digital Culture, Play, and Identity: A* World of Warcraft® *Reader*. Cambridge, MA: MIT Press.

Crawford, Chris. 1984. *The Art of Computer Game Design*. Accessed July 2, 2012. http://pdf.textfiles.com/books/cgd-crawford.pdf.

Crawford, Garry. 2011. *Video Gamers*. Abingdon, UK: Routledge.

Crawford, Garry, Victoria K. Gosling, and Ben Light. 2011. *Online Gaming in Context: The Social and Cultural Significance of Online Games*. New York: Routledge.

Csikszentmihalyi, Mihaly. 1990. *FLOW: The Psychology of Optimal Experience*. New York: Harper and Row.

Cuddon, J. A. 1999. *The Penguin Dictionary of Literary Terms and Literary Theory*. London: Penguin.

Debord, Guy. 1958/1981. Theory of the Dérive. In *Situationist International Anthology*, edited by Ken Knabb, 50–54. Berkeley, CA: Bureau of Public Secrets.

Delany, Paul, and George P. Landow. 1991. *Hypermedia and Literary Studies*. Cambridge, MA: MIT Press.

Derrida, Jacques. 1967. *De la Grammatologie*. Paris: Les Éditions de Minuit.

Derrida, Jacques. 1978. Structure, Sign, and Play in the Discourse of the Human Sciences. In *Writing and Difference*, edited by Jacques Derrida, 278–294. Chicago: University of Chicago Press.

Derrida, Jacques. 1983. *Dissemination*. Chicago: University of Chicago Press.

Destructoid.com. 2007. "Alarmingly These Are Not Lovesick Zombies: Well, They Aren't (I Think)." October 30. Accessed August 23, 2012. http://www.destructoid .com/alarmingly-these-are-not-lovesick-zombies-well-they-aren-t-i-think--51782 .phtml.

Detweiler, Robert. 1976. Games and Play in Modern American Fiction. *Contemporary Literature* 17 (1):44–62.

Dicks, Bella, Bruce Mason, Amanda Coffey, and Paul Atkinson. 2005. *Qualitative Research and Hypermedia: Ethnography for the Digital Age*. London: Sage.

Douglas, Jane Yellowlees. 1994. "How Do I Stop This Thing?": Closure and Indeterminacy in Interactive Narratives. In *Hyper/Text/Theory*, edited by George Landow, 159–188. Baltimore: Johns Hopkins University Press.

Douglass, Jeremy. 2007. Enlightening Interactive Fiction: Andrew Plotkin's *Shade*. In *Second Person: Role-Playing and Story in Games and Playable Media*, edited by Pat Harrigan and Noah Wardrip-Fruin, 129–136. Cambridge, MA: MIT Press.

Dovey, Jon, and Helen Kennedy. 2006. *Game Cultures: Computer Games as New Media*. Maidenhead, UK: Open University Press.

Dragona, Daphne. 2010. From Parasitism to Institutionalism: Risks and Tactics for Game-Based Art. In *Artists Re:thinking Games*, edited by Ruth Catlow, Marc Garrett, and Corrado Morgana, 26–32. Liverpool: FACT.

Dreaming Methods. 2010. "Consensus Trance II," instruction booklet. Accessed February 8, 2013. www.nightingalesplayground.com.

Dumitrica, Delia D. 2011. An Exploration of Cheating in a Virtual Gaming World. *Journal of Gaming and Virtual Worlds* 3 (1):21–36.

Dundes, Alan. 1989. *Little Red Riding Hood: A Casebook*. Madison: University of Wisconsin Press.

Eagleton, Terry. 2008. *Literary Theory: An Introduction*. Minneapolis: University of Minnesota Press.

Eastgate Systems. 2008. Catalogue entry for Richard Holeton's *Figurski at Findhorn on Acid*. Accessed August 8, 2012. http://www.eastgate.com/catalog/Figurski.html.

Edwards, Brian. 1998. *Theories of Play and Postmodern Fiction*. New York: Garland.

Egenfeldt-Nielsen, Simon, Jonas Heide Smith, and Susana Pajares Tosca. 2008. *Understanding Video Games: The Essential Introduction*. New York: Routledge.

Ehrmann, Jacques. 1968. Homo Ludens revisited. *Yale French Studies* 41:31–57.

Ensslin, Astrid. 2005. Women in Wasteland: Gendered Deserts in T. S. Eliot and Shelley Jackson. *Journal of Gender Studies* 14 (3):205–216.

Ensslin, Astrid. 2007. *Canonizing Hypertext: Explorations and Constructions*. London: Continuum.

Ensslin, Astrid. 2009. Respiratory Narrative: Multimodality and Cybernetic Corporeality in "Physio-Cybertext." In *New Perspectives on Narrative and Multimodality*, edited by Ruth Page, 155–165. London: Routledge.

Ensslin, Astrid. 2011a. *The Language of Gaming*. Basingstoke, UK: Palgrave Macmillan.

Ensslin, Astrid. 2011b. From (W)reader to Breather: Cybertextual Retro-Intentionalisation in Kate Pullinger et al.'s *Breathing Wall*. In *New Narratives: Stories and Storytelling in the Digital Age*, edited by Ruth Page and Bronwen Thomas, 138–152. Lincoln: University of Nebraska Press.

Ensslin, Astrid. 2012a. Computer Gaming. In *The Routledge Companion to Experimental Literature*, edited by Joe Bray, Alison Gibbons, and Brian McHale, 497–511. New York: Routledge.

Ensslin, Astrid. 2012b. "Locating the Literary in Electronic Ludicity: Jason Nelson's *evidence of everything exploding*." Paper presented at Electronic Literature Organization Conference 2012, Morgantown, West Virginia, June 22. Video available from *Literary Gaming* blog. Accessed July 24, 2012. http://literarygaming.blogspot.co.uk.

Ensslin, Astrid. 2014a. Hypertext/Hypertextuality. In *The Johns Hopkins Guide to Digital Media and Textuality*, edited by Marie-Laure Ryan, Lori Emerson, and Benjamin Robertson. Baltimore: Johns Hopkins University Press.

Ensslin, Astrid. 2014b. Toward Functional Ludo-Narrativism: Metaludicity, Allusive Fallacy and Illusory Agency in *The Path*. In *Analyzing Digital Fiction*, edited by Alice Bell, Astrid Ensslin, and Hans Rustad. New York: Routledge.

Ensslin, Astrid, and Alice Bell. 2007. *New Perspectives on Digital Literature: Criticism and Analysis*. Special Issue of *dichtung-digital* 37. Accessed July 23, 2012. http://www.dichtung-digital.org/Newsletter/2007/index.htm.

Ensslin, Astrid, and Alice Bell. 2012. "Click = Kill": Textual *You* in Ludic Digital Fiction. *Storyworlds* 4:49–74.

Eskelinen, Markku. 2012. *Cybertext Poetics: The Critical Landscape of New Media Literary Theory*. London: Continuum.

Esslin, Martin. 1986. Brecht and the Scientific Spirit of Playfulness. In *Auctor Ludens: Essays on Play in Literature*, edited by Gerald Guinness and Andrew Hurley, 25–36. Amsterdam: John Benjamins.

Fauth, Jurgen. 1995. "Poles in Your Face: The Promises and Pitfalls of Hyperfiction." *Blip Magazine* 1 (6). Accessed August 3, 2012. http://blipmagazine.net/backissues/1995/06-jurge.html.

Fizek, Sonia. 2012. "Pivoting the Player: A Methodological Toolkit for Player Character Research in Offline Role-Playing Games." Unpublished PhD dissertation, Bangor University, UK.

Flam, Jack D. 2003. *Primitivism and Twentieth-Century Art: A Documentary History*. Berkeley: University of California Press.

Flores, Leonardo. 2012. "'Chroma' by Erik Loyer." *I ⬛ E-Poetry*, February 19. Accessed April 19, 2013. http://leonardoflores.net/post/17858217982/chroma-by-erik-loyer.

Flusser, Vilèm. 1997. *Medienkultur*. Frankfurt am Main: Fischer.

Gallegos, Anthony. 2011. "To the Moon Review." IGN.com, November 29. Accessed April 3, 2013. http://uk.ign.com/articles/2011/11/30/to-the-moon-review.

Garrelts, Nate. 2006. *The Meaning and Culture of Grand Theft Auto: Critical Essays*. Jefferson, NC: McFarland & Company.

Gazzard, Alison. 2012. *Mazes in Videogames: Exploring Paths and Spaces*. Jefferson, NC: McFarland & Company.

Gee, James Paul. 2003. *What Video Games Have to Teach Us about Learning and Literacy*. New York: Palgrave Macmillan.

Gendolla, Peter, and Schäfer, Jörgen. 2007. *The Aesthetics of Net Literature: Writing, Reading and Playing in Programmable Media*. Bielefeld, Germany: transcript.

Genette, Gerard. 1980. *Narrative Discourse: An Essay in Method*. Translated by Jane E. Lewin. Ithaca, NY: Cornell University Press.

Genette, Gerard. 1997. *Paratexts: Thresholds of Interpretation*. Translated by Jane E. Lewin. Cambridge: Cambridge University Press.

Getsy, David J. 2011. *From Diversion to Subversion: Games, Play, and Twentieth-Century Art*. University Park: Pennsylvania State University Press.

Gezari, Janet K. 1971. "Game Fiction. The World of Play and the Novels of Vladimir Nabokov." Unpublished PhD dissertation, Yale University, Connecticut.

Gezari, Janet K. 1974. Roman et problème chez Nabokov. *Poétique* 17:96–113.

Glazier, Loss Pequeño. 2002. *Digital Poetics: The Making of E-Poetries*. Tuscaloosa: University of Alabama Press.

Grand Text Auto. 2003–2013. "About Grand Text Auto." Accessed August 20, 2013. http://grandtextauto.org/about.

Guinness, Gerald, and Andrew Hurley. 1986. *Auctor Ludens: Essays on Play in Literature*. Amsterdam: John Benjamins.

Harrigan, Pat, and Noah Wardrip-Fruin. 2007. *Second Person: Role-Playing and Story in Games and Playable Media*. Cambridge, MA: MIT Press.

Harrigan, Pat, and Noah Wardrip-Fruin. 2009. *Third Person: Authoring and Exploring Vast Narratives*. Cambridge, MA: MIT Press.

Hayles, N. Katherine. 2005. *My Mother Was a Computer: Digital Subjects and Literary Texts*. Chicago: University of Chicago Press.

Hayles, N. Katherine. 2007. Hyper and Deep Attention: The Generational Divide in Cognitive Modes. *Profession* 13:187–199.

Hayles, N. Katherine. 2008. *Electronic Literature: New Horizons for the Literary*. Notre Dame, IN: University of Notre Dame Press.

Hayles, N. Katherine and Nick Montfort. 2012. Interactive fiction. In *The Routledge Companion to Experimental Literature*, edited by Joe Bray, Alison Gibbons, and Brian McHale, 452–466. New York: Routledge.

Heckman, Davin. 2011. "Technics and Violence in Electronic Literature." *Culture Machine* 12: 1–14. Accessed January 11, 2013. http://www.culturemachine.net/index.php/cm/article/view/435.

Herman, David. 1994. Textual *You* and Double Deixis in Edna O'Brien's *A Pagan Place*. *Style* 28 (3):378–411.

Herman, David. 2002. *Story Logic: Problems and Possibilities of Narrative*. Lincoln: University of Nebraska Press.

Hutchinson, Peter. 1983. *Games Authors Play*. London: Methuen.

Huizinga, Johan. 1962. *Homo Ludens: A Study of the Play-Element in Culture*. Boston: Beacon Press.

Jackson, Shelley. n.d. "Stitch Bitch: The Patchwork Girl." MIT, Cambridge, MA. Accessed August 7, 2012. http://web.mit.edu/comm-forum/papers/jackson.html.

Jacobus, Kristen. 2010. "RedRidinghood." In *Electronic Literature Directory*, edited by Joseph Tabbi et al. Accessed April 3, 2013. http://directory.eliterature.org/node/402.

Jeanneret, Yves. 2000. *Y a-t-il vraiment des technologies de l'information?* Paris: Editions universitaires du Septentrion.

Jenkins, Henry. 2004. Game Design as Narrative Architecture. In *First Person: New Media as Story, Performance, and Game*, edited by Noah Wardrip-Fruin and Pat Harrigan, 118–130. Cambridge, MA: MIT Press.

Jenkins, Henry. 2006. *Convergence Culture: Where Old and New Media Collide*. New York: New York University Press.

Jones, Steven E. 2008. *The Meaning of Video Games: Gaming and Textual Strategies*. New York: Routledge.

Joyce, Michael. 1996. *Of Two Minds: Hypertext Pedagogy and Poetics*. Ann Arbor: University of Michigan Press.

Juul, Jesper. 2005. *Half-Real: Video Games between Real Rules and Fictional Worlds*. Cambridge, MA: MIT Press.

Juul, Jesper. 2010. *A Casual Revolution: Reinventing Video Games and Their Players*. Cambridge, MA: MIT Press.

Kac, Eduardo. 2007. *Media Poetry: An International Anthology*. Bristol, UK: Intellect.

Kant, Immanuel. 1911. *Critique of Aesthetic Judgement*. Translated by J. C. Meredith. Oxford: Clarendon.

Keep, Christopher, Tim McLaughlin, and Robin Parmar. 1993–2001. *The Electronic Labyrinth*. Accessed April 15, 2013. http://www2.iath.virginia.edu/elab/elab.html.

Klabbers, Jan H. G. 2009. *The Magic Circle: Principles of Gaming and Simulation*. 3rd ed. Rotterdam: Sense Publishers.

Kocher, Mela. 2007. The Ludoliterary Cycle: Analysis and Typology of Digital Games. In *The Aesthetics of Net Literature: Writing, Reading and Playing in Programmable Media*, edited by Peter Gendolla and Jörgen Schäfer, 107–120. Bielefeld, Germany: transcript.

Koskimaa, Raine. 1997/1998. "Visual Structuring of Hyperfiction Narratives." *Electronic Book Review* 6. Accessed August 3, 2012. http://www.altx.com/ebr/ebr6/6koskimaa/6koski.htm.

Kuhlen, Rainer. 1991. *Hypertext: Ein nicht-lineares Medium zwischen Buch und Wissensbank*. Berlin: Springer.

Kukkonen, Karin. 2011. Metalepsis in Popular Culture: An Introduction. In *Metalepsis in Popular Culture*, edited by Karin Kukkonen and Sonia Klimek, 1–21. Berlin: Walter de Gruyter.

Landow, George P. 1992. *Hypertext: The Convergence of Contemporary Critical Theory and Technology*. Baltimore: Johns Hopkins University Press.

Landow, George P. 1997. *Hypertext 2.0: The Convergence of Contemporary Critical Theory and Technology*. Baltimore: Johns Hopkins University Press.

Landow, George P. 2006. *Hypertext 3.0: New Media and Critical Theory in an Era of Globalization*. Baltimore: Johns Hopkins University Press.

Lanham, Richard. 1973. *Tristram Shandy: The Games of Pleasure*. Berkeley: University of California Press.

Lankoski, Petri, Annika Waern, Anne Mette Thorhauge, and Harko Verhagen. 2011. *Experiencing Games: Games, Play and Players*. Special issue of *Journal of Gaming and Virtual Worlds* 3 (3) (Winter).

Larsen, Deena. 2008. *Deena Larsen's Hypertext/New Media/Electronic Lit/Possibilities Addicts Attic*. Accessed August 2, 2012. http://www.deenalarsen.net.

Laxton, Susan. 2011. From Judgment to Process: The Modern Ludic Field. In *From Diversion to Subversion: Games, Play, and Twentieth-Century Art*, edited by David J. Getsy, 3–24. University Park: Pennsylvania State University Press.

Lewis, Philip E. 1968. La Rouchefoucauld: The Rationality of Play. *Yale French Studies* 41: 133-147.

Liede, Alfred. 1963. *Dichtung als Spiel: Studien zur Unsinnspoesie an den Grenzen der Sprache*. Berlin: de Gruyter.

Lister, Martin, Jon Dovey, Seth Giddings, Iain Grant, and Kieran Kelly. 2009. *New Media: A Critical Introduction*. 2nd ed. Abingdon, UK: Routledge.

Luce-Kapler, Rebecca, and Theresa Dobson. 2005. In Search of a Story: Reading and Writing E-Literature. *Reading Online* 8 (6). Accessed August 3, 2012. http://www.readingonline.org/articles/luce-kapler/.

MacCallum-Stewart, Esther, and Justin Parsler. 2007. "Illusory Agency in *Vampire: The Masquerade—Bloodlines*." *dichtung-digital* 37. Accessed January 11, 2013. http://dichtung-digital.de/2007/maccallumstewart_parsler.htm.

Martin, Tim. 2009. "Endpaper—Fiction Reaches a New Level." *The Telegraph*, May 7. Accessed April 2, 2013. http://www.telegraph.co.uk/culture/books/bookreviews/5291671/Endpaper-Fiction-reaches-a-new-level.html.

Mateas, Michael. 2004. A Preliminary Poetics for Interactive Drama and Games. In *First Person: New Media as Story, Performance, and Game*, edited by Noah Wardrip-Fruin and Pat Harrigan, 19–33. Cambridge, MA: MIT Press.

McDonough, Tom. 2002. Situationist Space. In *Guy Debord and the Situationist International*, edited by T. McDonough, 241–265. Cambridge, MA: MIT Press.

McGonigal, Jane. 2011. *Reality Is Broken: Why Games Make Us Better and How They Can Change the World*. New York: Penguin.

McHale, Brian. 1999. *Postmodernist Fiction*. London: Routledge.

Meades, Alan. 2013. Infectious Pleasures: Ethnographic Perspectives on the Production and Use of Illicit Videogame Modifications on the *Call of Duty* Franchise. *Journal of Gaming and Virtual Worlds* 5 (1):59–76.

Migros Museum für Gegenwartskunst. 2005. "Cory Archangel: Nerdzone Version 1." Accessed April 1, 2013. http://www.migrosmuseum.ch/en/exhibitions/exhibition-details/?tx_museumplus%5Bexhib%5D=88.

Milani, Abbas. 2008. *Eminent Persians: The Men and Women Who Made Modern Iran, 1941–1979.* Vol. 1. Syracuse, NY: Syracuse University Press.

Millard, David E., Nicholas M. Gibbins, Danius T. Michaelides, and Mark J. Weal. 2005. "Mind the Semantic Gap." In *Hypertext '05: Proceedings of the Sixteenth ACM Conference on Hypertext and Hypermedia*, edited by Siegfried Reich and Manolis Tzagarakis, 54–62. New York: ACM.

Miller, Nancy K. 1986. *The Poetics of Gender.* New York: Columbia University Press.

Millon, Marc. 1999. *Creative Content for the Web.* Exeter, UK: Intellect.

Montfort, Nick. 2003. *Twisty Little Passages: An Approach to Interactive Fiction.* Cambridge, MA: MIT Press.

Montfort, Nick. 2004. Interactive Fiction as "Story," "Game," "Storygame," "Novel," "World," "Literature," "Puzzle," "Problem," "Riddle," and "Machine." In *First Person: New Media as Story, Performance, and Game*, edited by Noah Wardrip-Fruin and Pat Harrigan, 310–317. Cambridge, MA: MIT Press.

Montfort, Nick, and Stuart Moulthrop. 2003. "Face It, Tiger, You Just Hit the Jackpot: Reading and Playing Cadre's *Varicella.*" *Fineart Forum* 17 (8) (August). Accessed August 1, 2012. http://nickm.com/if/Varicella.pdf.

Montola, Markus, Jaakko Stenros, and Annika Waern. 2009. *Pervasive Games: Theory and Design.* Amsterdam: Morgan Kaufmann.

Morgan, Wendy, and Richard Andrews. 1999. City of Text? Metaphors for Hypertext in Literary Education. *Changing English: Studies in Culture and Education* 6 (1):81–92.

Morgana, Corrado. 2010. Introduction: Artists Re:thinking Games. In *Artists Re:thinking Games*, edited by Ruth Catlow, Marc Garrett, and Corrado Morgana, 7–14. Liverpool: FACT.

Morris, Adalaide, and Thomas Swiss. 2006. *New Media Poetics: Contexts, Technotexts, and Theories.* Cambridge, MA: MIT Press.

Morrissette, Bruce. 1968. Games and Game Structures in Robbe-Grillet. *Yale French Studies* 41: 159–167.

Moulthrop, Stuart. 1991. Reading from the Map: Metonymy and Metaphor in the Fiction of Forking Paths. In *Hypermedia and Literary Studies*, edited by Paul Delany and George P. Landow, 119–132. Cambridge, MA: MIT Press.

Myers, David. 2012. "Circles Tend to Return." *Game Studies: The International Journal of Computer Game Research* 12 (2). Accessed April 23, 2013. http://gamestudies .org/1202/articles/myers_book_review.

Nietzsche, Friedrich. 1908/2004. *Ecce Homo*. Mineola, NY: Dover.

Nitsche, Michael. 2008. *Video Game Spaces: Image, Play, and Structure in 3D Worlds*. Cambridge, MA: MIT Press.

Paul, Christopher A. 2012. *Wordplay and the Discourse of Video Games: Analyzing Words, Design, and Play*. New York: Routledge.

Pettersson, Anders. 2000. *Verbal Art: A Philosophy of Literature and Literary Experience*. Montreal: McGill-Queen's University Press.

Picot, Edward. 2003. "What Makes Them Click?" Accessed April 30, 2010. http:// tracearchive.ntu.ac.uk/review/index.cfm?article=76.

Picot, Edward. 2009. "Play on Meaning?—Computer Games as Art." furtherfield.org, April 30. Accessed June 27, 2010. http://www.furtherfield.org/displayreview.php? review_id=345.

Pope, Rob. 2005. *Creativity: Theory, History, Practice*. Abingdon, UK: Routledge.

Prawer, Siegbert S. 1969. Recent German Language Games. In *Essays in German Language, Culture and Society*, edited by Siegbert S. Prawer, R. Hinton Thomas, and Leonard Forster, 69–83. London: University of London.

Pressman, Jessica. 2008. The Strategy of Digital Modernism: Young-Hae Chang Heavy Industries' *Dakota*. *Modern Fiction Studies* 54 (2):302–326.

Prince, Gerald. 1987. *A Dictionary of Narratology*. Lincoln: University of Nebraska Press.

Pullinger, Kate, and Chris Joseph. 2013. "Inanimate Alice—Homepage." Accessed February 11, 2013. http://www.inanimatealice.com.

Punday, Daniel. 2014. Seeing into the Worlds of Digital Fictions. In *Analyzing Digital Fiction*, edited by Alice Bell, Astrid Ensslin, and Hans K. Rustad. New York: Routledge.

Reichle, Marcus. 2012. *Die Welt des Mobile Gaming: Technik, Theorien, Ausblicke*. Saarbrücken: AV Akademikerverlag.

Rettberg, Scott. 2011. "Loss of Grasp—The Multimedia Work of Serge Bouchardon." *Necessary Fiction* 13, October 2011. Accessed January 11, 2013. http:// necessaryfiction.com/writerinres/LossofGraspI heMultimediaworkofSergeBouchar don.

Rettberg, Scott, and Patricia Tomaszek. 2010. "'Loss of Grasp,' A Performance by Serge Bouchardon." *Vimeo* clip. Accessed January 3, 2013. http://vimeo.com/ 15779853.

Ricardo, Francisco J. 2009. *Literary Art in Digital Performance: Case Studies in New Media Art and Criticism*. New York: Continuum.

Richardson, Brian. 2006. *Unnatural Voices: Extreme Narration in Modern and Contemporary Fiction*. Columbus: Ohio State University Press.

Rose, Michael. 2009. "Review: The Path (Tale of Tales)." *IndieGames: The Weblog*, March 21. Accessed April 1, 2013. http://www.indiegames.com/2009/03/review_the_path_tale_of_tales.html.

Rosenberg, Jim. 1996. The Structure of Hypertext Activity. In *Hypertext '96.*, 22–30. New York: ACM.

Rustad, Hans K. 2009. "A Four-Sided Model for Reading Hypertext Fiction." *Hyperrhiz: New Media Cultures* 6 (summer). Accessed August 3, 2012. http://www.hyperrhiz.net/hyperrhiz06/19-essays/80-a-four-sided-model.

Rustad, Hans K. 2012. *Digital Litteratur: En Innføring*. Oslo: Cappelen Damm Akademisk.

Ryan, Malcolm, and Brigid Costello. 2012. My Friend Scarlet: Interactive Tragedy in *The Path*. *Games and Culture* 7 (2):111–126.

Ryan, Marie-Laure. 1999. *Cyberspace Textuality: Computer Technology and Literary Theory*. Bloomington: Indiana University Press.

Ryan, Marie-Laure. 2006. *Avatars of Story*. Minneapolis: University of Minnesota Press.

Ryan, Marie-Laure. 2008. Interactive Narrative, Plot Types, and Interpersonal Relations. In *Interactive Storytelling: First Joint International Conference on Interactive Digital Storytelling, ICIDS 2008, Germany, November 2008, Proceedings*, edited by Ulrike Spierling and Nicolas Szilas, 6–13. Berlin: Springer.

Salen, Katie, and Eric Zimmerman. 2004. *Rules of Play: Game Design Fundamentals*. Cambridge, MA: MIT Press.

Samyn, Michael, and Auriea Harvey. 2012. "Postmortem: Tale of Tales' *The Path*." *Gamasutra*. Accessed April 1, 2013. http://www.gamasutra.com/view/feature/5902/postmortem_tale_of_tales_the_path.php?print=1.

Schäfer, Jörgen. 2009. Looking Behind the *Façade*: Playing and Performing an Interactive Drama. In *Literary Art in Digital Performance: Case Studies in New Media Art and Criticism*, edited by Francisco Ricardo, 143–161. New York: Continuum.

Schäfer, Jörgen, and Peter Gendolla. 2010. *Beyond the Screen: Transformations of Literary Structures, Interfaces and Genres*. Bielefeld, Germany: transcript.

Schiller, Friedrich. 1795/2006. *The Aesthetical Essays*. Project Gutenberg. Accessed July 13, 2012. http://www.gutenberg.org/files/6798/6798-h/6798-h.htm.

Schleiner, Anne-Marie. 2011. Dissolving the Magic Circle of Play: Lessons from Situationist Gaming. In *From Diversion to Subversion: Games, Play, and Twentieth-Century Art*, edited by David J. Getsy, 149–158. University Park: Pennsylvania State University Press.

Shaw, Evelyn S., and Joan S. Darling. 1986. *Female Strategies*. New York: Simon and Schuster.

Shklovsky, Viktor. 1917/1998. Art as Technique. In *Literary Theory: An Anthology*, edited by Julie Rivkin and Michael Ryan, 15–21. Malden, MA: Blackwell.

Short, Emily. 2000b. "Galatea Cheats and Walkthroughs." Accessed March 20, 2013. http://emshort.home.mindspring.com/cheats.htm.

Short, Emily. 2008. "Everybody Dies." *WebCite*, November 20. Accessed March 18, 2013. http://www.webcitation.org/query?url=http%3A%2F%2Fplaythisthing.com%2Feverybody-dies&date=2009-01-19.

Simanowski, Roberto. 2002. *Interfictions: Vom Schreiben im Netz*. Frankfurt am Main: Suhrkamp Verlag.

Simanowski, Roberto. 2011. *Digital Art and Meaning: Reading Kinetic Poetry, Text Machines, Mapping Art, and Interactive Installations*. Minneapolis: University of Minnesota Press.

Slethaug, Gordon E. 1993. Game Theory. In *The Encyclopedia of Contemporary Literary Theory*, edited by Irena R. Makaryk, 64–69. Toronto: University of Toronto Press.

Slocombe, Will. 2006. *Nihilism and the Sublime Postmodern: The (Hi)Story of a Difficult Relationship from Romanticism to Postmodernism*. London: Routledge.

Spariosu, Mihai. 1982. *Literature, Mimesis and Play: Essays in Literary Theory*. Tübingen, Germany: Gunter Narr.

Spariosu, Mihai. 1989. *Dionysus Reborn: Play and the Aesthetic Dimension in Modern Philosophical and Scientific Discourse*. Ithaca, NY: Cornell University Press.

Steel, D. A. 1971. *Lafcadio Ludens*: Ideas of Play and Levity in *Les Caves du Vatican*. *Modern Language Review* 66 (3):554–564.

Suits, Bernard. 1978/1990. *Grasshopper: Games, Life, and Utopia*. Boston: David R. Godine.

Suits, Bernard. 1978/2005. *Grasshopper: Games, Life, and Utopia*. Peterborough, Ontario: Broadview Press.

Tale of Tales. 2009b. *The Path*, instruction booklet. Accessed April 2, 2013. http://cdn.steampowered.com/Manuals/27000/ThePATH-UserManual.pdf?t=1360881193.

Tale of Tales. 2013. *The Path* website. Accessed August 12, 2011. http://tale-of-tales.com/ThePath.

Taylor, T. L. 2006. *Play Between Worlds: Exploring Online Game Culture*. Cambridge, MA: MIT Press.

thatgamecompany. 2013. "Flower." Accessed April 1, 2013. http://thatgamecompany .com/games/flower.

Tosca, Susana. 2014. *Amnesia, the Dark Descent*. The Player's Very Own Purgatory. In *Analyzing Digital Fiction*, edited by Alice Bell, Astrid Ensslin, and Hans K. Rustad. New York: Routledge.

Tribunella, Eric L. 2010. *Melancholia and Maturation: The Use of Trauma in American Children's Literature*. Knoxville: University of Tennessee Press.

Vaneigem, Raoul. 1967. *The Revolution of Everyday Life*. Accessed July 17, 2012. http://library.nothingness.org/articles/SI/en/pub_contents/5.

Van Looy, Jan, and Jan Baetens. 2003. *Close Reading New Media: Analyzing Electronic Literature*. Leuven, Belgium: Leuven University Press.

Walker Bynum, Caroline. 1991. *Fragmentation and Redemption: Essays on Gender and the Human Body in Medieval Religion*. New York: Zone Books.

Wardrip-Fruin, Noah. 2009. *Expressive Processing: Digital Fictions, Computer Games, and Software Studies*. Cambridge, MA: MIT Press.

Wardrip-Fruin, Noah, and Pat Harrigan. 2004. *First Person: New Media as Story, Performance, and Game*. Cambridge, MA: MIT Press.

Westecott, Emma. 2010. Playing with the Gothic: If You Go Down to the Woods Tonight . . . . In *Artists Re:thinking Games*, edited by R. Catlow, Marc Garrett, and Corrado Morgana, 78–81. Liverpool: FACT.

Wideman, Herbert H., Ronald D. Owston, Christine Brown, Andre Kushniruk, Francis Ho, and Kevin C. Pitts. 2007. Unpacking the Potential of Educational Gaming: A New Tool for Gaming Research. *Simulation & Gaming* 38 (1):10–30.

Wimsatt, W. K. 1973. Belinda Ludens: Strife and Play in the Rape of the Lock. *New Literary History* 4 (2):357–374.

Wittgenstein, Ludwig. 1953/2001. *Philosophical Investigations*. Oxford: Blackwell.

Ziegfeld, Richard. 1989. Interactive Fiction: A New Literary Genre? *New Literary History* 20 (2):341–372.

Zimmerman, Eric. 2004. Narrative, Interactivity, Play, and Games: Four Naughty Concepts in Need of Discipline. In *First Person: New Media as Story, Performance, and Game*, edited by Noah Wardrip-Fruin and Pat Harrigan, 154–164. Cambridge, MA: MIT Press.

Zipes, Jack. 1993. *The Trials & Tribulations of Little Red Riding Hood*. 2nd ed. New York: Routledge.

Glossary

Agon, the Greek word for "contest" or "struggle," is used by Roger Caillois (2001) to refer to competitive games, such as athletics and football. See also *alea*, *ilinx*, and *mimicry*.

Alea is Latin for "dice." Caillois (2001) uses this term to refer to games of chance, such as roulette and gambling.

An **anagram** is a word made of reassembled letters from another word (e.g., "dame" and "made").

Analepsis is a stylistic term for the more commonly used word flashback. It is the opposite of *prolepsis*.

Antiludic game or media design comprises a wide range of design techniques that are used to critique various aspects of game(r) culture, such as unreflected, fast-paced action and violence.

Art games are a type of independent game made by game designers that follow a mostly noncommercialist, avant-garde agenda that *détourns* aspects of mainstream game culture.

Auteur is a term derived from film culture and is mostly used to refer to a type of film that strongly reflects its director's personal "stamp," or audiovisual and narrative style. More recently, it has come to be used in the videogame industry to describe the style of a specific (lead) designer or design team.

Avatars are virtual bodies controlled by players that act as their embodied representatives in the game.

The German term **Bildungsroman** refers to a specific novelistic genre that typically features the educational, artistic, psychological, and/or moral development of a young protagonist.

Born digital refers to digital artifacts that require the specific interactive, multimodal, and executable qualities of digital media and their underlying source code in order to be produced and consumed.

Bricolage is used in visual arts theory to refer to artifacts that have been assembled from a wide range of diverse, everyday objects available to the artist at the time of production.

Carnivalesque is a term coined by Russian literary theorist Mikhail Bakhtin. It refers to a style of writing intended to subvert dominant culture and politics in a playful, satirical manner to instill a sense of chaos into orderly, regulated systems.

Cento is a Latin literary term ("patchwork cloak") that refers to poems entirely composed of passages of other writers' works.

Cognitive ludicity is used in this book to refer to literary and artistic structures that play with audience expectations and affect their mental (rather than kinetic and/or ludic-mechanic) interactions with a text.

Culinary is a critical concept coined by Bertolt Brecht for his theory of epic theater. It refers to the kind of passive, enjoyable entertainment provided by conventional theater, which doesn't impact the personal lives of the audience.

Deconstruction is a poststructuralist method of iconoclastic literary analysis, originally intended for debunking binary, hierarchical oppositions yet used more widely to critique traditional hermeneutic concepts of closure, harmony, and (unambiguous) meaning.

Dérive is, according to *Situationist* Guy Debord (1958/1981, 51), "a mode of experimental behaviour linked to the conditions of urban society: a technique of transient passage through varied ambiences."

Détournement is a *Situationist* concept combining appropriation and subversion. It refers to the exploration of new ways of using commodity goods and the values attached to them in the sense of "an all embracing reinsertion of things into play whereby play grasps and reunites beings and things" (Vaneigem 1967, n.p.).

Diegesis (Greek for "narration") is a narratological term referring to (1) the (fictional) world in which narrated events and situations take place, and (2) the telling as opposed to showing (*mimesis*) of a narrative (Prince 1987, 20).

Dingsymbol is a German literary term referring to objects that recur in fictional texts to communicate specific symbolical meanings.

Écriture féminine is a branch of feminist literary theory that emphasizes the distinctness of women's writing as well as the inscription of the female body as text.

Ekphrasis (Greek for "to speak out") is an ancient rhetorical term meaning the precise and eloquent verbal description of a visual object, experience, or person.

Embedded narratives in games are preprogrammed narrative elements, such as cutscenes and enemy encounters (Jenkins 2004).

Epitext is a type of *paratext* that includes the texts relating to but not physically accompanying another text, such as reviews, interviews, and diaries (Genette 1997).

Ergodicity (from the Greek "ergon," "piece of work," and "hodos," "path") is a specific hermeneutic quality ascribed to literary works that require "nontrivial effort" from readers "to traverse the text" (Aarseth 1997, 1).

Errata are revisions issued by a publisher after a book or computer program has been published. They tend to come in the form of loose sheets or software patches.

Extradiegetic is a narratological term meaning outside the narrative world. Its opposite is *intradiegetic*.

Game art is "any art in which digital games played a significant role in the creation, production, and/or display of the artwork. . . . The resulting artwork can exist as a game, painting, photograph, sound, animation, video, performance or gallery installation" (Bittanti and Quaranta 2006, 9).

Gamification refers to a widespread cultural trend in which gameplay and ludic mechanics are introduced into normally nonludic elements of society, such as business, education, and health.

Gesamtkunstwerk is an aesthetic concept associated with nineteenth-century German composer Richard Wagner, who used it to refer to a "total," "universal," or "ideal" work of art that integrates numerous or all individual arts (music, drama, fine arts, etc.).

Griefing is online harrassment.

Hacking is used in videogame (sub)culture to refer to (1) gamers' very own playful and creative ways of programming that often result in innovative, playable games and/or related digital media, and (2) illegal attempts to access, steal, and/or modify a game's source code.

Hacktivism is a blend between "hacker" and "activism" signifying political engagement using hacking methods.

Heterodiegetic narration refers to a style of verbal storytelling in which the narrator "is not a character in the situations and events recounted" (Prince 1987, 40; Genette 1980). See *homodiegetic narration*.

Hominidization is the evolutionary development from primates to humans.

Homodiegetic narration is a style of verbal storytelling in which the narrator is a character in the fictional world he or she presents (Genette 1980). See *heterodiegetic narration*.

Hypermedia is an overarching term used for multimodal digital literature that is made for on-screen interaction. Its most common form is digital fiction, such as

Flash, Java, or Shockwave fiction, but some multimodal *hypertexts* also come under this genre label.

Hypertext is an electronic text format that interlinks various types of digital files and documents into an interactive, associative network. Among its most important art forms are hypertext fiction and poetry.

Idée fixe is a musicological term signifying an important, recurrent motif in a composition.

Ilinx, in Caillois's (2001) ludology, refers to types of "play" that cause feelings of dizziness. Examples include dancing, swinging, whirling, and tightrope walking.

Implicature is a concept from linguistic pragmatics. It refers to meanings that are implied rather than explicated by an utterance and that have to be inferred from the context and rules of language use.

The **implied author** is different from the real, historical author of a work in that he or she has to be reconstructed from the text, and the implied author's intent and values may differ considerably across different works (see Booth 1983).

The **implied reader** is "the audience presupposed by a text" and "must be distinguished from its real reader" (Prince 1987, 43), whose values and opinions may differ considerably from those of the former.

Interactive Fiction is "a text-based narrative in which the user is offered navigational possibilities . . . , assets to pick up or refuse (such as a sword or key), virtual objects to view and manipulate, and a framework in which the user can win or lose" (Hayles and Montfort 2012, 452).

Intermedia is the term used by Fluxus artists to refer to their mixed-media artifacts and to question "the procedural and conceptual barriers between medium, genre, and media practices" (Braun and Gentès 2005).

Intradiegetic is a narratological term meaning inside the narrative world. Its opposite is *extradiegetic*.

Lexia is the term generally used to refer to an individual unit, or text chunk, of a *hypertext*. Lexias are displayed as text windows.

A **lipogram** is a text that deliberately excludes one or more alphabetic characters.

Ludicity (from the Latin "ludere," "to play") is a catch-all term for playfulness and game-ness, whereby games are understood to be a subform of play.

Ludic mechanics is the term used in this book to signify game-ness, which includes the rules underlying a game, its challenges, risks, actions, objectives, feedback and progress mechanisms, and its victory and termination conditions. In digital media, ludic mechanics includes the executable code that realizes these features.

Ludology is the study of games.

Ludus is the term used by Caillois (2001) to refer to rule-based gameplay.

Metafiction is, broadly speaking, fiction about fiction, including writerly processes as well as the norms and conventions of fiction writing.

Metalepsis (from the Greek "meta," "beyond," and "leipein," to "leave") is a narratological term denoting a jump across narrative worlds or ontological spheres (Kukkonen 2011, 1). "Jump" in this sense can refer to a full physical transgression, a way of transporting characters, narrators, or the audience into and out of diegetic levels, or ontological spheres or worlds, or just a quick "glance" across—for instance when a narrator or character briefly addresses a reader, viewer, or player.

Metaludic means "about" any aspect of games or play.

Metaludological means "about" any aspect of *ludology*.

Mimesis is, in its most traditional Aristotelian meaning, a term that refers to the showing as opposed to the telling (*diegesis*) of a narrative. Traditional mimetic arts are drama and painting, for example, whereas diegesis relates to fiction and poetry.

Mimicry is a collective term that Caillois (2001) uses to mean games of make-believe, such as masks, illusions, and spectacles.

Modding is a shortened form of "modifying" and refers to the purposeful manipulation of a game's source code.

Multimodality refers to the combination of various semiotic modes (e.g., image, sound, speech) to communicate complex meanings.

Multiperson narration is the combination of first, second, and third person narration to form a polyphony of narrative voices (Richardson 2006).

Paidia (from the Greek "pais," "child") is the term used by Caillois (2001) to refer to unstructured play as occurs most typically with children.

A **palimpsest** is a piece of parchment that has been written on and erased several times, thereby creating multiple layers of more or less visible and transparent text.

Paratext is the text, or rather the textual ecology, surrounding an artifact like a novel, film, or game, such as a title, blurb, reviews, interviews, and product websites (Genette 1997; Jones 2008; Ensslin 2011a). Paratext subdivides into *peritext* and *epitext* (Genette 1997).

Peritext is a type of *paratext* that includes the texts immediately surrounding a text, such as title, blurb, and contents page (Genette 1997).

Pervasive gaming is event-based gaming that blends virtual and physical game spaces. Typically, players use mobile devices to navigate, communicate, and solve tasks.

Physio-cybertexts are digital, ergodic texts that both integrate, through cybernetic interaction, and thematize and/or problematize functions and limitations of the human body (Ensslin 2009, 2011b).

The **play drive** is, according to Friedrich Schiller's aesthetic theory, the basic human need for play. It mediates between sensual and rational forces and enables mankind to develop aesthetic freedom.

Playerly is used in this book to refer to artifacts designed in such a way as to afford and demand close gameplay.

Procedural rhetoric is a term coined by Ian Bogost (2007). It refers to "the practice of using processes persuasively" (3). In particular, this relates to the ludic processes afforded by videogames' underlying algorithms and how they are used in some games to communicate to players moral, critical, satirical, etc. messages in an effective, convincing way.

Prolepsis is a stylistic term for the more commonly used word flashforward. It is the opposite of *analepsis*.

Readerly is used in this book to refer to artifacts designed in such a way as to afford and demand close reading.

Remediation (Bolter and Grusin 1999) refers to a process of refashioning that happens when older media appropriate elements of new media (such as Twitter feeds on television news) and vice versa (e.g., the use of the proscenium arch in early cinema).

Respawning refers to character rebirth after being killed in-game, whereby the game doesn't have to be started again from scratch.

Rhythmos is Greek for "rule, harmony, and rational order." This comes closest to Caillois's notion of *ludus*, rule-based gameplay, where the mechanics of rules, challenges, rewards, winning, and losing form the structural foundation of the player's activity.

Situationism is a theoretical and practical school of thought dating back to the Situationist International, an international political and artistic movement of the 1950s and 60s whose ideas were inspired by Marxism and early twentieth-century European avant-gardes. Among its key aesthetic concepts and methods are *dérive* and *détournement*.

Slow games are games that prevent players from engaging in fast-paced action, encouraging them to focus instead on exploration, meditation, and/or critical thought.

Story arc is a term used in game theory to refer to individual players' experiences of a videogame narrative. Due to the nonlinearity of this medium, story arcs tend to differ considerably between players. The term is also used to signify an extended storyline comprising numerous subcomponents, such as episodes in comics or television drama, or videogame levels.

Storyworlds are the audience's (readers', players', viewers', etc.) "mental models of who did what to and with whom, when, where, why, and in what fashion in the world" (Herman 2002, 5). In this book "storyworlds" and "fictional worlds" are used interchangeably.

Subludic meanings are meanings that lie beyond a game's surface. Like subtextual meanings, they have to be read into a game through processes of *implicature*.

Textual *you* (Herman 1994, 2002) is a narratological term referring to the various uses of the second person pronoun in English-medium narrative fiction. Among the most common uses are apostrophe (reader address) and second person narration.

Transmediation derives from Jenkins's (2006) concept of transmedia storytelling. It refers to the remediation and further development of existing narratives in the same or a different medium.

Unnatural narratives are fictional narratives that go against the rules of natural realism and conventional realistic storytelling and therefore have a defamiliarizing effect on the audience.

Unnatural narratology is the study of *unnatural narratives*.

Verba dicendi are reporting verbs such as "say," "argue," and "answer."

World play is a term used by Nietzsche in *Ecce Homo* (1908/2004) to refer to the perpetual recurrence of life and death, of individual creation and destruction, that constitutes human existence.

Wreader is a term coined by George P. Landow (1992) that blends *writer* and *reader* and means the convergence of the two roles in readers who cocreate textual meaning. The term is most widely used in postmodernism-inspired hypertext theory because readers of Storyspace hyperfiction are quite literally invited to add notes to preauthored hypertext, thereby becoming coauthors.

Zero-player games are games that require zero players. They are designed to be viewed rather than interacted with kinetically.

Index